Alice Paul and the
American Suffrage Campaign

Alice Paul and the American Suffrage Campaign

KATHERINE H. ADAMS
AND MICHAEL L. KEENE

University of Illinois Press

URBANA AND CHICAGO

Library of Congress Cataloging-in-Publication Data
Adams, Katherine H., 1954–
Alice Paul and the American suffrage campaign /
Katherine H. Adams and Michael L. Keene.
p.   cm.
Includes bibliographical references and index.
ISBN-13: 978-0-252-03220-2 (cloth : alk. paper)
ISBN-10: 0-252-03220-9
ISBN-13: 978-0-252-07471-4 (pbk. : alk. paper)
ISBN-10: 0-252-07471-8
1. Paul, Alice, 1885–1977.
2. Suffragists—United States—Biography.
3. Women—Suffrage—United States—History.
4. Women's rights—United States—History.
I. Keene, Michael L. II. Title.
HQ1413.P38A23   2008
324.6'23092—dc22 [B]   2007020859

KHA: For my wonderful god-child, Lillian Hodges Withers,
who will cast her first vote in 2018

MLK: For Maxine Hairston

Contents

Acknowledgments

Kate is writing her share of these acknowledgments at her father's house, to which she has fled from Hurricane Katrina. She would like to thank her father, James R. Hodges, and her son, Cole Adams, who both went with her to Washington to do research on this book and who are both fine companions to her now. She would like to also thank her sister and brother-in-law, Laura Hodges and Michael Rouse, for housing her during this storm and getting this manuscript to the press. Funding from her William and Audrey Hutchinson Professorship enabled her to spend the month in Washington; a fall sabbatical granted by Loyola University New Orleans enabled her to work with Mike on a first draft. She wishes to thank her chair, Mary McCay, as well as the interlibrary loan librarian at Loyola, Pat Doran, and reference librarian, Jim Hobbs, for their kind assistance. She would also like to thank Mary Sue Morrow of the University of Cincinnati, Erin O'Donnell of the University of Southern Mississippi, Leslie Parr of Loyola, and Bob Cleaver of Moorestown, New Jersey, for their knowledgeable contributions, although certainly all errors are the authors' own.

Mike joins Kate in thanking these contributors and would like to add to the list the reference department at the University of Tennessee library and the John C. Hodges Better English Fund.

Introduction

Who are the best known figures of the woman suffrage movement in the United States? Susan B. Anthony, Elizabeth Cady Stanton, and Lucretia Mott. They had all died by 1906, however, and women did not achieve the vote until 1920. Who, then, carried on their work and secured the passage of the Nineteenth Amendment? The most common answer would be Carrie Chapman Catt and Anna Howard Shaw, leaders of the largest suffrage organization, the National American Woman Suffrage Association (NAWSA), an amalgam of two associations that formed after the Civil War. After Anthony's death, Catt and Shaw led the difficult state-by-state fight for woman's enfranchisement through a national council and local affiliates that involved two million members.

This official story, depicting a triumphal march of early pioneers and later organizational leaders, appeared in many books by and about these women published before 1930. Friends and associates wrote laudatory biographies, such as Anna Davis Hallowell's *James and Lucretia Mott: Life and Letters* (1890) and Ida Husted Harper's *The Life and Work of Susan B. Anthony* (1898). The women themselves also wrote autobiographies and histories of the suffrage movement: Elizabeth Cady Stanton's *Eighty Years and More (1815–1897): Reminiscences of Elizabeth Cady Stanton* (1898), Anna Howard Shaw's *The Story of a Pioneer* (1915), and Carrie Chapman Catt's *Woman Suffrage and Politics: The Inner Story of the Suffrage Movement* (1923). Stanton and Anthony worked with Ida Husted Harper, NAWSA's historian, on a six-volume *History of Woman Suffrage,* published between 1881 and 1922, which featured the contributions of the first leaders along with NAWSA's yearly progress. Following the lead of these biographies and histories, subsequent publications told the same two-part story. Books with all-encompassing titles like *American Feminists* (Riegel, 1963), *The Woman Movement: Feminism in the United States and England* (O'Neill, 1969), and *One Half the People: The Fight for Woman Suffrage* (Scott and Scott, 1975), as well as many textbooks, repeat this familiar construction of women's history.

After these women, and especially the first inspirational group, became the accepted figures of the American suffrage movement, they gained further status through official forms of commemoration. For example, a portrait monument of Mott, Stanton, and Anthony was placed in the Crypt of the Capitol, the large circular area on the first floor, on February 15, 1921, Susan B. Anthony's birthday. This statue is now in the Rotunda. The U.S. Postal Service issued stamps featuring Susan B. Anthony in 1936 and 1955, and one featuring Stanton, Mott, and Catt in 1948. And in 1979 the Susan B. Anthony dollar appeared.

This concern for official forms of commemoration, like the written histories, began with NAWSA leaders themselves. To insure the position of first-generation heroes and NAWSA's connection to them, the organization hired a sculptor to create portrait busts. Adelaide Johnson of Illinois made busts of Susan B. Anthony and Elizabeth Cady Stanton after visiting with them, and she created a bust of Lucretia Mott from a photograph. But, when Johnson delivered her products, NAWSA officials were displeased with the work and placed it in storage. It remained there until Alice Paul of the National Woman's Party (NWP) got permission to use the rejected statues and spoke to Johnson about donating them to the Capitol. Instead of deeding these busts to the NWP, Johnson decided to go to Italy for Carrara marble to make a new statue that depicts the three suffrage pioneers, with Lucretia Mott in front, followed by Elizabeth Cady Stanton and Susan B. Anthony. An unfinished portion of marble at the back of the statue represents women leaders of the future.

Today, when visitors see this statue at the Capitol, they may wonder about this blank piece of marble at the back. When they read that the statue was donated by Alice Paul and the National Woman's Party, this name and this group may draw a similar blank. In fact, in the accepted history of the American campaign for woman's suffrage, Alice Paul is the undelineated one, a woman whose story has never been fully incorporated into the official two-part version of the campaign for the vote.

During the years in which Paul worked for a federal amendment, 1912 to 1920, she was certainly not an unknown advocate. Instead, she was perhaps the one securing the most national attention. To this campaign she brought a superior education in political reform. She grew up in Moorestown, New

The portrait monument. Sculptor Adelaide Johnson, Dora Lewis of the NWP, and Jane Addams posing in front of the statue of pioneer suffragists in the U.S. Capitol.

Jersey, a small Quaker community, and before she came to Washington, she graduated from Swarthmore College, obtained masters and doctoral degrees in political science at the University of Pennsylvania, and studied in England at the Woodbrooke Quaker Study Centre and the London School of Economics. In London, she also worked with the Pankhursts and their

Women's Social and Political Union (WSPU), planning meetings, questioning politicians, and hunger striking in jail to contribute to the English campaign for suffrage.

From the time that she moved to Washington, in December of 1912, Alice Paul devoted all of her time to achieving a federal amendment, which she thought was the most direct route to suffrage for American women. With Jane Addams's help, she talked NAWSA into appointing her as head of an inactive subcommittee charged with introducing a federal suffrage amendment in the legislature each year, something that had been a ceremonial function because NAWSA was emphasizing state-by-state campaigns. Instead of accepting that limited goal, Paul created an active Congressional Committee in 1913, formed a Congressional Union (CU) later that same year to expand her campaign throughout the nation, separated her group from NAWSA in 1914, and then instituted a National Woman's Party in 1916. The NWP first involved members from states where women could vote but later involved women from all states, working together to achieve a federal amendment. Although many suffragists preferred state work, Paul insisted that her organizations' only focus would be the plainly written Susan B. Anthony Amendment: "Article—Section 1. The right of citizens of the United States to vote shall not be denied or abridged by the United States or any State on account of sex. Section 2. Congress shall have power, by appropriate legislation, to enforce the provisions of this article." This legislation would signal the country's recognition of women's equal status, in all states, for all elections, concerning all issues.

As head of these organizations formed to achieve a federal amendment, Paul planned a series of actions that shocked the government, the press, and even fellow suffragists. In states where women had the vote, her adherents conducted boycott campaigns against Wilson and other Democrats because this majority party opposed a federal amendment. In Washington, they lobbied legislators each day, picketed the White House and the Capitol, burned Wilson's speeches on democracy, and then burned him in effigy. As the prison sentences resulting from these actions stretched from a day to seven months, with Paul placed in a psychiatric ward to demonstrate—or cause—her mental instability, these women chose to initiate hunger strikes that led to force-feeding, with tubes shoved down their mouths and noses. On one "Night of Terror," November 15, 1917, they were beaten, pulled down halls by their hair, and handcuffed to beds.

As suffrage moved toward passage, newspapers recognized these women's sacrifice and their impact on the nation's politicians and public. J. D. Barry in the *New York Telegram* wrote on May 17, 1918, that "The militant wing of the Suffragists has performed a big service. But for its enterprise and daring suffrage would not have had nearly so wide a publicity during the past few years or made nearly so urgent an appeal." The *Cambden* (New Jersey) *Courier* said of these women: "They have made it their business to stir things up. Anything from a street row to a riot was to be regarded as good advertising for the cause. And they certainly 'put it over,' for it was they who helped put through the House of Representatives the resolution calling for a suffrage amendment to the Constitution" ("Honor Badge"). Even the antisuffragist *New York Times* chronicled their jail experiences daily and admitted that Alice Paul's willingness to die in jail had changed the nation's opinion of suffrage and suffragists ("Force Yard of Jail"). And Carrie Chapman Catt, who disapproved of Paul's aggressive tactics, was willing to admit privately, to her state suffrage association presidents, that "there is no doubt but that the Congressional Union has pushed the Federal Amendment to the front, no matter what anybody says about it" (Letter to Presidents).

As soon as the amendment was ratified, however, Paul began to recede from the public construction of the suffrage campaign. She did not seek to have her own story told, as did Mott, Stanton, Anthony, Catt, and Shaw. Instead she immediately turned her attention to an Equal Rights Amendment, the official version of which she authored in 1923. Paul was not interested in providing the details of her suffrage campaign, and no other group had a reason to do so. She represented what was always a minority of suffrage advocates; her story disparaged both Democrats and Republicans and revealed dirty truths about American police and jails as well as the president. The official removal of her story was in fact beginning before the campaign ended. When Wilson finally advocated suffrage as a war measure in Congress in September of 1918, he insisted that "the voices of foolish and intemperate agitators do not reach me at all," castigating the NWP even as he took the action that it had sought so fervently. When Secretary of State Bainbridge Colby signed the amendment into law at his home on August 26, 1920, he denied Paul's requests that her representatives be present.

It has been within only the last twenty years that historians have begun to reconsider the established version of the suffrage campaign as solely Anthony's and NAWSA's story. Two books, Christine A. Lunardini's *From Equal Suffrage to Equal Rights: Alice Paul and the National Woman's Party, 1910–1928* (1986) and Linda Ford's *Iron-Jawed Angels: The Suffrage Militancy of the National Woman's Party, 1912–1920* (1991), provide a fuller picture of the NWP's activities. A recent HBO film, *Iron-Jawed Angels,* directed by Katia von Garnier and written by Sally Robinson, depicted the activism of Alice Paul and her comrade Lucy Burns.

With the party and Paul beginning to secure attention, it is time for a thorough consideration of her campaign theory and practice. To further fill in the blank space of Alice Paul, this book will consider two intertwined features of her suffrage campaign: her reliance on nonviolence and her use of visual rhetoric.

Like the *New York Telegram* reporter in 1918 and Linda Ford in 1991, many writers have labeled Paul as "militant," and she has frequently been compared to the Pankhursts and the WSPU, a group for whom militancy included violence to persons and property. But Paul was a Quaker, and her goal was to establish a campaign grounded in nonviolence. Led by her own religion, she established the first successful nonviolent campaign for social reform in the United States, experimenting with the same techniques that Gandhi employed in South Africa and India. In the early years of the eighteenth century, Quaker William Penn had difficulty attempting to enact nonviolent principles in a large, contentious colony with American Indians on its borders; William Lloyd Garrison and many Quakers ultimately abandoned nonviolent principles and supported both John Brown's actions at Harper's Ferry and civil war. Paul, however, steadfastly relied on the principles of nonviolence, even when her colleagues in England abandoned this methodology and other American suffragists allowed World War I to dictate contrary choices. The many histories of nonviolent campaigns do not mention Paul, but she adhered to that ideology, one involving not just pacifism but a concern for instigating change by first effecting it within an organization's members and a belief in the equality of the activist and the established power.[1]

The book's second, related focus concerns the type of campaign Paul instigated to enact these principles. When Paul surveyed the American suffrage scene after she returned from England in 1910, she felt that she was encountering a bankrupt movement, its older leaders dead and its state campaigns failing. As she indicated in letters to fellow suffragists, she thought that NAWSA's reliance on writing and speaking—on journals, letters, pamphlets, meetings, and conferences—would never succeed. Instead, along with planning for speeches and meetings, she mounted a dramatic visual campaign, involving photographs, cartoons, parades, boycotts, car and train trips, picketing, and hunger striking in jail. For a small group of women to reach a large nation, she believed, there must be daily actions that symbolized their intelligence, independence, and responsibility—their right to be voting citizens. She intended this nonviolent visual rhetoric, writ large by the press coverage it engendered, not only to appeal to emotions such as pity, love, and fear but to create a persuasive logical argument concerning the rights of citizens and the attributes of women.

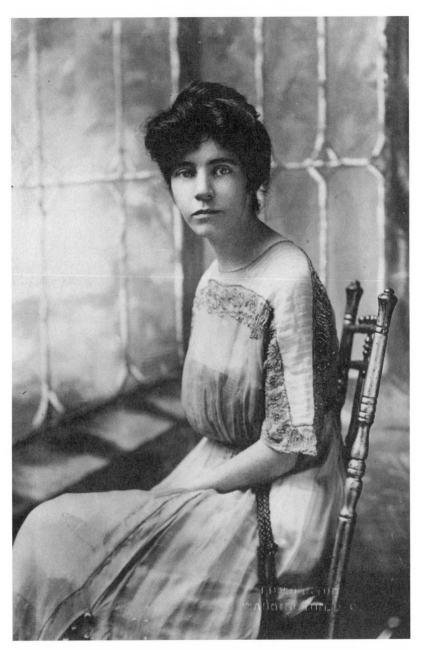

Alice Paul. Circa 1915.

The term *visual rhetoric* has been recently featured in books, journal articles, and conference papers because it gives scholars a means of looking at the persuasive techniques involved in Web sites, business reports, advertising, museum displays, political campaigns, television coverage of war, and film and video.[2] Although definitions of this term vary, it generally refers to the persuasive impact of visual images in combination with the written and spoken word. Thus it stems from Kenneth Burke's definition of rhetoric as both verbal and non-verbal discourse, "symbolic action" that is designed to elicit a "response." Its successful use frequently involves what Chaim Perelman and Lucie Olbrechts-Tyteca discuss as creating a physical "presence" at a point of conflict, a method referred to as "witnessing" in the Quaker tradition (116–18). It may also involve the presentation of vivid information, of positive values, of cultural icons, and of striking comparisons (Hill, Foss). In Alice Paul's campaign, we encounter an unprecedented expert use of such varied visual rhetoric, one intended, at different times and for different audiences, to engage, to shock, to thrill, to shame, to pressure, and to convince. And this rhetoric, involving the communication possibilities of the new century, drew its power from principles of nonviolence: Paul repeatedly used all available means to place her group at the scene of conflict, where they could use their bodies to literally "stand up" against degradation, inequality, and violence.

To create a full picture of Alice Paul's theory and practice, the chapters that follow first consider her training in nonviolence and then turn to the specifics of her campaign to change the United States. The first chapter focuses on her early life—the foundations of her rhetoric in her Quaker upbringing, in her education, and in her association with the Pankhursts. A discussion of nonviolence follows to place Paul within that powerful reform tradition. Then subsequent chapters consider the various forms of visual rhetoric Paul employed and the rationale behind them, from traditional methods to the very controversial, through which she created her own highly influential version of nonviolent activism, one that exploited new forms of mass persuasion to forge a new status for women.

Notes

1. In *Nonviolent Power: Active and Passive Resistance in America* (1972), Judith Stiehm argues that between William Lloyd Garrison and Martin Luther King, "the doctrine of nonviolence might be said to have been on a one-hundred-year leave of absence from the United States while it affected Russia and Europe through Tolstoy and Asia through Gandhi" (6). In *The Handbook of Non-Violence* (1986), Robert Seeley traces a line from Thoreau to Gandhi to Martin Luther King (208, 300). James C. Juhnke and Carol M. Hunter's 2001 book with the seeming all-inclusive title of *The Missing Peace: The Search*

for Nonviolent Alternatives in United States History covers the abolition movement, labor strikes, and civil rights, but excludes Paul.

2. A recent book provides definitions and an overview of research on visual rhetoric: Charles A. Hill and Marguerite Helmers, *Defining Visual Rhetorics* (2004). Various articles also provide specific applications: for example, of the rhetoric of digital environments (Hocks), photojournalism (Lucaites and Hariman), war memorials (Taylor), political theatre (Demo), and presidential campaigns (Kiewe).

1. Alice Paul's Formation as Activist

In December of 1912, Alice Paul boarded a train in Philadelphia to move to Washington, D.C. She was on her way there to represent the National American Woman Suffrage Association (NAWSA) in Congress as chair of its Congressional Committee and thus as its official advocate of a federal suffrage amendment. At age twenty-seven, she went alone, with no place secured either to live or to work, and with a ten-dollar budget from NAWSA and an agreement that she would not ask for more. The association had been loath to trust her with this job; only Jane Addams's argument for her selection had curbed President Anna Howard Shaw's objections to this too young and too militant woman who had been jailed in England with the Pankhursts. (One contemporary journalist commented on this hesitancy, "Above all, Dr. Shaw wanted no wildness in her ranks" [Faber 126].) Starting that December, at a time when the suffrage effort was in a stagnant period following the deaths of leaders Lucy Stone, Elizabeth Cady Stanton, and Susan B. Anthony, and the failure of many state campaigns, Paul began to mount her own nonviolent campaign, one involving a visual rhetoric shaped by her Quaker upbringing, her extensive education, and her suffrage experience in England.

Alice Paul's Quaker Roots

Alice Stokes Paul traced her background on both sides to Quakers who had worked for governmental reform. "I have practically no ancestor who wasn't a Quaker," she declared in a 1972/1973 interview with oral historian Amelia Fry: "My father and mother were, and their fathers and mothers were." On her mother's side, one English ancestor was William Crispin, who helped

William Penn with plans for a Quaker colony in the new world (Dunn and Dunn 47). On her father's side, Hannah Feake became a Quaker minister and married fellow Quaker John Bowne of New York in 1656. Hearing that the Bownes were holding Quaker meetings in their home, Governor Stuyvesant had John arrested and banished to Holland, where he was able to convince the Estates General to force an end to this interference with religious freedom; Hannah conducted secret meetings during his absence and later worked with her husband to involve others in their faith (*Flushing Remonstrance*).

By the time of Alice Paul's birth, her staunchly Quaker family, proud of its activist past, had been in New Jersey and Pennsylvania for many generations. She was born on January 11, 1885, in Moorestown, New Jersey, a Quaker village in Burlington County about fourteen miles from Philadelphia across the Delaware River. Her father, William M. Paul, owned a large farm there and was president of the Burlington County Trust Company. As a farmer and banker, he adhered to long traditions within the Society of Friends, who in seventeenth- and eighteenth-century England had often combined farm income with business employment because they could not take government jobs or pursue a university education to support their families (Vipont 146–47). During Paul's childhood, Moorestown had two congregations or "meetings," one for the more traditional, rural, and separatist Hicksite group and one for the more modern and urban Orthodox group. As a family of farmers and traditional Quakers, the Pauls were Hicksites, putting emphasis on inner strength, a separate community, and quietism, a calm and reserved approach to everyday life.

As confirmed Hicksites living in a Quaker village, the Pauls followed Quaker traditions in their home, community life, and educational choices. Like their neighbors, they dressed plainly, used *thee* and *thou* in their speech, and had no music in their home. The family went to the local Hicksite meeting each Sunday, and the children attended the Hicksite Friends school on Chester Avenue, which had built a new brick building in 1880 and opened the area's first kindergarten in 1883. This thriving school encouraged serious habits of reading and reflection, which led Paul to the library the school shared with the meeting: "And I read just endlessly, ceaselessly, almost every book it seems! We had a Friends library there in the meeting house, and I took out every book in the library" (Fry).

In this small world of home, school, and meeting, Paul was imbued with the tenets of the Quaker faith. The Society had begun in England over two hundred years earlier when George Fox, in 1647, began preaching the doctrine of "Christ within" or "inner light." Fox traveled throughout England, forming small groups that chose to abandon traditional forms of worship and concentrate on "the pure knowledge of God and of Christ alone, without the help of any man, book or writing." These groups vested power not in clergy, religious rituals, or stories of the historical Jesus, but in personal experience of the Holy Spirit or the inner light, a transforming form of communion that silent reflection made possible (*Faith and Practice* 1).

At the earliest meetings of Fox's adherents, as in the Moorestown meeting Paul's family attended, members were encouraged to make the choice of a "testimony" or reform goal, which George Fox described in 1656 as being "valiant for the Truth upon earth" (*Faith and Practice* 7). To follow the true path of Jesus, members would endeavor to improve the lives of their fellows, changing the temporal world by their work for social justice. The Quaker testimony thus provided "a way of redeeming the world," not "a ladder for climbing out of it" (W. R. Miller 27). In this quest for justice, the means would be every bit as crucial as the end. For Quakers, the one right means was "witnessing," as Fox defined it: "Be patterns, be examples in all countries, places, islands, nations, wherever you come; that your carriage and life may preach among all sorts of people, and to them" (*Faith and Practice* 7). Real change, Fox advised, would be accomplished not by arguing, intimidating, or controlling. Instead, the Quaker's actions would serve as an example on which others might focus their own inner light and energy. "Being-with-others" through daily work—in an urban neighborhood, for example, or in a clinic, business, or home—would demonstrate respect and provide help while enabling a group to plan larger efforts that would reap larger benefits.

This Quaker emphasis on service and a serious life purpose influenced all of Paul's siblings. Alice was the oldest of four children. Her younger sister Helen graduated from Wellesley, where she became a "student volunteer," a member of an organization that trained young people for foreign service. After graduation, she attempted to join a group of missionaries headed to China, following a Quaker path forged by Robert John Davidson and Mary J. Davidson in 1886, but she was too young (Vipont 214–15). Instead, she went to the University of Pennsylvania for graduate study in Chinese to further prepare herself for a trip abroad. But while she was at the university, she became interested in Christian Science and eventually founded a Christian Science church in Moorestown. The younger of Paul's brothers, Parry, went to the University of Wisconsin to study engineering and then joined the Friends Service Committee to teach the use of tractors to the Russians, participating in a tradition of Friends' activism in Russia that had begun when Quakers William Allen and Stephen Grellet traveled there in 1818 to work in educational and agricultural reform movements (Vipont 194). Only brother

William missed this dedication to religious reform and instead served community and family needs. After studying at Rutgers College and the Cornell School of Agriculture, he inherited part of his father's farmland and served on the board of directors of the bank, taking over management of the family's financial interests after his father's death, a more restricted but still crucial form of Quaker service.

Besides asking for a commitment to a testimony and to witnessing, the Quaker tradition, as established by Fox and his wife Margaret Fell and practiced by the Pauls, included a commitment to women's equality. At sessions held every two weeks in most congregations, women discussed church accounts and records, philanthropic efforts, and the proper behavior of members. Quakers believed this organizational structure encouraged women's rhetorical openness and activism and thus expanded their influence in the larger group. Women also became traveling ministers, going out to faraway sites to interact with established groups and to form new meetings, often at great physical risk. These traveling ministers joined in the silent services and met with members afterwards, generally to offer organizational help and to share their personal commitments rather than to formally preach or lecture (Bacon, *Mothers of Feminism* 7, 23).

This women's rights tradition within Quakerism, so influential to Alice Paul, had flourished in the United States from the colonial period. In 1656, Englishwomen Mary Fisher and Ann Austin landed in Boston, and Elizabeth Harris traveled to Virginia to share the Quaker message. Throughout the eighteenth century, women from the colonies traveled to Europe, taking great risks to interact with other Quakers. Susanna Morris of Bucks County, Pennsylvania, for example, made three trips to England, during which she was shipwrecked three times. Charity Cook, Sarah Harrison, and Mary Swett went to prison in Friedberg, Germany, in 1798, for attempting to hold a Quaker meeting there (Bacon, *Mothers of Feminism* 37). These women left home alone and in groups, with men and without, with a "traveling minute" or authorization from their local meetings.

Although most Quaker women married, singleness did not carry a negative connotation for Quaker women involved in service and reform. Unmarried Quakers were well represented among women activists, social workers, doctors, scientists, and entrepreneurs. In 1895 Lillian Wald established the Nurses' Settlement house at 225 Henry Street in New York City (Stoneburner 46–47). In the same time period, Anna Elizabeth Broomall worked as an obstetrician and medical educator; Mary Elizabeth Garrett endowed colleges that, frequently under pressure as at Johns Hopkins Medical School, provided education opportunities for women as well as men; M. Carey Thomas served as president of Bryn Mawr College; and Grace Abbott helped administrate the federal Children's Bureau and became a specialist in child labor law.

Swarthmore

By the time Alice Paul finished high school, she had become attracted to the choice of a single life imbued with a meaningful testimony that would improve women's lives, but finding a more specific goal and means would take several years. At age sixteen, in 1901, she enrolled at Swarthmore College, a Quaker school that her mother's father had helped to found and that her mother, Tacie Parry Paul, attended before her marriage. It was named for Margaret Fell's home in England, which had served as a meeting spot for the Society's earliest members.

Philadelphia Hicksite Friends founded the college in 1869 as one of the first to offer equal educational opportunities to men and women (Walton 4–5). From its beginning, the school endeavored to isolate young Quakers from the outside world, providing a setting where they could develop their own inner light (Enion 74). Its founders felt that this combination of a separate space and a rigorous education would prepare graduates to form testimonies that would help shape their nation. The school especially stressed science education to equip students with the tools for contributing to an industrializing America, a more modern and practical approach to undergraduate education than was occurring in many older private colleges. From its beginning, Swarthmore continued to grow and build, from eighty-two students in 1880 to 163 in 1890, while maintaining the small average class size (of just 10.5) that enabled students to interact with the faculty and their classmates and thus forge their own meaningful futures (Walton 13; Enion 82). In Paul's sophomore year, the school initiated a particularly noteworthy period of formation when Joseph Swain from Indiana University became its president, hired more and better faculty members, launched a building program, and further enlarged the student body.

While Alice Paul attended this Quaker college, she considered several choices that might define her future. Paul chose biology for her major because this subject provided an intellectual challenge, but she did not find her answer by studying biology. Like most other women students of the time, she then imagined that her calling might be teaching, making a difference by modeling positive values and intellectual discipline for young people. In fact, most female Swarthmore graduates, whatever their major, worked as teachers, at least until they married and had children: "over 80 percent of the women graduates and about 7 percent of the men from 1869–89" chose this path (Enion 79–80). But Paul viewed this career as filled with the daily frustrations of repetitive lessons, uninspired pupils, and intellectual loneliness; she was not convinced that her involvement in this profession could lead to any real change in society. She thought that teaching might have to be her future, but she felt less than thrilled at the prospect.

During her senior year, Professor Robert Clarkson Brooks sent her in a new direction—into the service work that also inspired Helen and Parry Paul. Brooks, one of the new hires made by President Swain, taught a seminar-style course in political science and economics that offered her "a great joy" during that year (Fry). Then thirty years old, Brooks had finished his dissertation at Cornell University the year before and was involved in sociological research on urban life. His publications included an 1890 study of the age of marriage in slums and nonslums, research that concentrated on the effect of poverty on a woman's choices. In his senior seminars, he established a close group that he expected to question America's received truths about class and gender, following a tradition of advanced work which, as Brooks wrote, Joseph Swain was trying to establish across campus: "Even for a small college there was close contact and cordial good feeling to an unusual degree between instructors and students, especially in advanced courses. Most important of all, the faculty was by no means satisfied by the progress already achieved, and individual experiments with groups of five or six advanced students, somewhat similar to honors work, were being made in several departments" (Walton 29).

At the end of the year, Brooks helped Paul to avoid the teaching profession and establish her own path of activism by nominating her for a fellowship from the College Settlement Association of America. Paul thus spent 1905–1906 at a settlement located at 95 Rivington Street in New York City. The College Settlement Association had been founded in 1887 by graduates of Smith, Bryn Mawr, and Wellesley, including Jean Fine, Helen Rand, and Vida Scudder. Within a few years, women from Swarthmore, Radcliffe, Brooklyn's Packer Institute, and Barnard had become residents at settlement houses in New York, Boston, Philadelphia, and other cities. To provide "uplifting influences" in the slums of New York as in the other cities, these college graduates established homes that could serve as meeting centers for local residents, especially young working women and mothers. These women were divided up into "clubs" and given instruction in homemaking skills, in the arts of singing, gymnastics, and dancing, and in high school subjects (Garbus).

From Rivington Street to Woodbrooke

What Paul found appealing at Rivington Street was the actual interaction—the opportunity for Quaker witnessing—that the work entailed. But a year there made clear to her the limitations of such philanthropy. "I knew in a very short time I was never going to be a social worker," she later recalled, "because I could see that social workers were not doing much good in the world . . . you knew you couldn't change the situation by social work" (Fry). She began viewing such charitable involvements as a stopgap that did not alter inequities and that, in fact, might be viewed as participation in a corrupt system. As a Quaker seeking her own testimony, she wanted to participate in changing the system, not just ameliorating or masking its worst results.

As Paul would do throughout her life, she immediately sought the education that could further elucidate the problems of the practical work on which she had embarked. When she began settlement work, she also enrolled in the School of Philanthropy, now the School of Social Work, at Columbia University, a certificate program from which she graduated in 1906. Then, not only to learn practical techniques of working with the poor but instead to study the institutional structures that created their plight, she enrolled at the University of Pennsylvania in the fall of 1906. Studying political science, sociology, and economics, she received a master's degree in the fall of 1907.

After completing these two graduate programs, Paul sought more training in the Quaker path of activism. She applied for a scholarship to the Woodbrooke Quaker Study Centre in England, where she enrolled in the fall of 1907. Woodbrooke, the former home of Sir George Cadbury, had become a Quaker center in 1903. Its founders felt that, as young Friends secured an education to enter professions, they were abandoning the traditional commitment to a personal testimony and thus to activism. John Willem Rowntree, one of these founders, expected this school to answer a key question for the future: "How can we maintain a free ministry among busy men who feel the exacting toll of increasing commercial competition?" (Wood, "Origins" 17).

When Paul attended in 1907, Woodbrooke had forty-one students of different ages and nationalities. The group, of whom over a third were women, had silent devotion each morning, then lectures and community-forming games. The short courses, without exams or elaborate syllabi, covered Quaker history and the Bible; current laws, economic trends, and moral codes that a Quaker might be required to analyze and change; and the best practical means of enabling that change. The Director of Studies, Rufus Harris, "was resolved that Woodbrooke should not be an introverted Quaker institution" but a place from which new, influential styles of living would emanate (Wood, "First Director of Studies" 29).

While Paul was at Woodbrooke furthering her knowledge of Quaker approaches to social activism, she took courses at the University of Birmingham to continue her study of the social sciences. During 1908 and 1909 she also attended the School of Economics in London. There, Paul heard lectures by

Sidney and Beatrice Webb, who had started the school in 1894 to further the Fabian Society's "evolutionary rather than revolutionary" approach to socialism (Radice 56). Sydney Webb had been conducting research and was giving lectures on the inequality of wages in England; Beatrice Webb had been studying women's plight in factory sweatshops and was then a member of a Royal Commission formed to revise the 1834 Poor Law, work that she discussed frequently with students. Echoing a conclusion that Paul had made on Rivington Street, Beatrice Webb declared that she wanted "to stem the tide of philanthropic impulse" and focus attention instead on the social change possible only through equal legal status for all citizens (Radice 161).

At the London School, Paul also studied with Edward Westermarck, a Dutch anthropologist whose *The History of Human Marriage* (1891) and *The Origin and Development of the Moral Ideas* (2 vols., 1908 and 1912) focused on the temporal and need-based nature of supposedly fixed cultural values. Concerning marriage, for example, he demonstrated the variability of rules governing the appropriate age, the approved number of wives, the significance of promiscuity, and the stigma of separation or divorce. In his books and class lectures, he also examined the disparity among accepted definitions of a good or desirable woman. He argued that in some primitive cultures women were ceded more respect for their intellectual and physical abilities than were women in civilized cultures, in which the decreased need for women's labor had led to desirability being vested in "a slight, dainty, and relatively feeble creature." His analysis especially concentrated on the Victorian vision of a silent woman sitting pristinely in a well-appointed drawing room: delicate beauty, he argued, was the main signifier of her marital and even her moral superiority. In examining changing expectations for women, Westermarck noted that "in every society the traditional notions as to what is good or bad, obligatory or indifferent, are commonly accepted by the mass of people without further reflection." But a "scrutinising and enlightened judge," what Paul herself was endeavoring to become, could analyze and reject social mores since they were not eternal or god-given values even if they seemed so to the unquestioning majority (*History of Human Marriage* 661).

While she was taking classes at Woodbrooke, Birmingham, and the London School of Economics, Paul returned to social work because it provided a place to stay and an income, but these experiences only confirmed the misgivings she had at Rivington Street. She first lived in the Quaker-run Summer Lane Settlement in Birmingham, and then in a settlement house in London's impoverished Dalston area. Again, and like Beatrice Webb, she viewed philanthropic efforts as too little, too late: "My main impression of poverty work was the hopelessness of it all. . . . It seems we were always burying children" (Fry).

The Pankhursts

Paul found no new meaning in charity work in London, but it was there that she would ultimately embark on another form of testimony. It began when she attended a rally led by Christabel Pankhurst on the subject of votes for women. During this speech at the University of Birmingham, the men in the audience shouted Pankhurst down. Although she finally finished her talk, the other speakers could not continue, and the meeting ended in chaos. As Paul would soon learn, such abuse of suffragists was occurring all over England. Press stories commonly reported, and added to, the cruel epithets hurled at these activists: they were "warped old maids," "destroyers of the family," "the shrieking sisterhood," "viragoes," and "disappointed cast-offs of the marriage market" (Ramelson 171).

As Paul began studying the English suffrage campaign, she recognized that it involved women who, instead of accepting or ameliorating the status quo, were taking risks each day to advocate legal and social change. She felt an immediate attraction: "You know if you feel some group that's your group is the underdog you want to try to help; it's natural I guess for everybody. . . . When I saw this outbreak of hostility, I thought, 'That's one group now I want to throw in all the strength I can give to help'. . . . She [Christabel Pankhurst] and the other young women who spoke with her—they were all three young girls—they had anyway one heart and soul convert—I don't know how many others they had. That was myself" (Fry). Under Christabel Pankhurst's influence, Paul became a "heart and soul convert" not to the ideal of suffrage, which she had always believed in, but to daily involvement in the campaign. Her church and her family endorsed the right of women to vote: "I know my father believed and my mother believed in and supported the suffrage movement, and I remember my mother taking me to suffrage meetings held in the home of a Quaker family that lived not far from us." But only now did she view suffrage as the issue that could lead her beyond social work and academic study to systemic reform: "It was one thing that had to be done, I guess that's how I thought" (Fry). The struggle for suffrage, Paul recognized, could enable poor as well as rich women to alter their own situations, to become citizens who would not need anybody's charity. Suffrage would be her one testimony, her means of achieving social reform, for which her knowledge of political science, economics, legal rights, and Quaker activism prepared her well.

To learn more about this issue and the English campaign, Paul quickly joined the Women's Social and Political Union (WSPU) and started attending weekly meetings. Through this suffrage association, she was able to contribute her efforts immediately while also evaluating an array of rhetorical strategies that she could employ in the United States. The WSPU had started in Manchester as a local unit of the Women's Franchise League, an established suffrage organization. When Emmeline Pankhurst, Christabel's mother, moved to London and into a large home on Russell Square in 1889, she began holding meetings there to protest the league's lack of activity and its exclusion of married women from its bid for suffrage. Pankhurst's separate WSPU, founded in 1903, worked to achieve voting rights for all women through a more aggressive campaign supported by a growing number of dedicated activists or "suffragettes," as these radical adherents were soon dubbed by the press. During the elections of 1905–06, the WSPU began a long-term policy of opposing the candidates of the party in power, regardless of its general platform, since no English party then supported the extension of the franchise to women. In February 1907, on the day after Parliament opened, the organization hired Caxton Hall for meetings of what would become a regular "Woman's Parliament," where members discussed strategy and from which they marched to the House of Commons for protest meetings. In 1907–08, the WSPU estimated that it organized more than five thousand small and large meetings. In 1908, for a huge Chelsea demonstration, seven thousand women marched in white to Hyde Park, with 250,000 spectators watching. These public events often led to arrests and prison terms and thus to more press coverage of the cause. In 1906–07, suffragist imprisonments totaled 191 weeks; in 1907–08, 350 weeks (E. S. Pankhurst, *Suffragette Movement* 223, 275–85).

As Paul became involved with this dedicated group, she worried about her own ability to make a meaningful contribution. She felt then, as she did in college and throughout her life, that public speaking was not her greatest strength. At Swarthmore, she had a small role in a performance of *Hamlet*. She also joined the debating team, through which she met Mabel Vernon, who later worked diligently with Paul as an officer of the Congressional Union (CU) and the National Woman's Party (NWP). When Paul was chosen Ivy Poet and thus had to read an original composition at commencement, "with all the alumni present and all the college present," she wrote the poem with the help of a teacher. Then she turned to Mabel for help with the harder part of this requirement: "So then I thought, 'Well, I've done all I can on composing, and now the awful problem, with my complete lack of oratorical knowledge or any oratorical power, how will I deliver it outdoors to all these people?' So then I went to Mabel Vernon. . . . And I said, 'Now will you train me so I can deliver my poem?' So she undertook very religiously to have me practice and practice and practice my poem. So when the day came—I think she had gotten me up to a point where probably people could hear me—and this great audience [was there, and] I gave my little Ivy Poem" (Fry).

In London, Paul's sense of inadequacy continued as she approached the daunting task of daily one-to-one confrontations on the streets. At the School of Economics, she met Rachel Barrett, an ardent worker for the WSPU, who asked Paul to join her in selling the suffrage magazine *Votes for Women* on the street. Given the public animosity toward the suffrage campaign, this was indeed a difficult form of one-to-one persuasion. The suffragist often had to stand in the gutter to avoid being arrested on the charge of obstruction of the pavement; elderly men yelled out "sex filth"; factory workers threw rotten fruits and vegetables (Richardson 11–13). When Paul accompanied Barrett, she found this method of direct appeal quite frightening: "I remember how very bold and good she was and how very timid and unsuccessful I was, standing beside her trying to ask people to buy *Votes for Women*. So contrary to my nature really. I didn't seem to be very brave by nature" (Fry).

In these first outings with the WSPU, Paul continued to question not only her skill at one-to-one persuasion but also at speaking before a large group. Recounting a meeting in Bermondsey where the WSPU protested the antisuf-frage stance of Lloyd George, Chancellor of the Exchequer, Paul remembered her fear of mounting a platform and addressing a crowd. Each person who got up to speak was instantly arrested, "so when it came my time to get up and make a speech, my heart was calm because I knew I wouldn't have to make the terrible speech, which was the thing that worried me more than anything else. So I was immediately arrested. And that's the first time I was in prison" (Fry). On that night, Paul clearly preferred arrest to public speaking.

Although recognizing her own limitations, Paul began to see that real persuasive power did not always stem from the traditional public speaking that she preferred to avoid. She clearly saw that a great speaker could stir an audience to action. At a large procession in Hyde Park, for example, the speech given by Lady Emmeline Pethick-Lawrence confirmed her respect for strong verbal rhetoric: "I was standing there right at her feet. Just by chance. I didn't know where I was going. . . . And I was *thrilled* beyond *words* by this *marvelous* speech. She was a great, great speaker I thought." But in Bermondsey, the event's effect lay not in the words spoken, but in the crowd's seeing each woman stand forth and face arrest before she could utter a word, a visual demonstration of civil rights denied, one in which Paul participated without speaking: "Imagine I, knowing hardly anything about speaking at all! . . . But I learned then that you didn't have to be an eloquent speaker as I thought you might have to be and I knew I would never be" (Fry). As Paul participated in more WSPU events, she was quickly exposed to other scenes of dramatically staged action. With one hundred other women, she marched as part of a deputation to see Prime Minister Herbert Henry Asquith. Emmeline

Pankhurst led the procession through the streets of London from Caxton Hall to Parliament; there the marchers were stopped, arrested, and loaded in police vans before a large protesting crowd. At this stirring event, Paul met Lucy Burns, a suffragist activist who would become her companion throughout the entire campaign in the United States. Born in Brooklyn, Burns graduated from Vassar in 1902, studied at Yale in 1902–03 and at the University of Berlin in 1908–09, and joined the WSPU in London in 1909 to help with the English effort but also to prepare for a role in the American campaign (Bland 6–7). At this event, Paul and Burns together witnessed the persuasive effect of visual rhetoric.

During Paul's further involvement with the Pankhursts, with Lucy Burns joining her, she moved beyond serving as one of a large group of demonstrators and began organizing events and campaign offices. When Emmeline Pankhurst went to Scotland to expand the movement there, Paul and Burns accompanied her as assistants. They set up a headquarters in Edinburgh and planned a procession there featuring beautiful costumes and music, with a well-publicized tableau that brought out viewers who might have ignored a program of speeches. They then moved out to Dundee and other towns, recruiting supporters who could form local networks and plan their own visual events. When Winston Churchill, then a cabinet member and president of the board of trade, held a meeting in Dundee, they protested outside along with local women who were learning about direct political action.

After serving as a member of the group and as an organizer, Paul began to take the rhetorical lead in symbolic actions. From their headquarters in Edinburgh, suffragists made plans for accosting Sir Edward Grey, a member of the cabinet and minister of foreign affairs, as he spoke at Berwick-upon-Tweed, a town on the border with England. For a week they met in small groups on street corners to acquaint people with why they were protesting against this cabinet member. At the meeting, as Grey discussed the government's proposed legislation that would lead to future prosperity, Paul stood up as planned and said, "Well, these are very wonderful ideals, but couldn't you extend them to women?" As the suffragists expected, the police immediately took her by the arms and led her out of the meeting, walking her through the streets to the police station where she was arrested, with a large audience of townspeople viewing this public silencing. This well-planned visual rhetoric led to the desired outcome: an increase in press coverage and in public sympathy.

At subsequent events, Paul took even greater risks to use symbolic action to expose the government's perfidy and the plight of women. On August 20, 1909, Lord Crewe, Liberal Party member of the House of Lords, spoke at St. Andrew's Hall in Glasgow. Before the police guards came on duty, Paul

Lucy Burns. Photo printed in the *Suffragist*, Dec. 25, 1915.

climbed to the roof of the building in the hope of speaking from there to those who would be standing outside waiting for the meeting to begin. When she was discovered and the police forced her to descend, she was cheered by a crowd of spectators and workmen, one of whom explained that he had called the police only because he thought she needed help. Later the women tried to force their way into the hall, with the crowd's help, but officers used truncheons to beat them back. When the police attempted to make arrests, "the women were rescued from their clutches again and again" by sympathetic bystanders. Eventually Emmeline Pankhurst's daughter Adela, along with Margaret Smith, Lucy Burns, and Paul was taken into custody, but the crowds outside the police station continued to shout for their release (E. S. Pankhurst, *Suffragette* 416–17). All parts of this scene were reported in newspapers and repeated in WSPU meetings to emphasize the women's dedication and their current position, on the roof and in the jail, as political outsiders.

When these suffragists returned to London, they continued their well-planned confrontations between women and the government that did not represent them. On November 9, 1909, Lord Mayor's Day, when the Lord Mayor of London was having a banquet in the Guild Hall for cabinet ministers, Alice Paul again led the WSPU's response. She and Amelia Brown disguised themselves as cleaning women and, carrying buckets and brushes, entered the building with the rest of the staff at 9:00 a.m. They hid themselves until evening and then "took their stand" in the gallery outside the Banqueting Hall. When Prime Minister Asquith was about to speak, Brown broke a pane of stained glass with her shoe to get attention, and they both cried out "votes for women." Both were arrested and sent to prison for one month's hard labor when they refused to pay fines and damages.

As Emmeline Pankhurst directed, Paul adopted a new rhetorical strategy from within jail by demanding to be treated as a political prisoner. In many European countries political prisoners were granted a special status: they were not searched upon arrest, not housed with the rest of the prisoner population, not required to wear prison garb, and not force-fed if they engaged in hunger strikes. At an international prison conference in London in 1872, the Italian government declared that "persons guilty of offences not implying great moral perversity should be kept in simple detention, apart from common criminals"; Germany recognized this principle in its designation of *Custodia Honesta*. In England, the Prison Act of 1877 declared that a political prisoner would be ceded special treatment as a "misdemeanant of the first class." This act resulted in special treatment for some prisoners. In the House of Commons in 1889, for example, Herbert Gladstone's appeal for its application resulted in special treatment for Irish political offenders. Suffragists, however, were not generally ceded this special status; individual prison wardens could make their own decisions about treatment of these prisoners. When a London jail warden denied Paul's claim to political-prisoner status, she refused to put on prison clothes. When the prison matrons were unable to forcibly undress her, they called in male guards for help, shocking impropriety and bodily facts for which the WSPU sought extensive press coverage.

To further protest their unjust incarceration and denial of political-prisoner status, at Emmeline Pankhurst's request Alice Paul and Amelia Brown took the next rhetorical step, a well-publicized hunger strike. In June of 1909, Marion Wallace Dunlop, a sculptor, had become the first WSPU hunger striker. By that fall, many imprisoned suffragists were initiating hunger strikes to publicize their mistreatment and obtain quick releases from wardens who feared the public response to middle-class women becoming sick or dying in prison. Paul had refused food after two earlier arrests, and these hunger strikes had led to her release, but this time her incarceration continued for the full month: the warden relied on force-feeding to keep her healthy enough to remain there. Although prison doctors maintained that this procedure was humane, an attempt to help the prisoner sustain her strength, Paul and many other prisoners found it a gruesome torture, as she described after she returned home: "When the forcible feedings were ordered I was taken from my bed, carried to another room and forced into a chair, bound with sheets and sat upon bodily by a fat murderer, whose duty it was to keep me still. Then the prison doctor, assisted by two woman attendants, placed a rubber tube up my nostrils and pumped liquid food through it into the stomach. Twice a day for a month . . . this was done" ("Alice Paul Talks"). After she returned home, Paul further recalled these horrors in a speech given at the Cooper Union auditorium in New York: "They tied us down with bonds around our legs, chests, and necks. Then the doctors and warders held us down and forced a tube five or six feet long, about the size of a finger, through the nostrils to the stomach. . . . It always caused my nose to bleed and brought out a perspiration all over me. I had fits of trembling, and I never went through the experience without weeping and sometimes crying aloud" ("Suffragette Tells"). As a result of hunger striking and this harsh treatment, Amelia Brown got severe gastritis; Paul was carried out from the prison in a weakened state on December 9, 1909, and went to the home of a friend, where a doctor tended her (E. S. Pankhurst, *Suffragette* 460).

Back to Moorestown and Philadelphia

After her long incarceration and recovery, Paul returned home in January of 1910 to further restore her health, continue her education, and make plans for her own suffrage campaign in the United States. She decided to devote herself to one cause, embracing it as a testimony, as Quakers were urged to do at Woodbrooke. Whereas Susan B. Anthony had worked for suffrage along with married women's property rights and the abolition of slavery and Emmeline Pankhurst was trying to reform the British party system as well as its voting laws, Paul planned to devote her entire energy to achieving this one goal. At that time, she viewed NAWSA, like the Women's Franchise League in England, as a group that kept giving the same speeches and waiting for men to recognize their worth. She wanted to rely less on meetings and speeches and more on a visual rhetoric that would portray women as independent and equal citizens.

When Paul came home, she recognized that her tie to the Pankhursts and her time in jail gave her access to the media and to women that she would not otherwise have had since she had no experience in American organizations. The *Woman's Journal* recorded the attention paid to her arrival on January 20: "As Miss Paul tripped down the gangplank of the Haverford in her trim brown tailormade suit, she had scarcely time to greet her mother and younger brother when a crowd of newspaper men and photographers rushed up and plied her with questions" ("Miss Alice Paul Returns"). Speaking offers followed. Though still preferring to avoid public speaking, she knew that speeches to large audiences could establish a clear role for her in the suffrage movement.

As she gave interviews and accepted speaking engagements, Paul immediately tried to change the subject from the Pankhursts to a new type of American campaign. On February 5, 1910, in Moorestown, New Jersey, for example, she spoke to a crowd of five hundred who came to hear her because of the announced topic of "The Militant Suffrage Movement in England." Although Paul began by mentioning the infamous window breaking and force-feeding, she quickly moved to the full array of rhetorical techniques—public questioning of officials, marches, and jail sentences—that could achieve suffrage in the United States. To connect the suffrage campaign with the best American traditions, she associated its activists with heroes of American democracy: they were resistors to tyranny, like George Washington, Ben Franklin, and Thomas Jefferson. For this largely Quaker audience, she thus positioned suffrage as a noble testimony, the key social reform of her generation. In this speech and others that followed, she used her notoriety to secure an audience but quickly abandoned the position of Pankhurst disciple as she refigured suffrage within her own religious background and her own country's history.

In a speech at the Haverford Summer School in July, given to a Quaker audience to celebrate Woodbrooke Day, Paul again situated activism within the tradition of Quaker testimony and further constructed herself as a leader, like a traveling minister, who could shape an American suffrage campaign that would draw on the best Quaker values. Assuming the role of her teachers at Woodbrooke, she lamented that many Quaker meetings were losing touch with pressing social problems: "[W]e are so introspective, so absorbed in developing our own characters into perfect flowers that we have no time for the great social movements that are bent on making such development possible for all. As we look at the placid, comfortable attitude with which Friends regard the social ills about them, it seems indeed a far cry to the aggressive vigor with which the early Friends challenged the evils of their time." She continued by claiming that many Quakers felt that they did not need to assume an activist stance because they had missed the great campaigns like abolition. To the contrary, she argued, these "stirring times" engendered just as great a "need for workers." Suffrage could be the Quakers' opportunity to reassume their best identity, and Paul could help them to embrace that testimony and become witnesses for that cause.

In this speech, as Paul situated suffrage as the key form of activism required of her generation, she developed an argument that built upon her judgments of social work. She argued on Woodbrooke Day, as she would continue to do, that this legal reform—unlike settlement houses—could lead to real change for the poor. The lower classes, she told the group, were lumping the Society of Friends in with other churches as "the stronghold of hypocrisy and oppression," and further participation in philanthropy would not alter that evaluation. Through work for suffrage, she maintained, the Friends could truly impact the world "where children are toiling at an age when they ought to be living with fairy tales" and "where women are employed at machines of such a character that three months of the work means the forfeiture of the power of motherhood." Meaningful social change would begin to occur when women had the right to vote, Paul argued, because then they could advocate for themselves and for the needs of children and families. She maintained that the Quakers in her audience, by choosing this testimony over philanthropic efforts, could change the public attitude toward their church and achieve a new sense of moral and social purpose ("Church and Social Problems" 514–15).

In 1910, as Paul began establishing herself as an activist leader within the Quaker tradition, she decided to extend her academic training in social policy by seeking a doctoral degree. She re-enrolled at the University of Pennsylvania, where she had received a master's degree in 1907, again to study the social sciences. Her master's thesis, "Towards Equality," had concerned the legal inequalities faced by women in Pennsylvania at the beginning of the twentieth century. In 1912 she completed her dissertation, "The Legal Position of Women in Pennsylvania," which provided a history of women's legal status in Pennsylvania as an example of larger patterns throughout the United States.

This dissertation's text is an odd mixture of typing and handwriting, with source attributions missing and plenty of mistakes—as though it were written quickly as Paul worked through her own thinking, further developing arguments about the need for systemic legal reform, not social work or well-intentioned philanthropy, to change the lives of American women. In creating this review of women's legal rights, Paul envisioned an audience not solely of Quakers and not of men, but of American women of all religions and classes. As she would on many subsequent occasions, she argued that only suffrage would lead to real change in women's position in society. Women had the responsibility, to themselves and their society, to press for this right until it was won, regardless of the circumstances prevailing in any time period. Here she recognized that reformers often made the mistake of succumbing to other priorities, as many suffragists had during and after the Civil War: "Many of the abolitionists felt, however, that the agitation for woman suffrage at that moment, would, by complicating the situation, postpone the enfranchisement of the Negro, which then seemed more possible of achievement than did the enfranchisement of women. The woman suffrage forces were consequently weakened by the standing aloof of a number who took this point of view" (145). She argued further, forecasting her own plans, that one person could create tremendous progress. Her example here was Pennsylvanian Carrie S. Burnham, who tried to vote in 1871 and then brought an unsuccessful suit after being refused, acting "on her own initiative and quite independently of any suffrage organization" (151). Her singular awe-inspiring action, Paul argued, led to increased membership in state suffrage organizations and to a suffrage amendment being considered in the Pennsylvania state legislature in 1883.

As Paul positioned suffrage as the key issue of her time, she also carefully considered the "enemy," again developing arguments that she used throughout the campaign. Like Edward Westermarck, she believed that both men and women were caught in a social system that made the temporal seem eternal. In the search for equal rights, "in no sense has this course of development been marked by a sex struggle. . . . It has not been characterized by a conscious desire on the part of man to keep the other sex in a state of subjection, for his own gratification and emolument" (258). Instead, both sexes were controlled by the roles that civilized society asked them to play; and both were degraded by this system of domination and dependence. Men, then, did not need to be judged as the enemy—or as the superior group. Both men and women had to work toward a more equitable society, and that work had to begin with women's achievement of full suffrage.

From 1910 to 1912, while Paul formulated her own arguments and built her reputation within academic and Quaker communities, she also began taking a leadership role in local suffrage work, returning to many of the rhetorical choices she had witnessed in England and experimenting with new ones. In Philadelphia, she volunteered to chair a new committee on street meetings and began holding them twice a week, working with local suffragist Carolyn Katzenstein. They began by hiring a one-horse cart and sandwich stand, transformed with placards into a suffrage stand, which they brought to many locations where they spoke to larger and larger audiences. On September 30, 1911, a crowd of over two thousand gathered in Independence Square to hear eighteen speakers, including Paul, NAWSA president Anna Howard Shaw, journalist Rheta Childe Dorr, and civil-rights attorney Inez Milholland, who had spoken with Paul at the Cooper Union meeting when Paul returned from London. "It was utterly, I thought, a thrilling meeting," she recalled (Fry). At a rally on November 26, another large crowd came to hear Emmeline Pankhurst, who was visiting with Paul during a speaking tour of the United States (Katzenstein; Krone 27–30).

On to Washington

Although these experiences allowed Paul to continue with meaningful suffrage work, she realized that the kind of fundamental social change that she envisioned, and for which she was seeking a leadership role, could not occur in Philadelphia. In December of 1910 her suffrage work secured her an invitation to the national NAWSA convention in Washington, where she got to know some of the leaders of the movement. At a November 1912 national board meeting, Paul agreed to move to Washington that December to work on securing a federal suffrage amendment, in what the board viewed as a minimal role because NAWSA was concentrating its efforts in the states. As chair of NAWSA's Congressional Committee, which she would later rename the Congressional Union (CU) and then the National Woman's Party (NWP), Paul was replacing Elizabeth Kent, wife of a congressman from California, who didn't want to continue with this frustrating task of trying to get a suffrage amendment introduced into the Congress each year. Paul secured a headquarters for her Congressional Committee in a basement room at 1420 F Street Northwest, a site she found through the Quaker journal, *Friend's Intelligence,* and rented using her family's money: "I went into a little friendly boarding house . . . right next to the Quaker meeting house and everybody there, I guess, was a Quaker or in some way connected with them" (Fry). Lucy Burns joined her there in January.

With a substantial record of education and activism, Paul was ready in December of 1912 to begin her own campaign for suffrage, led by her own sense of Quaker testimony and witnessing. While she was still in college, she had realized she wanted to embrace a testimony that would alter the social and political status of women. After college she quickly decided that such change could not occur through philanthropic efforts. She carefully studied women's place in society and the history of women's legal rights and came to believe that legal and economic injustice stemmed not from eternal values but from a society's temporal definitions and needs. She envisioned a suffrage campaign not as simply a means to an end—getting the vote—but as an opportunity to change first women's thinking about themselves and then their status as American citizens. Unlike many NAWSA leaders, she believed this change should occur not at the state level but at the federal level, so that all American women working together would achieve a nationally recognized political and social status, signed into law in the nation's capital. Paul envisioned a powerful rhetoric, one not just of speeches but of action, that would draw on the best Quaker traditions to change minds and ultimately change American society.

2. The Commitment to Nonviolence

As Alice Paul began her suffrage work in Washington in December of 1912, she did so with a strong sense of testimony. Through her extensive experience with philanthropic work and her education in women's history, she had come to realize that she did not want to limit her life's work to helping working-class women cope with their poverty or to joining middle-class women in their slow-moving organizations. Her testimony was to involve *creating change*—not just ameliorating or bemoaning the results of an unjust status quo. To achieve this change, she would rely on the tradition of nonviolence.

Social Change through Quaker Witnessing

As she began formulating her campaign, Paul did so imbued with a belief that not only her cause but also her method should reflect a moral calling. And that method would be witnessing, standing with others each day, fully involved in a campaign infused with the philosophical choice of nonviolence. As her colleague Doris Stevens wrote in July 1919, Paul had carefully planned her own approach to social reform, which she called "passive opposition" and "passive resistance," by studying earlier advocates of this methodology: "It was deliberate. It was based on well established political and military strategy, and upon a deep knowledge of the history of all reform movements" ("Militant Campaign" 8).

From childhood, Alice Paul had been immersed in the Quaker tradition of nonviolence, a key part of George Fox's creed. In her hometown, Quakers lauded William Penn's creation of Pennsylvania as a separate space for pacifism. In 1681, soon after receiving the land in a grant from Charles II as payment of a debt that the king owed his father, Penn wrote a letter to the American Indian chiefs in the area, a text that every Quaker knew. In it, he cited the psychology behind the escalation of hostilities between colonists and the native population—and introduced the Quaker solution for such violence. "I am very sensible of the Unkindness and Injustice that hath been too much exercised towards you by the People of these Parts of the World," he wrote. "But I am not such a Man, as is well known in my own Country; I have great Love and Regard towards you, and I desire to win and gain your Love and Friendship, by a kind, Just, and Peaceable Life" (122). For the Quakers with whom Paul grew up, Penn's short tenure in the colony, noted for democratic government and for peace with the native peoples, was an essential part of a cherished past.

Paul also learned as a child that during the American Revolution most Quakers respected their faith's injunctions against bearing arms or paying for soldier-substitutes. During the war, countless draft-age Friends were arrested and jailed throughout the colonies; two Quakers in Lancaster, Pennsylvania, remained in prison for over two years (Goodell 19). During the War of 1812, Quakers again maintained their peace witness. Only in the South, where support for the war was strongest, were they imprisoned as a result, but even throughout the East they had to contend with property seizures and large fines (DeBenedetti 21–29).

When the Civil War was declared, most Quakers refused to serve, but some did decide to join in the Union's cause. In 1854, Angelina Grimke Weld discussed the controversial choice that many Quakers would make: "to choose between two evils, and all that we can do is take the *least,* and baptize liberty in blood, if it must be so." William Lloyd Garrison, a Baptist with Quaker leanings, also became an advocate of warfare. His associate Henry Wright declared that the sin of slavery "is to be taken away, not by Christ, but by John Brown" (DeBenedetti 55).

With members departing for war, both Hicksite and Orthodox meetings became "distracted and divided" concerning their testimony of nonviolence (DeBenedetti 62). In Philadelphia a study group appointed by the Orthodox Twelfth Street meeting recognized in April 1861 that the war was creating a crisis in the Quaker faith and in the local membership (Bacon, *In the Shadow* 12). After the war, the Philadelphia Race Street (Hicksite) meeting chose to readmit those members who had fought if they publicly apologized for violating the peace testimony, but the Twelfth Street meeting disowned eleven members who had been drafted or volunteered for duty (Bacon, *In the Shadow* 12, 37). In Moorestown, the Hicksite meeting did not force anyone to "be read out" because of their participation in the war, but the issue of war service caused great consternation within the group (Cleaver).

In 1868 the Pennsylvania Yearly Hicksite Meeting, a state-wide assembly of which Paul's congregation was a member, promulgated a new *Rules of Discipline* to stress the crucial "unity of faith and practice" that had to be reinstated after such a group-rending crisis (3). This document reminded members that that they must decline any government role "the duties of which are inconsistent with our religious principles," and that "Friends are exhorted faithfully to adhere to our ancient testimony against war and fightings" (24, 111). Such strict pronouncements only added to the discussion about the conflict between ideals and actions, a discussion that was still going on in Paul's community during her childhood.

Thoreau

In addition to these issues and documents continuing to receive attention in Paul's Moorestown meeting, Paul was also exposed to the theory of nonviolence as well as its contradictory applications through her schoolwork. In the late nineteenth century, Henry David Thoreau's "Civil Disobedience" (1849), in which he advocated nonviolent opposition to an American government that allowed slavery and was waging the Mexican War, was a widely read and discussed essay, quite influential in New England and in the Quaker community. As teacher Mary Fisher wrote in *A General Survey of American Literature* (1899), Thoreau's works were key classroom texts for understanding the "thoroughgoing optimism" and "deep and steady faith in the ultimate victory of good over evil" that defined American literature and values (31). William Cairns, literature historian at the University of Wisconsin, wrote in *A History of American Literature* (1912) that Thoreau "is one of the few American writers whose fame has steadily increased. His contemporaries refused to take him seriously, or buy his books. Later generations have been glad to collect and publish all his available writings" (242). Paul was certainly a student of a later generation, learning about nonviolence as both a Quaker and an American.

In "Civil Disobedience," Thoreau presents passive resistance as the appropriate response to a government whose dictates interfere with the individual's sense of right and wrong. He asks questions that became Paul's: "Can there not be a government in which majorities do not virtually decide right and wrong, but conscience?—in which majorities decide only those questions to which the rule of expediency is applicable? Must the citizen ever for a moment, or in the least agree, resign his conscience to the legislator?" (204).

Thoreau believed that individuals had the responsibility to reject those government sanctions that they judged immoral, and that ultimately citizens would be better off without any government to hinder the dictates of their conscience. As if voicing a warning to Paul, he recognized the high price that determined resisters face: "A few, as heroes, patriots, martyrs, reformers in the great sense, and men, serve the state with their consciences also, and so necessarily resist it for the most part; and they are commonly treated as enemies by it" (205). Like Garrison and many Quakers, Thoreau found the Civil War a very difficult case, and his writing about it proves that his civil disobedience was not always a route of nonviolence. Although he advocated passive resistance to unjust laws, Thoreau ultimately endorsed the Civil War and, in "A Plea for Captain John Brown" (1859), defended the raid on Harper's Ferry. This seeming inconsistency in his thinking only added to the public discussion of his life and work.

Tolstoy

Although Alice Paul learned about Thoreau's contradictory commitment to nonviolence through her church and school, she became acquainted with Tolstoy in graduate school and at Woodbrooke. His essay with the good Quaker title of *The Kingdom of God Is within You* was first published in London and New York in 1894 and went through twenty-two English editions by 1905. In this text, Tolstoy argues that people can become stuck in a violent system and thus ruin their basic nature: "A man cannot but suffer when his whole life is defined beforehand for him by laws, which he must obey under threat of punishment, though he does not believe in their wisdom or justice, and often clearly perceives their injustice, cruelty, and artificiality" (122). The elemental hypocrisy with which people live causes them to endorse institutional wrongdoing: war, capital punishment, colonialization. To move beyond the current inequalities and cruelties and to achieve a world led by Christian principles, Tolstoy argues, people must abandon their corrupt governments. Then, they could reorganize the world on a stateless basis, as a nonviolent society in which men and women could realize their full potential as loving human beings. For Tolstoy, only nonviolent resistance to the daily tyranny of institutionalized injustice would be the appropriate tool for achieving change (A. N. Wilson 408–11; Brock 185–87).

Many Americans, both those who visited Russia and others who read Tolstoy's works, were influenced by his commitment to nonviolence and social change. In the United States, as in Russia, there were separatist Tolstoyan communes, such as the "Christian Commonwealth" set up by Ralph

Albertson in Georgia. Many reformers, including William Dean Howells and Ernest H. Crosby, found his ideas seminal to their own thinking, as did Quaker activists like Paul's brother Parry, who worked in Russia for the Friends Committee. Jane Addams, founder of Hull House, visited Yasnaya Polyana in 1896, read all of Tolstoy's works that she could find in French and English, and made pilgrimages to the Russian communes (Brock 299).

From Thoreau's and Tolstoy's works and from news articles about the communes, Paul encountered influential thinkers who questioned government structures and planned for a more equitable, nonviolent society. Paul found their goals and methods attractive, but, unlike Thoreau and Tolstoy's disciples, she was not working toward any form of withdrawal or separate existence and certainly not toward an end of government. Instead, she was working toward women's assumption of an equal status in government and in society. And, unlike Thoreau and Tolstoy, she sought not to philosophize or suggest long-range possibilities, but to form an immediate plan of action.

Gandhi

Alice Paul was not the only activist of this time who was attracted to the Quaker tradition, to Thoreau, and to Tolstoy; who defined a campaign through reference to the Pankhursts; and who searched out new means of applying nonviolent ideals. Mohandas Gandhi operated under the same influences, and his choices often mirrored Paul's. In 1891, working as a legal advisor for an Indian firm in South Africa, Gandhi found himself treated as a second-class citizen, as a member of an inferior race. In 1896, after being attacked and beaten by white South Africans, he began advocating passive resistance. Part of the inspiration for this policy, he claimed, came from *ahimsa*, an advocacy of nonviolence shared by Buddhism and Hinduism, based in the belief that no individual has absolute knowledge of truth and therefore no one should use force to make others forgo their own vision of it. As he attempted to influence fellow Indians and English authorities, he frequently evoked the authority of Tolstoy and Thoreau. While he was in South Africa, in fact, he wrote that *The Kingdom of God Is within You* had made the deepest impression on him of the formative works on nonviolence and that he also admired Thoreau's "Civil Disobedience" (A. N. Wilson 411).

In 1906 the South African government's actions led to an extension of Gandhi's commitment to nonviolent reform. On August 22, the *Government Gazette* in the Transvaal published the Draft Asiatic Law Amendment Ordinance, requiring that all Indians, Arabs, and Turks register with the government, have their fingerprints made, and allow officers to make lists of their scars and other identification marks. Failure to comply could lead to fines, imprisonment, or deportation. Through the press, Gandhi announced a mass meeting of three thousand Transvaal Indians on September 11, calling for resistance to this new ordinance through civil disobedience (Dalton 14). At one stage in the protest, influenced by his meetings and the resultant press attention, over 2,500 Indians were serving prison terms for refusing to register their fingerprints and bodies.

Gandhi and the Pankhursts

As Gandhi took on this campaign, he formed his own application of nonviolent theory. Although he frequently referred to Thoreau and Tolstoy to defend his decisions, he also made rhetorical use of Emmeline Pankhurst to explain what his choices were not. Gandhi met Pankhurst in 1906 when he was in England from October to December to protest the Ordinance. In 1909, when he traveled to London to discuss the status of Indians in the new Union of South Africa, he met with her again, perhaps even meeting Alice Paul in Pankhurst's company (Green 167–91; Wolpert 74).

When Paul was in England, and much more so afterwards, the Pankhursts were turning away from a purely nonviolent approach—involving marches, boycotts, and noncooperation with police—to some uses of violence. The first window breakers had been Mary Leigh and Edith New, who acted on their own on August 22, 1908, throwing two stones through a window of the prime minister's house. By the time Paul and Amelia Brown broke a stained glass window at the Lord Mayor's banquet in the Guild Hall, on November 9, 1909, this technique had become commonplace. As time passed without demands being met, the Pankhursts initiated more violent alternatives. After strident antisuffragist Winston Churchill became an influential Labour Party official as First Lord of the Admiralty in 1911, he frequently became their target. In a train station, for example, Theresa Garnett struck him with a riding switch. Assaults on property also occurred. On December 15, 1911, Emily Wilding Davison was arrested for thrusting a piece of linen, on fire and saturated with paraffin, into a public mailbox (E. S. Pankhurst, *Suffragette Movement* 286–87). Other suffragists began using chemicals to blow up mailboxes and gates. On a Sunday in March of 1912, nurse Ellen Pitfield entered the General Post Office with a basket of wood shavings, lit the basket, ran outside, broke a window, and gave herself up to a policeman.

In July of 1912 suffragists also began setting fire to empty buildings that housed governmental leaders or events. The first attempt at such serious arson occurred at Nuneham House, the residence of antisuffrage minister

Lewis Harcourt. After that, Gladys Evans and Mary Leigh set fire to the Theatre Royal, where Prime Minister Henry Asquith was slated to speak. As the audience was leaving a play there, Leigh poured gas on the curtains of a box, set fire to them, and flung a flaming chair over the edge of the box into the orchestra while Evans set fire to the carpet. Further actions included setting golf courses on fire, breaking a great number of windows in the best shops of the West End, smashing porcelains in the British Museum, clipping telegraph wires, slashing train cushions, and sending red pepper and snuff in packages to cabinet ministers (Purvis).

As WSPU leaders embraced such violence, they were publicly reconstructing the meaning of their earlier nonviolent choices. In the news and at meetings, they began discussing the earlier reliance on parades, aggressive questioning, arrests, and hunger strikes as only preliminary techniques of the powerless, choices they no longer had to rely on since their strength and numbers had grown. With more powerful weapons at their disposal and attention greeting their every move, they would continue with this more aggressive approach until Parliament was forced to submit.

The widespread press coverage of this new violence in England provided Gandhi with an opportunity for publicly defining his own nonviolence: for him, that commitment did not represent a temporary expediency of the weak but an enduring choice for seeking justice. In South Africa, even some supporters of Gandhi viewed his plan of passive resistance as the only choice of a disenfranchised group. A sympathetic British magistrate, William Hosken, discussed Gandhi's passive resistance as the Indians' only choice in a terrible situation: "The Transvaal Indians have had recourse to passive resistance when all other means of securing redress proved to be of no avail. They do not enjoy the franchise. Numerically, they are only a few. They are weak and have no arms. Therefore they have taken to passive resistance which is a weapon of the weak" (Gandhi, *Satyagraha in South Africa* 111). When Hosken expressed this "sympathetic" judgment, Gandhi realized that he needed to refute it, to separate his actions from any tradition of "the weak." He did so through comparisons to the Pankhursts.

As he examined the suffragists' decisions, he wrote that he admired their determination but disapproved of their use of violence, an expedient and temporary choice, without philosophical grounding and thus with no chance for success. To identify and strengthen his own movement, Gandhi invented a new term, abandoning the phrase "passive resistance," which suffragists used for their acceptance of abuse from crowds and from police. Gandhi suggested his new terminology in a speech given in response to Hosken's characterization of his methods, as he later recalled: "In contradicting Mr.

Hosken, I defined our passive resistance as 'soul force.' I saw at this meeting that a use of the phrase 'passive resistance' was apt to give rise to terrible misunderstanding" (*Satyagraha in South Africa* 111). Gandhi's "satyagraha," or "soul force," depicts nonviolence as a determined choice made from a strong commitment to justice and respect for humanity, a choice his group would never abandon.

While Gandhi endeavored to separate his own satyagraha from any temporary device or form of weakness, he also commented extensively on the Pankhursts' use of violence, again to distance their political choices from his own. In fact, Gandhi perhaps exaggerated the role of violence in the English movement to create a contrast to his own developing campaign: "The Suffragist movement did not eschew the use of physical force. Some suffragists fired buildings and even assaulted men. I do not think they ever intended to kill any one. But they did intend to thrash people when an opportunity occurred." In comparison, he claimed, "brute force had absolutely no place in the Indian movement in any circumstance" (*Satyagraha in South Africa* 112–13). For Gandhi, this contrast was essential to nonviolent philosophy and action.

View of Friend and Foe

As Gandhi studied the Pankhursts and their violence against English rulers, he carefully considered the relationship between persecuted and persecutor in his own approach, developing ideals and strategies that Paul would also adopt. In Gandhi's satyagraha, it is not the enemy who should face pain and fear. Instead, the participants themselves must be prepared to endure physical suffering: his adherents would risk their own safety and even sacrifice their lives to prove that government policies were unjust and could not continue. The goal of these repeated risks would be not to defeat enemies but to convince them of the rightness of the cause. In *Nonviolent Power: Active and Passive Resistance in America,* Judith Stiehm describes this nonviolent commitment: "First, the resister risks death instead of threatening it; second, the leader goes to jail rather than the follower; and third, success is measured by what the resister actually gains and not by what he costs his opponent" (xi). After fully analyzing the relationship between resister and opponent, Stiehm further tallies the cost of success: "In nonviolent resistance, the 'winner' frequently suffers more than the 'loser' because he offers his own life instead of trying to take the life of others. Nonviolent resistance can be relatively cheap while being absolutely costly" (69). But, as Richard Gregg asserted in *The Power of Non-Violence,* no other method holds out the possibility of "a solution under which both parties can have complete self-respect and mutual respect" (54).

Given its possible requirement of long-term sacrifice, Gandhi described his version of nonviolence as an undertaking requiring a greater level of inner strength and self-control than would a quick call to arms. To persevere in such a campaign, participants would have to develop their own self-government and self-knowledge, traits that he labeled as "swaraj," a personal power that "liberates one from the sort of fear and insecurity that fuels both a desire to dominate or be dominated" (Dalton 7). This swaraj, Gandhi argued, would enable Indians to embrace the self-sacrifice that satyagraha would require: "Fostering the idea of strength, we grow stronger and stronger every day. With the increase in our strength, our Satyagraha too becomes more effective and we would never be casting about for an opportunity to give it up" (*Satyagraha in South Africa* 114). In *Gandhi: The Traditional Roots of Charisma*, Susanne Rudolph and Lloyd Rudolph maintain that Gandhi's true power stemmed from this insistence on changing the Indian's sense of self: "repairing wounds in self-esteem inflicted by generations of imperial subjection, restoring courage and potency, recruiting and mobilizing new constituencies and leaders, helping India to acquire national coherence" (3). They argue further that, for Gandhi, establishing a belief in the Indians' own personal strength was especially important because many of his countrymen had internalized the traditional British view—that Indians were naturally obsequious, compliant, and fearful, in need of outside governance. As colonized men and women, they had long experienced "a sense of impotence combined with the moral unworthiness arising with impotence"; thus the first step in a campaign for independence would be developing their self-respect, or swaraj (13).

Methodologies of Nonviolence

Once they were imbued with a new level of strength and self-respect, Gandhi believed, Indians would be ready to employ powerful techniques of nonviolence. As sociologist Clarence Marsh Case wrote in *Non-Violent Coercion: A Study in Methods of Social Pressure* in 1923, such a campaign could include an array of methodologies: persuasion by argument or noncooperation, strikes, boycotts, suffering, and hunger strikes. In 1959, Gene Sharp, senior scholar at the Albert Einstein Institution, listed leafleting, picketing, and marches; refusal to participate in unjust policies like slavery, taxes, or wars; economic and industrial noncooperation acts like labor strikes and consumer boycotts; and nonviolent direct action in the form of blockages and sit-ins. As William R. Miller described in *Nonviolence: A Christian Interpretation* in 1964, an over-all strategy would involve these techniques being carried out through "strategic leadership analogous to a military general staff" and "disciplined nonviolent cadres" (64).

Such definitions in research studies seem to stem from Gandhi's campaigns in South Africa and in India. In South Africa Gandhi encouraged Indians to form their own congress and begin redefining their rights as citizens. He initiated noncooperation as he encouraged them to refuse bodily inspections and to submit peacefully to the resulting imprisonment. In 1913 he launched a strike of two thousand Indian miners, thus educating the government on these workers' economic importance as well as their political determination. Gandhi's nonviolence in India had several stages—starting with work in the legislature; then speeches and meetings; then the announcement of a new, more confrontational stage; and then well-planned acts of nonviolence. In 1919, when the English established the Rowlatt Acts, peacetime extensions of wartime emergency measures giving colonial authorities powers to quell revolutionary activity by searching and arresting citizens without warrant, detaining them without trial, and trying them without juries, Indians protested by following Gandhi's call for a nationwide cessation of work and by staging large meetings. After soldiers fired into an unarmed crowd of ten thousand in Amritsar, killing at least four hundred and wounding twelve hundred, millions of Indians began to participate in Gandhi's nonviolent campaign: they resigned from public office, boycotted the law courts, withdrew their children from public schools, blocked the streets by squatting there, instituted a boycott of British goods, and revived cottage industries (Gandhi, "Living on Spinning").

Nonviolence and the American Suffrage Movement

In the same period that Gandhi established his civil rights campaigns in South Africa and in India, Alice Paul was forging her own testimony and methodologies in the United States, following the same creed of nonviolence that was a part of her religion and that she, like Gandhi, had learned more about in Thoreau and Tolstoy. She thought of women, like Indians, as living under an unjust tyrannical government, as being viewed as obsequious and dependent, as having little control over their own lives, and as frequently believing men's negative judgments of them. Like Gandhi, she began by holding meetings and forming a strong group, imbued with what Gandhi termed swaraj, and then she moved to controversial means of nonviolent protest. As she wrote to John E. Nordquit of the Socialist Party in July of 1913, she was leading a "great National movement," one that must be rooted in a "process of Moral Evolution" and that would involve a series of difficult risks to achieve the goal of equality.

Alice Paul's Complex Relationship with the Pankhursts

Though she respected and learned from the Pankhursts, Alice Paul, like Gandhi, did not make the same choices the Pankhursts did. They used violence to advocate for their social program, and they supported English and American entrance into World War I: Paul did neither. Unlike Gandhi, however, Paul did not exploit the Pankhursts to publicly define her thinking. Throughout her career, Paul never criticized Emmeline and Christabel Pankhurst: these were her mentors, her compatriots in the quest for international suffrage. In November 1913 when Emmeline Pankhurst spoke in Washington, Alice Paul told audience members that they may have read "distorted accounts in the daily papers" about this controversial leader but they would go away "with hearty sympathy—like mine." Emmeline Pankhurst began her address by voicing her pride in Paul and Lucy Burns: "In a way, they are my children" (Congressional Union Pamphlet).

Paul's continuing support of the Pankhursts led to a confusion between their drive for suffrage and hers. In fact, it led to just the type of linking by the press and public that Gandhi strove so assiduously to avoid. Throughout her quest for suffrage, Paul was publicly associated with the Pankhursts and labeled with their "militancy," a word used to describe all sorts of behavior considered inappropriate for women, whether violent or nonviolent. From the beginning of Paul's campaign, her opponents used this comparison to vilify her. In a press release on February 1, 1914, Ruth Hanna McCormick, an influential NAWSA officer, declared that Paul's organization had set suffrage back ten years: "It is militant clean through and its executive committee knows nothing of the meaning of American affairs. Miss Alice Paul and Miss Lucy Burns, president and vice-president of the Union, have both been trained under the militant methods of Mrs. Pankhurst. . . . These methods may go in England, but they are no good here." The *Remonstrance against Woman Suffrage,* a monthly of the antisuffrage movement, commented that the "Congressional Union, which owes its origin and its present leadership to immediate disciples of Mrs. Pankhurst, is committed to an American adaptation of the Pankhurst methods. It is intensely radical in its ideals and practices. It wants to smash things" ("Armed Truce"). In the *New York Times,* which opposed both state and federal suffrage, Mrs. Arthur Dodge of the National Association Opposed to Woman Suffrage stated of Paul's opposition of Democratic candidates in the 1914 election campaign that "It is quite appropriate that this fresh evidence of militancy in the United States should be coupled with the names of American women who are closely identified with the English militants," a group that the *Times* here referred to as "English 'Furies'" ("Attacks Belmont Meeting").

Only infrequently, and particularly when she was being disparaged for picketing the White House during wartime, did Paul and her supporters stress the differences between these two approaches to "militancy" and thus define their own work. Regarding her determination in 1914 to begin holding the Democratic Party responsible for denying women the vote, Paul described the distinct features of her militancy at an organizing conference and in many circular letters: "It is not militant in the sense that it means physical violence. It is militant only in the sense that it is strong, positive and energetic" (Report of the Congressional Union). In an article for *La Follette's Magazine,* reprinted in Paul's journal, the *Suffragist,* in October of 1917, Belle Case La Follette wrote that "It should be remembered that the Congressional Union has never been militant in the English sense. They have not violated the law nor committed violence. They have been aggressive, forceful, indefatigable, unafraid" ("Justice for Pickets"). In "The Militant Campaign," after making a list of bayonets, machine guns, and other weapons that men used to fight for liberty, Doris Stevens commented that "We could and would not fight with such weapons" (9). As Paul reviewed the entire effort in a 1921 report for her officers, she again made the contrast: "The struggle in England has gotten down to a physical fight. Here our fight is simply a political one" (*National Woman's Party 1921 Report*).

Rejecting Violence

Though a comparison of tactics of Paul's CU and the Pankhursts' WSPU was made frequently in the press and Paul rarely challenged it, this association was certainly not an accurate one. In fact, during the entire American campaign, there were only two "violent" incidents, both involving only window breaking. Paul used these incidents in her publicity, but explained them simply as a spontaneous response to stifling air and closed spaces, an indication of the suffragists' bravery and solidarity even during the most tyrannical of government actions, not as a harbinger of any other form of violence.

In the *Suffragist* in November of 1917, picket Florence Brewer Boeckel reported that when Paul entered prison for a seven-month sentence, she was immediately greeted by her fellow pickets crying, "We want air, air" because of the foul air in the abandoned jail in which they were housed. First, she opened a nearby window, Boeckel continued, emphasizing Paul's physical vulnerability: "Two six-foot men came up to ninety-five pound Alice Paul and tried to take the rope away from her. It broke in her hand. The window banged to and the guards began carrying Miss Paul to her cell." But then, to protect her troops, Paul took action: "Deep in the pocket of the coat she had worn to jail she had one book, a little brown volume of Browning's poems, which she had brought to read during her seven months. Like a flash, before her cell door was closed, she seized her book and with desperate sure aim threw it through that high round window" ("Why They Put"). In a much later interview, Paul said that Boeckel invented the picturesque detail of the Browning volume to emphasize Paul's scholarly and nonviolent nature: she had actually broken the window with a bowl, certainly an instrument more likely to crack glass (Gallagher 92).

A year later, as reported in the *Suffragist* in October of 1918, another window-breaking incident occurred when a police captain detained Paul and her picketing group in the Capitol, treating them roughly as he deposited them within a small cloak room and refusing to state the charges: "When he insisted loudly that 'You can't come out here. You can't see no one. It don't make any difference about the law. We're managing this now in our own way,' the women surprised him by showing that they *can* step into the hallway, for in a flash several of them broke the glass of the doors which the police have kept locked and guarded since the moment of our arrival" ("Preserving the Peace"). In the *Suffragist,* the event appeared as a natural reaction of a strong-willed person, but not part of any program of violence.

The Qualities of the Leader

In creating a plan for achieving social justice through nonviolence, Paul, like Gandhi, was led forward by a strong sense of personal strength and determination. She talked her way into a Washington appointment; she separated from NAWSA when it questioned her tactics; and she weathered the resignations of members who disapproved of her boycott of Democratic candidates, her picketing, and her burning of the president in effigy. In a letter to suffragist Eunice R. Oberly on March 6, 1914, Paul maintained that she and Lucy Burns started their federal work alone, "with no one in the country, as far as we know, believing that the time had come for it to be undertaken." Replying to a claim that she was overestimating her number of followers, she asserted, "We would go on just as serenely if we were only nine, as if we had a thousand women ready to help us, because we are sure that we are right."

Suffrage publications and conference presentations often stressed this fierce determination—to demonstrate the commitment of the woman at the helm and thus of the entire group. On January 10, 1914, in a *Suffragist* article detailing plans for an executive committee, its leader is referred to as having "a sturdy Quaker ancestry behind her that does not know the word 'failure'" ("The Executive Committee" 5). In the Closing Session of the Woman's Party Convention in 1916, Mrs. A. D. Ascough, a delegate from Connecticut, spoke from the floor, asking Paul to come forward after the following encomium: "It is to her clear vision, to her genius, that is due the launching of this great new Woman's Party. . . . She has been a tireless leader. She has given her life to this work, and she has inspired in all of us not only enthusiasm and loyalty, but a deep personal devotion" ("Closing Session"). In "The Militant Campaign," Doris Stevens wrote of Paul as "that unparalleled organizing genius and political strategist, Miss Alice Paul, the frail little Quaker scholar who has inspired the profoundest respect in the breasts of the enemies of suffrage and the warmest devotion and admiration among friends" (8).

In private letters and discussions, many volunteers also commented on Paul's powerful intensity, as one new organizer described it: "And then Miss Paul sent for you. I will never forget that first interview. Miss Paul sat at a desk in a room seemingly completely dark except for a small desk lamp. Later in reliving it I felt she deliberately created an atmosphere of the tough executive. There was no subtlety about her. Direct, blunt, she asked why I wanted to do this. She wanted to probe sufficiently without wasting time, to discover if I had any weaknesses and to what extent she and the movement could depend on me" (Fry and Ingersoll [I] 49–50). Another worker wrote of Paul's ability to draw her in: "I cannot say that I personally like to do the things that Alice Paul set us to do, but . . . I helped to picket the White House, to keep the watchfires burning near Suffrage Headquarters and to pester congressmen and senators and did my little best to swell all sorts of parades and demonstrations" (Fry and Ingersoll [II]).

Such strong direction and devotion insured the loyalty of many adherents, but could also be maddening for them. One organizer in Denver in 1915 complained about the lack of financial support and the difficulty of forming local organizations. She was short on funds, spending the last of her own cash, when she wrote to a fellow organizer: "Miss Paul neither eats and many times I do not believe she sleeps, but if she does she dreams about the Federal Amendment. But you know that we cannot all eat and sleep the Federal Amendment, especially in a strange community where one's bills have to be paid and it would be pretty cold sleeping under the Federal Amendment at present" (Organizer in Denver). Although she complained, the letter writer stayed at her post.

Paul's expectation of sacrifice and endless determination to secure a federal amendment did drive some supporters away. Like Gandhi, she would not alter her course to placate unhappy adherents: she was moving forward following the dictates of her own testimony. In January of 1914, a group led by Ivy Kellerman-Reed, a suffragist from Ohio, decided that "the members of the Union have, so far as we can discover, no voice in vote whatever, and we, as American women, strongly object to this condition of affairs, which is anomalous in [an] organization avowedly seeking to obtain for women the right to vote." They disliked arbitrary methods extolled by "an autocratic chairman and a committee independent of, and not responsible to, the members of said Congressional Union." They asked that Paul consider reorganizing the CU along representative lines with elective offices, a constitution, and by-laws approved by the majority of members, with any new policy approved by vote of the total membership (Hitchcock; Zimmerman 95). In response, Paul made clear that members would never have a voice in electing officers, and there would never be any accounting of money received or spent. Members should accept these terms or withdraw, she argued, because "It is better, as far as getting the vote is concerned I believe to have a small united group than an immense debating society" (Letter to Eunice R. Oberly). As a result of this ongoing debate, a small group concluded that their only choice was to resign. Charlotte A. Whitney, a prominent California suffragist, submitted her resignation in a letter to Elizabeth Kent: "I take this step because the Congressional Union is an autocratic organization with its control entirely in the hands of one woman. The Susan B. Anthony amendment and the whole suffrage movement stands for democracy, and work for it should seek to awaken and quicken women to a sense of responsibility and solidarity, based upon individual and social justice, but the Congressional Union is submerging the individuality of the worker into a blind following under hypnotic leadership. The spirit underlying the work and methods is 'the king can do no wrong,' and the cause must be won regardless of the method employed." Although adherents would leave at other points, most CU members admired Paul's commitment and results and felt inspired by her activism (Hitchcock). Certainly her group, growing from a Congressional Committee in Washington to a Congressional Union and a National Woman's Party (NWP) with supporters across the nation, never rivaled NAWSA in size. Paul's organization seems to have never had more than seventy thousand members, a number that was reduced to fifty thousand during the picketing in 1917 (Josephson 94). Low numbers did not overly concern Paul; what she sought was a dedicated and moveable force that would embrace her one testimony.

For the Group: A New Sense of Self

Though Paul relied on a personal testimony and sought only a small cadre of devoted adherents, she worked hard to recruit and maintain this self-sacrificing group by emphasizing that all efforts had to be based in a new sense of self. In 1910 Paul commented that the Pankhursts' Women's Social and Political Union (WSPU) had, when its focus was still on nonviolent means, provided an opportunity for women to "throw off their mental bondage. It had kindled in their hearts a great spirit of rebellion against their subjection. It has developed a self-respect, a respect for their sex, unknown before. On all hands one hears it said: 'A new race of women is developing before our eyes'—a type which has discarded the old ideal of the physical, and mental, and moral dependence, and has substituted the ideal of strength" ("Woman Suffrage Movement" 27). Paul envisioned her own continuing commitment to nonviolence as the means to create "a new race of women" whose self-respect would spur each action. While Gandhi was attempting to end the stereotype of Indians as obsequious and weak, in need of leadership from British officials, Paul was trying to alter the prevailing view of women: as weak, insufficiently educated, hysterical or temperamental, dependent on men, and not worthy of the vote. Instead of being hampered by actual limitations, Paul believed, women were hampered by inaccurate views of their own capabilities. With a new sense of self-respect, they could achieve all: they could become American heroes. In an article that Paul helped colleague Mary Beard prepare for *Pearson's Magazine* in the fall of 1913 (one that was not accepted for publication), they compared the hero's welcome given in the United States to Hungarian revolutionary Louis Kossuth in 1851 with the lack of respect ceded to suffragists by the usual "We" of society, men and women who accepted traditional definitions: "We refuse to accept female heroes. . . . What is feminine is hysterical, frenzied, or just idiotic—in a man's world. A man's world merely! Ah, ye men who think only the thoughts of your world! And ye women who think only the thoughts of men! May the time come soon when you may be able to think your own thoughts!" ("Have Americans Lost"). For Paul, women first had to stop believing false views of themselves, and then they could be equal members of a democracy and even its heroes.

As her group worked for suffrage, Paul argued that self-respectful women merited it as citizens: they were not to seek the vote as a favor or reward from men. She frequently claimed that "the majority of American women—brave, hardworking, wonderful women" lived under "a grave delusion": that they needed to prove themselves worthy of the right to vote. In that judgment, they were mistaken. When in 1915 William Jennings Bryan, who had just resigned as Wilson's Secretary of State, told her advisory council to have patience, that suffrage was one of his political children, and that they could trust him to oppose Wilson on suffrage just as he had on warfare, the *Suffragist* declared in an ironic tone, "How comforting it is to women to know that their right to self-government is viewed by Mr. Bryan with so fatherly an eye, which will watch with benevolence its slow growth to maturity." To the contrary, instead of relying on him or anyone else, they planned to move forward through their own initiatives ("Mr. Bryan").

Paul felt that as she helped women recognize their own strengths and thus their ability to wage a nonviolent campaign, she would be relying on their own best instincts. Throughout her life, Paul seemed to view women not as the weaker but as the more responsible sex, well able to persevere, solve problems, remain calm in adversity, and care for others. Like Harriot Stanton Blatch, daughter of Elizabeth Cady Stanton who worked with English suffragists in the late 1880s and formed the Women's Political Union in New York in 1908, she believed that women were especially well suited for the long-term goals and risks of nonviolence. Blatch proclaimed about gender definition: "Men's idea was different. They could not ask for the vote for village constables without getting into a brawl over it. Their democracy grew by riots, revolutions, wars. Women conquered in peace and quiet, with some fun, right off their own bat. If that was not a new idea, I do not think there has been one" (Blatch and Lutz 192). For Paul, women's positive attributes had too frequently gone untapped as they passively accepted their culture's dichotomies and judgments. Her "new idea" was for women to recognize their own strengths and invest them in a nonviolent style of political action.

To enable women to achieve a new level of self-respect or swaraj, Paul insisted that they plan, carry out, and publicize their events without male help, just as Gandhi wanted Indians to act together without sympathetic British or Americans taking leadership roles. Men joined in a few parades, and many individuals, such as Dudley Field Malone, made important contributions to her efforts, but the CU, and later, the NWP prohibited men from membership. During the picketing, especially, Paul would not allow men to participate. In September of 1917 it was suggested that men join the lines, but Paul vetoed the idea, saying there were not enough of them "willing to make a show" (Letter to H. E. Brennan; Emory). Although being joined by a few men might not have lessened the overall effect, she wanted this to be a women's "show," a manifestation of their own swaraj and abilities.

Like Gandhi, Paul believed that as she enabled participants to reach a new level of self-respect, they could work together at changing the level of respect accorded them by their adversaries. As her group participated in the full array of nonviolent activities, they did so, like Gandhi, with a specific view of their opponent: their essential job was not to hurt him but to educate him, so he would come to respect them and advocate their cause. William R. Miller comments on the difficult compromises faced by resisters as they attempt to deal positively with their opponents: "Our job is not to wheedle or to bluff, but to show him that we are responsible persons seeking a change of conditions to which the opponent's social structure can adjust, and that we have adequate support for a course of action that will deepen and prolong the conflict" (146). When Paul's deputation went to Wilson in March of 1913 after the pre-inaugural parade, he claimed that he didn't know enough about the issue to make a decision. In response, she started an educational campaign, sending deputations and delivering petitions to explain their priorities and illustrate their determination. He changed his response several times, primarily claiming after 1914 that he did not control his party but only followed its lead and that he could not turn his attention away from war. Paul knew he led his party in all issues—its tariff legislation, position on Panama Canal tolls, advocacy of presidential primaries, and war. Her picketing in front of the president's home in 1917 was aimed squarely at Wilson as an individual. If someone to whom you owed a debt stood outside your home, she argued, you might object, get irritated, call names, even call the police: "But the scandal would be out," and "Perhaps even against your will you would yield." Picketing thus pointed to the fact that Wilson "owed a just bill," a phrase echoed in Martin Luther King's assertion in front of the Lincoln Memorial that his people had been written a check marked "insufficient funds" and had come to collect on it (Stevens, "Militant Campaign" 9). Even as her techniques grew more aggressive, Paul stressed their educational purpose, as lessons that she had to make more visually dramatic as Democrats did not respond. In 1918, when Paul was asked if the pickets had irritated the president, her reply was that "They were not intended to irritate. They were intended to arouse and enlighten," but such a construction was certainly hard to maintain with the press and with Wilson ("Pickets at the White House").

Although Paul intended her techniques to be positive and forward-looking, her aggressive forays were not always received as such. Like Gandhi, she could seem difficult and threatening, not educational at all. A December 1915 *Suffragist* article, concerning parades and meetings but also lobbying and the boycott of Democrats, described the shock and anger elicited by her aggressive explanations and demands: "Is it to be wondered at that politicians were puzzled at first by this new development in the suffrage question, that after years upon years of please politely phrased, they doubted their senses and lost their tempers when they found themselves face to face with a protest couched in words of political power? All other mysteries of woman faded before this last one, that she should stop asking her 'friends' to give, and attempt, herself, to get" ("Hearing before the House" 5).

As Paul's clashes with Wilson and the legislature escalated, she was keeping her movement in the public eye, but she also risked alienating those with the power to pass the bill. Increasingly strong nonviolent rhetoric could have the wrong effect, as William R. Miller notes: if campaigners "embarrass the opponent and throw him off balance," they could "antagonize the opponent and destroy rather than establish rapport." A too-threatening approach might, in fact, give him the upper hand: "If we confront him with overbearing boldness, he will exaggerate the threat we pose to the status quo" (144). A seeming departure from a traditional nonviolent rhetoric of "conversion" to a rhetoric of "coercion," as April Carter argued in a 1962 pamphlet called *Direct Action*, could thus undermine a campaign since it might create more publicity but also more animosity. Paul, like Gandhi, conducted her campaign on that edge, trying as much as possible to demonstrate strength and gain publicity without courting unnecessary conflicts that might completely alienate the opposition.

A Variety of Persuasive Techniques

With a difficult president to convince, as well as the legislature and American women themselves, Paul, like Gandhi, viewed a nonviolent campaign as requiring a remarkable combination of persuasive techniques, all documented by the press to increase their influence, some involving more physical risk and some more risk of humiliating or alienating the opponent. In a 1916 *Everybody's Magazine* article that discussed Paul's "combination of reckless advertising and of canny politicianeering" through which "the suffrage Federal amendment has been taken out of cold-storage and made to sizzle," the writer recognized that Americans had been witnessing a rhetorical campaign of wide scope: the fact that Paul "is not really a first-class platform speaker," which she had recognized at Swarthmore, had not hindered this public performance in any way ("New Leader").

Throughout the campaign, although she gave many talks herself, Paul sent other women, like Lucy Burns, Inez Milholland, Mabel Vernon, and Elsie Hill, to make stirring speeches at big-city conferences and small-town volunteer drives. But like Gandhi in South Africa and India, as the months and years went by, she also moved to more hazardous and attention-getting visual acts of nonviolence. As William R. Miller comments about this path,

"The general pattern moves by stages from moderate to extreme forms of conventional action and then from moderate to extreme forms of nonviolent action. This movement carries with it a quickening of pace and tempo. As it goes toward the extreme it becomes riskier, harder to sustain. Greater demands are placed upon morale, courage, physical energy and discipline" (70). In 1915 Paul went from parades to a variety of big events, such as setting up a booth at the world's fair and recruiting women to make a much publicized car trip from the fairgrounds in California to Washington, D.C. In 1914 and 1916, she instituted boycotts, asking women across the country to vote against Democrats, who were opposing a federal amendment. In 1917, she asked her participants to stand in picket lines, steadfastly facing arrests and abuse from crowds. In a Washington courtroom, they refused to say their names and questioned the judges' right to sentence them because they did not possess full American citizenship. In prison, they initiated hunger strikes and refused to participate in work details. When picketing and jail terms did not bring suffrage, they burned the president's words, burned the president in effigy, and declared themselves political prisoners of a tyrannical government.

Paul knew, as did Gandhi, that such extreme rhetoric required large-scale media attention to be truly effective. By 1916, journalist Rheta Childe Dorr, the first editor of the *Suffragist,* claimed that the CU was "quite as widely advertised as Barnum's circus in its best days." Throughout the campaign, "publicity was its first weapon" (*Woman of Fifty* 298, 286–87). This was clearly understood by Louisine Havemeyer, a colleague of Paul's and a sugar millionaire who was the first major American collector of French impressionism and an important figure of the New York social scene. Paul sent her out with other women who had been to prison for the cause, leading Havemeyer to comment that "Publicity is the great active agency, always publicity, publicity! You must keep your cause always before the public, and in some way or another you must get the public interested in your cause" (661).

* * *

In the tradition of nonviolence in the United States, after the philosophical essays of Thoreau, after the failed attempts of abolitionists at a nonviolent campaign, and after the creation of separatist Tolstoyan communes, there was Alice Paul. She created a campaign of nonviolent advocacy, not to beg for the vote but to demonstrate, first to women themselves and then to the power elite and the public, that women had the right to full citizenry. Her nonviolent boycotts, picketing, and hunger strikes led to an ongoing association of Paul and her organization with the Pankhursts, but Paul was no more a follower of the Pankhursts than was Gandhi. From her first days in Washington, facing many forms of opposition, she developed her own multifaceted campaign of nonviolence, influenced by her religion and by Thoreau and Tolstoy. Like Gandhi, she sought equal rights by fostering individual strength, determination, and courage—the font from which all progress flowed. Also like Gandhi, Paul believed that nonviolent rhetoric could first change her adherents' self-image and then their status in society—thus changing everything about the world in which they lived.

3. Reaching the Group through Words and Pictures

In 1913 the women's suffrage movement in the United States was dispersed over a large country, with countless groups functioning separately and with many of them discouraged by state defeats. In the spring of that year, as Alice Paul developed plans for her campaign, she sought a means of convincing these suffragists of the primacy of a federal amendment, of involving them in the successes possible through nonviolent action, and of acquainting them with the particulars of each upcoming event, a forum where she could use written and visual arguments to define her goals while promulgating an affirmative vision of women's abilities and their future. Starting a new publication would give her an opportunity to work through her own attitudes about suffrage and to communicate them forcefully, thus encouraging immediate positive action toward a federal amendment.

A Carefully Engineered Text

As she made plans for a journal in the summer of 1913, Paul demonstrated what would be a frequent behavior: seeming accommodation. When Paul presented NAWSA board members with her plans for a new journal, one which they feared might compete with their own *Woman's Journal,* they wanted to wait until the board meeting in September and the annual convention in December to consider her plans. Paul did not want to wait, and she certainly did not want to put her idea before a group that might turn it down as a damaging form of competition or duplication.

That summer Alice Paul replied to NAWSA executives by claiming she would be publishing not a "journal" but a small "weekly bulletin" to replace the frequent circular letters that kept NAWSA members informed of the Congressional Committee's work for a federal amendment. This defining of her proposed publication, she wrote on June 28 to Mary Beard, who had edited the journal *Woman Voter* in New York, "is the most politic thing to do, because it will secure us the cooperation of the National Board, and also obviate the hostility which would come to us from the followers of the Journal, if we started the paper on a large scale." In response, NAWSA board member Mary Ware Dennett informed Paul that she would approve such a bulletin because it would not compete with the *Woman's Journal.*

Regardless of what Paul promised Dennett, she intended to publish a regular journal, not a newspaper or circular letter. She did carefully consider comparisons to the *Woman's Journal,* but her true goal was to create a more substantial product. The *Woman's Journal,* published from 1870 to 1917 and succeeded by the *Woman Citizen* from 1917 to 1927, was the most widely distributed suffrage journal in the United States. Begun as a more conservative counterpart to Susan B. Anthony's *Revolution,* it boasted an impressive list of editors, including Lucy Stone, William Lloyd Garrison, Henry Blackwell, T. W. Higginson, and Julia Ward Howe, whose participation helped assure a wide readership. Circulation was two thousand in 1909, four thousand in 1910, fifteen thousand in 1911, and twenty thousand in 1913 (Ryan 23). Beginning in 1900, it had been affiliated with NAWSA (Huxman 87–91). Its suffrage coverage generally involved short pieces: notes on state work, progress in other countries, the achievements of participants, and college activities. Though suffrage was its mainstay, the journal also printed regular columns unrelated to suffrage, with titles like "Gossips and Gleanings," "Humorous," "Children's Column," and "Concerning Women," as well as poetry, short stories, and book reviews. The journal's headnote described the general aims: it was "devoted to the interests of woman—to her educational, industrial, legal and political equality, and especially to her right of suffrage." Its tone and subject matter were middle-class (or higher) and educated; it did not concern the realities faced by working-class women.

Paul envisioned her journal as separate not because it would be a smaller planning document, but because it would embrace a different purpose and content. Lucy Burns wrote to a friend in April of 1914 about what she and Paul viewed as a clear demarcation: "I do not see why sentiment for the *Woman's Journal* should stand in our way at all, as the papers do not interfere with each other, and there is no reason why people should not take both, as they are very different, and both useful in their own sphere" (Letter to Emily Perry). To work toward her one testimony, Paul planned to center her journal on a federal amendment, avoiding other issues of interest to women. Her title choice of the *Suffragist* would indicate this more limited focus. She also envisioned her coverage of suffrage as political or instrumental rather than broadly educational. Paul thought that her articles would succeed primarily with those who did not need basic information or education; they had already signed on for a suffrage campaign. Thus, this journal would not argue for suffrage as did the *Woman's Journal;* instead, it would convince readers that a federal amendment was the best route to suffrage and enable them to attain it. This group, these readers, didn't need to keep discussing the goal; they needed to view themselves as already on the path to its achievement.

In the first issue (November 15, 1913), to establish this separate identity for the journal, Paul stresses the audience and purpose as different from those of any other suffrage periodical. Her signed foreword, on the front cover, connects the paper to her national goal of securing federal action: "The purpose of this paper is to aid in securing an amendment to the Constitution of the United States enfranchising the women of the whole country." This first issue makes clear who her audience is not. In a salutatory, she declares that this publication will not provide an historical overview or general arguments for the uninitiated (whom she thinks no longer exist anyway): "There is not one single literate person, now in doubt, who can not easily and cheaply inform himself fully as to the merits of woman suffrage. It is a subject infinitely more familiar to voters than the tariff, the currency, or conservation. Therefore, we declare that woman suffrage has passed beyond propaganda and has reached the political stage." In the first pages of this issue, Paul continues to emphasize the word *political* as describing her purpose instead of the more traditional *educational.* Suffrage, the salutatory declares, has "reached its political stage"; suffrage is "purely a political issue" ("Congressional Union for Woman Suffrage").

In the editorials in the first issue, as in subsequent ones, Paul also makes clear not just that her readers have embraced woman's suffrage as a goal, know the facts of the campaign, and espouse a federal solution: she also posits the attitude that informs their nonviolent work. Paul constructs her reader as a woman who is confidently moving forward: her self-respect, unity with other women, and determination will enable her to soon obtain the goal. Paul's first editorial, "A Federal Amendment Now," forecasts imminent victory: "Women are continually being told that their enfranchisement is only a matter of time. Naturally, then, the only question that should interest them is, 'What time?' To that question suffragists have only one answer, 'Now.'" Throughout the years, whatever the difficulties and disappointments, Paul continues to focus on positive plans and signs of success, so crucial to keeping people involved and confident of victory. The self-respect and ability—the swaraj—of the suffragist for whom the journal is named is ultimately the key to success and the subject of Paul's journal.

To engender self-respect and secure a federal amendment, Paul wanted the *Suffragist* to differ from the *Woman's Journal* in physical appearance, by being not less but much more. From its beginning, the *Journal* resembled a city newspaper with four to eight pages, four columns, small print, no white space, and only one picture at the top center of the first page. Whatever had been promised, from its beginning the *Suffragist* was certainly more: its eight pages, sixteen during important conferences and events, began with a front cover with a cartoon and title, followed by short and long articles on the campaign. This formally written weekly journal measured eleven by fourteen inches, like many other weeklies of the period and certainly not like any newspaper or circular letter. The *Suffragist,* in fact, looked similar to the English movement's *Suffragette,* a journal of a similar size and length which also had a cartoon and title page, notes, and longer articles. During that summer of planning, Paul's staff carefully studied the English paper. Such a comparison was appropriately made only by the journal's staff and not by the general public; Paul was trying to forge her own campaign and to dissociate herself from the Pankhursts.

For her national readership headed together toward a federal amendment, Paul chose a substantial publication with several clearly delineated sections that combined visual with verbal rhetoric to persuade women and move them to action. In the first issue, Paul established a standard table of contents that remained little changed throughout the years: a cartoon or picture on the front cover; a page of "News Notes of the Week"; a credits page that contained an editorial; middle pages with news stories and photographs concerning meetings, parades, or state efforts; a treasurer's report citing recent gifts and a total of funds; and a back cover with subscription information along with small boxed ads. Beginning on January 31, 1914, the last pages also included, usually once a month, paragraphs of praise for CU activities, which were quoted from large and small newspapers across the country and listed under the heading "Comments of the Press." Paul believed that this structure gave her journal the substantial look of a well-established publication, and the various sections enabled her to espouse her own opinions, lavish attention on successful events, feature positive press coverage, and stress her large membership and financial solvency.

Although Paul believed that reading this well-structured publication would substantially affect women, she thought that selling it would be beneficial as well. In the summer and fall of 1913, Paul used the quest for subscribers to foster activism. In circular letters, she asked fifty people to each secure a hundred subscribers. Beginning with the first issue, she sponsored letter campaigns, sidewalk sales, and promotions at meetings to secure additional subscribers. A woman's ability to sell the magazine and subscriptions indicated her potential ability to succeed at other tasks, as Paul wrote to Emily Perry on March 12, 1914, about a Rhode Island volunteer: "We can tell what she is like by the results which she is able to get in those lines; we could then, perhaps, take her as a salaried organizer so that she could give all her time to the work." Repeatedly in the journal, editors reminded readers that it was their "duty" to expand circulation as "nothing helps more than this in getting people to understand what the Woman's Party is doing and planning." The editors also wanted legislators to have copies, and they posited readers as able to put this journal on their desks: "They need the *Suffragist* badly. Their speeches show that they do not understand politics from the women's point of view, President Wilson should by all means receive the paper. What New Jersey woman will subscribe for the President? Every member of the Cabinet needs the *Suffragist,* especially the Secretary of War and the Navy. We call upon the women to send the paper to every member of the Administration and of Congress" ("Publisher's Note"). By December 1913, the magazine claimed at least twelve hundred paid subscribers (Lunardini 39); in 1918, regular subscription was ten thousand (Baumgartner 47; Masel-Walters 68). Publishing circulation numbers and repeatedly discussing five thousand new members made the journal—and hence the movement—seem ever more influential.

In her first choice of editor, Paul revealed her desire to create a well-written and well-respected weekly journal. As the work progressed, her relationship with this editor also demonstrated the strength of her belief in one testimony: regardless of disagreements or even the facts of any given matter, the journal must always emphasize women's belief in themselves and in forward progress.

In 1913 Paul asked Rheta Childe Dorr to take on the role of editor, choosing the American journalist with perhaps the greatest knowledge of women's rights. Dorr began her career in 1902 at the *New York Evening Post,* covering women's clubs and charity work as well as writing a series on women's work in factories. In 1906 she went to Europe and began sending in articles on European politics; she met Christabel Pankhurst and other suffrage leaders in London. In 1908 she returned to New York to write freelance articles for the *Sun,* and then for the women's page of the *Tribune* and the *Post* (Ross 112–14). In 1909 she worked as a laundress, seamstress, and factory hand while taking courses at the College Settlement on Rivington Street, where Paul had worked three years earlier, and she published the results of her ethnographic research in *Everybody's Magazine* and other periodicals. She then wrote for

Hampton's, a short-lived reform magazine, from 1909 to 1912; she published some of her articles from this journal in anthology form in *What Eight Million Women Want* (1910). In 1912, on a second trip to Europe, she reported on Emmeline Pankhurst for *Good Housekeeping* and helped Pankhurst organize her autobiography, *My Own Story.*

Besides being an experienced advocate of women's rights, Dorr shared with Paul the belief that gaining the vote was essential for obtaining real citizenship. In *What Eight Million Women Want,* Dorr wrote that women's continuous service to their country brought them no respect: "It is a fact in this country, although every one knows that women own property, pay taxes, successfully manage their own business affairs, and do an astonishing amount of community work as well, no one ever thinks of them as citizens" (290). She argued that the belief in men as protectors was "a sentimental kind of delusion," one that women's recent activism had revealed: "When they got out into the world of action, when they began to ask for something more substantial than bonbons, the club women found that the American man was not so very generous after all" (291). Entering the world of work, she noted, had brought many women to the suffrage cause: "The first woman who followed her spinning-wheel out of her home into the factory was the natural ancestress of the first woman who demanded the ballot" (317).

When Dorr worked on a pamphlet for NAWSA in 1912, she was "discouraged by the slow and academic methods," and came to believe that Paul and Burns, the true successors of Susan B. Anthony, had the practical program for success (*Woman of Fifty* 281). At the *Suffragist,* Dorr quickly got to work creating a strong sense of forward movement: "I published in the paper every scrap of news, and there was always news, accounts of the deputations we sent to the president and aggressive editorials." Dorr worked long hours with Paul, who contributed most of the editorials and some of the articles.

Although Dorr was listed as editor, Paul did not grant her true editorial control. On April 21, 1914, after five months of working together, Dorr wrote to Paul complaining that Paul had gone into the office right before a deadline, shut the door, and made changes to the editorial page without consultation. Dorr asserted in this letter that although she would have been glad to consider changes together, what Paul had done was intolerable: "But nobody has a right to lay hands on a single piece of copy without the editor's permission, much less edit, erase or change without consulting the editor. For me, for instance, to give the business manager one set of directions and for you to countermand those directions is simply unbearable. For you to rush off with the [editorial] page, lock yourself in and me out, and finally refuse to allow the page to go to the printer is simply to treat me with contempt." At this juncture, Dorr resigned. She remained on the masthead as editor until June 6, 1914, but she refused to work on another issue. In resigning, Dorr made clear that her decision was not based on this one experience. What she had wanted was an objective newspaper, with editorials, certainly, but otherwise with factual accounts of both successes and failures. She saw that Paul wanted something else, an organ for her nonviolent approach, one that might bend the facts to convince women to join in: "You want a little newspaper to advertise the Union. A paper to be written by yourself, with the assistance of a good hack writer. A paper to come out at your convenience, and at intervals, regular if possible, but nothing to be sacrificed to regularity. I want a paper that will stand with any journal of its kind edited by first class men. . . . I have no idea of sacrificing my reputation as a serious journalist, which is exactly what I am doing in editing—or pretending to edit—a paper which is run in this fashion" (Letter to Alice Paul).

In the editorials to which Dorr objected, the ones Paul had rewritten after Dorr had approved other copy, Paul makes strong positive statements that would not bear close factual scrutiny. In the first, "Platform Pledges," she motivates readers through a bandwagon appeal, exaggerating the movement's strength in that most vexing of regions, the South: "Woman suffrage has taken possession of the country. Even the last strongholds of resistance have succumbed. Not a Southern State that has not a strong suffrage group. In old New Orleans, in San Antonio, in a dozen other southern cities the women are holding street meetings in listening, approving crowds." Although she does not quite claim that majorities in these southern states support the amendment, she comes close to doing so, a proclamation untrue then and still untrue when suffrage was ratified in 1920.

In the second editorial on April 18, Paul rearranges facts again, this time to simplify a complex situation and thus rally her troops around the one acceptable choice of an amendment. Her subject here is the Shafroth-Palmer Amendment, which Senator John Shafroth of Colorado had introduced into Congress on March 2. This amendment asserted that when suffragists in any state could secure a petition with signatures of eight percent of the voters in the last election, that state would hold a referendum on woman's suffrage and change state law to abide by the vote. Supporters thought this bill would be acceptable to states-rights Democrats and would enable suffrage workers to appeal directly to voters, circumventing conservative state legislators (Lunardini 55). This NAWSA-backed attempt to convince Congress to endorse separate state votes seemed to Paul only to delay suffrage endlessly, relegating it to a "dim and speculative future." Fighting for this amendment's passage, she would frequently claim, would not give any woman the vote and would divide those legislators who supported suffrage. In this editorial, she creates an argument she used frequently, that the Shafroth-Palmer Amendment arose solely from congressional malevolence and had no suffragists' support: "The Congressional Union wishes to make clear to members of Congress that suffragists refuse to accept the Shafroth-Palmer Resolution as a substitute for a direct suffrage measure" ("Members of Congress and Suffrage"). Here again, and without consultation with Dorr, Paul chose persuasion over accuracy, casting all suffragists in opposition to this evil plot when support for the Shafroth was actually coming from NAWSA.

In letters to influential friends and supporters, Paul immediately began shaping Dorr's departure so that it would not detract from the movement's progress. To colleague Dora Lewis in Philadelphia on June 1, 1914, she wrote that Dorr's resigning would save a hundred dollars a month—the letter doesn't mention any conflict. Mary Beard's June 24 reply to a similar letter from Paul reveals that she had heard of no disagreements but assumed that Dorr just didn't want to work hard enough: "I am sorry you are left entirely with the Suffragist on your hands but I fancy Mrs. Dorr really helped very little. It is so hard to know about people until one lives with them. Bluff dominates too much everywhere."

Although Dorr and Paul could not run a paper together, Dorr remained a supporter of Paul's campaign. On June 30, 1914, she led a deputation of five hundred members of the General Federation of Women's Clubs (GFWC) to present a suffrage resolution to the president. She also accepted a place on Paul's advisory council. In her autobiography, she described this movement with the highest of praise: "To my mind this six-years campaign, conceived by Alice Paul and Lucy Burns, and carried on with skill and amazing courage by thousands of women in every part of the country, stands out as one of the immense achievements of my time" (*Woman of Fifty* 303–04).

After Dorr left, Paul and Burns took on all of the editorial work and writing responsibilities. During the 1916 election campaign, when Burns was campaigning in the West, Paul worked from Chicago, not only writing the editorials but also assembling the entire contents of the paper, as she later recalled: "I remember I just didn't see how I could do it. I decided that I would stay up all night every other night; one night I would go to sleep, and the next night—because all through the day you were having telephone [calls], you were having people, and you couldn't do anything—so at night when everybody had gone and the charwomen came in to clean the building and so on I would work on the Suffragist" (Fry).

As she looked for a woman to take over this busy job, Paul did not again pursue a well-known feminist or journalist to be editor, but instead selected

Suffragist cover for Nov. 22, 1913. Drawing by Will H. Chandlee. Liberty comes to Washington D.C.

women from within the NWP ranks—campaigners who would enable Paul to turn out a clearly written and beautifully illustrated magazine, but one that would always serve her goals. Vivian Pierce and Pauline Clarke served as editors in 1917 and 1918, Clara Wold in the late fall of 1918, and Sue White in 1919. In these hires, Alice Paul sought journalism experience while making sure that each new editor's first concern, as she planned for every page of the *Suffragist,* was not editorial control of the journal, but what was best for the campaign.

The Cover Cartoons

From the beginning, the cover of the *Suffragist* carried the journal's title and either a picture from a recent event or, much more commonly, a full-page cartoon. Some of the cartoons were reprinted from other newspapers, but most were drawn by the magazine's own cartoonists. Will H. Chandlee, a well-known Washington artist, donated two of the first: one for the November 22, 1913, issue, featuring a suffragist standing before the Capitol building, appearing both dignified and imploring in a flowing toga, a classical image that would become a common feature; and one for November 29, 1913, of the spirit forms of Anthony and Stanton, looking on as delegates came to the NAWSA national convention. Nina Van Loon drew ten cartoons in early 1914. Several were in a style that, in 1925, cartoonists Julian De Miskey and H. O. Hofman made an identifier of a new magazine, the *New Yorker*—simple figures, a minimum of lines, all smooth curves. Van Loon's first, from January 3, 1914, introduces the tall dandy with spats, tails, a walking stick, a cigarette in a holder, and a top hat. The caption is "Anti Suffragist: 'I am utterly opposed to Woman Suffrage.'" Another, on March 7, 1914, shows three of these sparely drawn city men, labeled Progressive, Democrat, and Republican. Each is pointing a finger at the other two; papers in their pockets are labeled "promises"; the caption reads, "Tell *him* to do it." In these cartoons and others, Van Loon uses this male type to satirize the injustice of aristocrats who would not willingly extend their own rights to women.

Although these cartoonists helped to establish the magazine's cover as a site of social critique, the themes and tones of the weekly cover were fully established by Nina Allender, who took over on June 6, 1914. Allender, who was from Topeka, Kansas, began working for the Treasury Department in Washington, D.C., and became active in a local arts club after her husband left her. She held office in several suffrage organizations and served as president of the Stanton Club, the largest suffrage organization in the district, while also working full time. In 1912 she went to Ohio to lobby for a state referendum, an effort that failed. She then became an enthusiastic Congressional Committee member, and Paul talked her into regular cartooning.

Allender's cartoons, quintessentially visual rhetoric within a written medium, quickly secured their own readership and admirers. An excerpt from the *Forecast,* printed along with her picture in February of 1915, noted that she often created "an argument more forceful than could be put into words" ("Artist's Work"). As an article commented a year later, "More than one bubble of opposition has been pricked by Mrs. Allender's cartoons, when long and tedious arguments would have failed to clear it out of the air" ("Cartooning for the *Suffragist*"). In her 1920 autobiography, fellow suffragist Inez Haynes Irwin captured Allender's method and her strong connection with an audience of women. In these few sentences she also focuses on the political slant of the magazine, especially its front cover: "She has a keen political sense. She has translated this aspect of the feminist movement in terms that women alone can best appreciate. Her work is full of the intimate everyday details of the woman's life from her little girlhood to her old age. And she translates that existence with a woman's vivacity and a woman's sense of humor; a humor which plays keenly and gracefully about masculine insensibility; a humor as realistic, but as archly un-bitter as that of Jane Austen. It would be impossible for any man to have done Mrs. Allender's work. A woman speaking to women, about women, in the language of women" (*Story of Alice Paul* 48). Allender's cartoons spoke to women, as Irwin claimed, by showing their vulnerability in their current state but also their great capacity for strength and action. Allender embraced traditional notions of women as objects of courtship, homemakers, and childraisers at the same time that she created new notions of women—as highly competent citizens and workers, aware of the wider world. She also compared the needs of women from all classes, positioning suffrage as not just a middle-class concern. These various forms of contrast, of shifting expectations and priorities, create irony in the cartoons and are thus the source of much of their power.

One of the strongest themes in Allender's work is that working and poor women need suffrage, and that the campaign involves them as well as middle- or upper-class women. To emphasize that theme, Allender manipulated the readers' expectations that she would make a solely middle-class appeal. In her June 6, 1914, cartoon, for example, the caption "The Summer Campaign" might be assumed to mean the suffrage work that Eastern leisure-class women could undertake during their summer vacations on Long Island or in the Hamptons. What her picture shows is one of these affluent women holding a suitcase while watching a long line of women workers heading into the factories. Her August 29 cartoon again shows the long line to the factory, now as background to a poor mother of five standing in front of a shack where her children watch her leave for work. Here the ironic heading is "Woman's Place is in the Home." If this mother stayed in the home, the traditional site of womanly behavior, her family would starve. In these cartoons, creating strong contrasts based on class, poor women have no protectors: they need the protection of the vote.

The Suffragist

WEEKLY ORGAN OF THE
CONGRESSIONAL UNION FOR WOMAN SUFFRAGE

JUNE 13, 1914

The Inspiration of the Suffrage Workers

Suffragist cover for June 13, 1914. Cartoon by Nina Allender. Caption: "The Inspiration of the Suffrage Workers." As in Allender's first cartoon (June 6, 1914), working women and poor women are in the spotlight.

Throughout the summer of 1914, as Allender focused on struggling, un-protected mothers, her primary audience continued to be middle- and up-per-class readers who could work to help these women. Poor women were constructed primarily as subject, not as reader. The cartoon from June 13, 1914, features the caption "The Inspiration of Suffrage Workers," and shows a young mother with two children standing in front of a Hogarthian scene of rooms to let, open garbage cans, hungry people, and a booth where the wealthy go to hire servants. This woman inspires "suffrage workers"; she is not constructed as one of them. On July 25, another long line is featured, this time of women and children leaving the factories. The captions are "Child Saving Is Woman's Work" and "Organize to Save the Children—Join the Congressional Union." Again the "woman" doing the work of saving these children might not be an overwhelmed laborer, but a middle- or upper-class woman who should forgo her volunteer work in settlement houses and instead should work on securing the vote and thereby securing political equality for all women. In 1914 Paul and Allender assumed that the journal's readership was primarily educated and affluent women, but they would extend their journal audience and organizational membership by 1917 and 1918.

In the fall of 1914, well before the United States entered the war but with war in the nation's consciousness, Allender also created contrasts that involved soldiers on the battlefield. In these cartoons, she showed women making their way alone, as war widows. Her October 3, 1914, cartoon, captioned "After the Battle," depicts a woman and a child being attacked by a huge vulture while men lie dead around her. Her October 17, 1914, cartoon depicts a kneeling woman left alone with two children who are accosted by skeletal faces labeled "Poverty," "Sorrow," "Starvation," and "Greed." An inset shows a dead man on a battlefield being brought a wreath labeled "Glory" by another spectre. These cartoons communicate the possibility that any woman, not just a poor wife, could be left destitute if her husband goes off to the glorious fight and does not return. The message was clear: a war widow would need suffrage to secure the legal rights necessary to protect herself. The negative side of "glory" could be the shocking effect on those left behind.

Many cartoons from 1914 feature the urban woman struggling alone, with no sure means of supporting children. Paul, of course, did not want too many depictions of women who looked weak or desperate. To develop their self-respect, women needed to view themselves as strong and able, attributes that Allender portrayed by creating a contrasting reality, of women who worked outside in a rural landscape. Such figures helped to refute the common argu-ment that women didn't deserve full citizenship because they didn't defend the nation in wars or do the nation's work. Allender's November 14, 1914, cartoon shows two muscular farm women who, judging from their clothes, may have been from Denmark, where women were gradually being given the vote and would achieve full suffrage in 1915. The pair controls an ox and follows him with a plow; the ironic caption is "Women Cannot Fight." Clearly these two strong women are winning a fight each day on their farm and could do so in the armed forces. An election year cartoon from September 2, 1916, shows two strong women in outdoor garb with a donkey, the Democratic and states' rights symbol, between them. The western suffragist, with her lasso in the air, tells her eastern counterpart, "Don't be discouraged; I'll fix him!" Here, the argument is for women's ability to alter an election by casting their votes as a group; muscular women are controlling lassoes and domesticating the Democratic donkey. These cartoons create a contrast to traditional images of women as weak or helpless, making an argument based to some extent on a threat: these women can control ropes and plows and can exercise control in politics; thus, no party should underestimate their determination to get the vote or their ability to use it against a party that has denied their rights.

Whereas such cartoons emphasized women's strength and confidence, others satirized men's assumptions of superiority and reverence. These cartoons shared a humor of deprecation, a contrast of how women were expected to react to men and how they actually did. The April 12, 1919, cartoon, for example, shows a mother writing at her desk and a daughter on the floor reading a newspaper that has headlines of "The League of Nations" and "Women Arrested for Freedom." They have this conversation:

> "Mother, What is a League of Nations?"
> "Oh, Just a Bunch of MEN"

The intimidating powerbrokers that suffragists must oppose are here just "a Bunch of MEN." This casual undercutting of men's assumed superiority, presented in talk among women and girls, was also shown in other cartoons. The July 10, 1915, cartoon depicts a younger and older woman lighting fireworks together. The caption compares male opposition to suffrage to so much noise:

> "EXPLODING OPPOSITION"
> First Suffragist: "What a noise they make!"
> Second Suffragist: "And that's all!"

On May 19, 1917, the cartoon featured an Uncle Sam figure, blackened from sliding down the chimney and holding bags labeled "Democracy." A child has run to her mother, and the caption is their conversation:

Suffragist cover for Sept. 2, 1916. Cartoon by Nina Allender. Caption: "Western Voter (to Eastern Suffragist): 'Don't be discouraged; I'll fix him!'" This cartoon concerns a boycott of Democrats while also emphasizing women's strength and independence.

"LOST ILLUSIONS"

"Mother, Isn't There Any Santa Claus?"

"No, Dear. It's Only Your Uncle Dressed Up."

The male legislators holding onto democracy are just pretenders. To cede them mythic status is to participate in a destructive and childish illusion. In all of these cartoons, in fact, women recognize that men are not supernatural, and can be opposed.

In featuring women's privately expressed judgments of men's inanities, Allender used both Uncle Sam and President Wilson to give a specific face to the opposition. Uncle Sam was already a well-known symbol of the government before James Montgomery Flagg depicted him in "I Want You" recruiting posters in 1917. Allender primarily portrayed him as a symbol of American policies that did not favor women, of the government's repeated hypocrisies and denials. Her March 20, 1915, cartoon depicts him sitting disgusted behind a desk while a woman with two children points out how little of the federal budget goes to child services. In the August 11, 1917, cartoon, he holds a banner declaring "Democracy for the World" in his right hand, while behind him he restrains a suffragist with his left hand. She holds up a sign that says "Democracy Begins at Home." The caption, "Uncle Sam: If I could only keep my left hand from knowing what my right hand is doing!" creates a cynical reworking of the advice on charity in Matthew 6:3. Such cartoons turned Uncle Sam into an authoritarian hypocrite who speaks for democracy but offers half the nation's citizens no role in it.

As the counterpart to these Uncle Sam cartoons, Allender's portrayals of President Wilson constructed him as tyrannical while also satirizing his particular traits. In these cartoons, he is thin and dour, disapproving, even cruel. In a cartoon on April 1, 1916, as an old bespectacled schoolteacher behind a desk coated with spider webs, Wilson keeps a young girl after school, an image symbolizing the House's postponement of a vote on suffrage. The former teacher clearly believes that all women have inferior intellects and are thus controllable. In a July 1, 1916, cartoon, Wilson, as a dour shopkeeper, watches a young woman leave his store and then addresses his clerk:

"LOSING A CUSTOMER"

Manager Wilson: "What's the matter with her?"

Clerk: "She demands the Anthony label, *and will accept no substitute!*"

Such a cartoon showed the possible economic cost for Wilson and his party if they continued to oppose suffrage: the canned goods left unpurchased on the counter all have donkey labels. In these cartoons and others, Wilson was

Suffragist cover for Aug. 11, 1917. Cartoon by Nina Allender. Caption: "Uncle Sam: 'If I could only keep my left hand from knowing what my right hand is doing!'" Uncle Sam is shown here as an authoritarian hypocrite.

the nineteenth-century authoritarian, dressed in an old-fashioned suit, wearing pinching glasses, and having a thin, disapproving face; in the twentieth century, however, Wilson's control was slipping away.

In these cartoons involving Wilson and Uncle Sam and in many others, Allender portrayed women surrounded by the commodities of their own existences. They thus assumed power, as in the rejection of the canned goods, by extending their own daily commonsense decision making. Even the simplest details of home life take on new power and meaning in Allender's work. In the March 30, 1918, cartoon, for example, a woman is in her kitchen, stirring a pot labeled "1918 Elections," while outside the house Democratic senators argue about other issues, such as the eight-hour workday and daylight savings time. In the caption, the woman says: "If he doesn't stop talking and come in *his dinner will be spoiled!*" The woman is holding a spoon labeled "Woman's Votes," showing that she is fully capable of planning dinner and of planning a national boycott of Democrats. The cartoon for September 13, 1919, shows a woman using a long fork to get an olive from a jar labeled "Governor Brand Olives." The caption, "If I get the first one—the rest is easy," compares getting the first olive out of the jar to the work of convincing one governor to call a legislative session for a suffrage vote; once this initial task is complete, all the rest of the olives or governors will follow. In these cartoons, comparing women's daily chores to their work for suffrage provided humor and encouragement while puncturing the power bubble of the men they opposed.

As she considered the details of women's lives, Allender also included cartoons concerning sexual flirtation, using the trappings of "getting a man" to satirize the requirements of getting the vote. In her March 13, 1915, cartoon, a small inset shows a state-suffrage supporter in a simple dress, while in the middle a larger woman spreads a giant skirt that says "National Constitutional Amendment." Under the heading of "Changing Fashions," a man representing Congress wipes his brow, saying, "She Used to Be Satisfied with So Little," satirizing men's exasperation over women's greater expectations—a federal amendment instead of state legislation. Though men may regret that women want full rights for all citizens, other cartoons argue, they will be forced to "court" women with power. The January 22, 1916, cartoon, for example, again depicts the competition between two women for a man's attention. Here the popular woman is the one from the West, with "votes" written on her fan, whereas the eastern woman, from a nonsuffrage state, sits all alone, as "The Wall-Flower." On May 31, 1919, by which time both parties had approved the amendment and both were increasingly concerned about securing women's votes in 1920, the cartoon shows one woman and two men who seek her. Now the woman stands between two older men, labeled "Democrat" and

"Republican," both holding out their arms for her and both saying "May I Have the Honor?" These cartoons created humor by recognizing the power games of courtship and of politics, as well as women's repositioning as a group that could choose instead of waiting to be chosen.

In many of these cartoons, Allender created a similar rendering of the woman for whom the journal is named, "The Suffragist," a figure that Paul also put on billboards and handbills during the 1916 election. This woman has dark hair and a round face; she is thin and conservatively dressed in current styles; she always looks intelligent and fully engaged. In fact, she has many of the physical traits of Alice Paul. By relying on this character, who appeared at one time or another as a member of all classes, Nina Allender made suffragists look attractive and young. She realized, as Paul did from her studies with Edward Westermarck and her experiences with parading, that it was the better-looking, more youthful woman who symbolized promise and strength and who would be judged as morally superior. Between 1912 and 1920, Allender aged this woman somewhat, perhaps from her late twenties to her thirties and forties, giving her a sharper nose and better clothing. In making these alterations, she may have been depicting women as less vulnerable, as becoming more assured campaigners and citizens each year. This Allender image, in both its younger and older versions, contrasts starkly with the older, forbidding suffragist found in even supportive cartoons from other journals and certainly in antisuffrage cartoons.

In a few cartoons, the suffragist is also portrayed as a child, showing the politicians' tendency to regard her as one and to inflict arbitrary rules and discipline. A September 30, 1916, Allender cartoon, for example, depicts Wilson in vest and tails, arbitrarily drawing a circle around a girl from New Jersey, who is quite prissy with her petticoats, ringlets, and parasol. He is choosing the girl from the state where he had cast a vote for suffrage. Outside the circle stand poorer girls from the middle states, southern states, and New England— the girls who would not get the vote from Wilson because he was not supporting a federal amendment. Wilson's selection of an affluent "good girl"—an infantilized woman—and his denial of the others demonstrate the arbitrariness of his own choices and of women's waiting to be picked by him. In the December 26, 1914, cartoon, a child sits alone in a dark fireplace waiting for Santa to bring her a federal amendment, dramatizing again the futility of trying to be a good girl who would get suffrage as a present for good behavior.

Allender also used the child metaphor to show women changing from dependents into fearless adults. In an April 22, 1916, cartoon, Little Miss Moffitt sits holding a bowl full of four million votes from the states where women were already enfranchised. She brandishes her spoon at the spider

FIVE CENTS

WEEKLY ORGAN OF THE
CONGRESSIONAL UNION FOR WOMAN SUFFRAGE
AND OF THE NATIONAL WOMAN'S PARTY

SEPTEMBER 30, 1916

Mr. Wilson Believes in Woman Suffrage for New Jersey

Suffragist cover for Sept. 30, 1916. Cartoon by Nina Allender. Caption: "Mr. Wilson Believes in Woman Suffrage for New Jersey." The President is playing with an affluent "good girl"—an infantilized woman—and leaving the others out.

sent by the Judiciary Committee, the powerful group that could persuade the Rules Committee to approve suffrage for a vote in the House. The scene has the following caption, underlining the difference between this "Miss" and a woman/child:

> Little Miss Moffitt,
> Sat on a Tuffit,
> Eating her curds and whey;
> There came a great spider
> And sat down beside her,
> DID IT FRIGHTEN MISS MOFFITT AWAY?
> IT DID NOT!

Here the capital letters indicate another refusal to accept myths of strength and weakness. This spider, like men throwing fireworks or choosing one child/woman over another, does not threaten a "new Miss Moffitt" at all.

In 1917 as picketers began standing at the White House, Allender abandoned her usual combination of picture plus caption and used a combination of cartoon figures, banners, and captions to create several layers of contrast and irony. In that year, as Wilson became a wartime president, the cartoons no longer satirized him as an individual. Instead, like the picketing itself, they focused on his declarations about democracy, especially on their lack of meaning at home. In Allender's June 2, 1917, cartoon, a well-dressed suffragist holds a banner quoting Wilson's declaration-of-war speech to Congress, in which he argued that Americans were willing to fight for democracy, "for the right of those who submit to authority to have a voice in their own governments." The caption "Insulting the President?" refers to the irony of suffragists facing intense criticism for holding these banners and for expecting these principles to apply to American women. In a November 3, 1917, cartoon, three women stare out from their jail cells, holding onto the bars; their banner stands in front of them: "Mr. President, what will you do for woman suffrage?" The cartoon points to the irony that arresting women was all he would do for suffrage. The caption makes his own hypocrisies even clearer: "President Wilson says, 'Godspeed to the cause.'" In each of these cartoons, the banner itself wielded rhetorical power, as on the picket line, bringing Wilson's failures as the world's democratic leader into sharp relief. Here the triple commentary of picture, caption, and banner recreated the ironies of women's limited citizenship.

As violence began to occur on the picket line in the fall of 1917 and more and more women were jailed, Allender portrayed these scenes with varying constructions of the pickets' enemies. Some of the cartoons depicted soldiers and sailors accosting women on the lines and at their headquarters. In the September 8, 1917, cartoon, a sailor holds a suffragist by the throat and threatens her with a long stick, while a policeman, labeled "The Good Natured Police," looks on complacently. Her banner, Wilson's famous "Make the World Safe for Democracy," is on the ground. This picture emphasized the disjunction between what the banner said and what American authorities were doing. The caption added another level of irony in its referral to these men's status as fighters: "'First to Fight' (Government Recruiting Poster Slogan)."

In wartime, though, any denunciation of American troops could lead to negative associations for suffragists. Thus, on October 6, 1917, Allender chose a different tack, presenting a completely fanciful scene of soldiers supporting the campaign. A spiritlike woman holding the banner "We Shall Fight for Democracy at Home" marches at the front of a huge line of soldiers. The captions show the soldiers' personal commitment to her cause:

> First Drafted Man—My Wife is in Prison for Democracy.
> Second Drafted Man—My Mother is in Prison for Democracy.
> Third Drafted Man—My Sister is in Prison for Democracy.

The cartoon is titled "The Spirit from Occoquan," the infamous workhouse prison where so many suffragist pickets, including Alice Paul, were incarcerated. In such cartoons, less truthful but more common than those in which soldiers appear as opponents, Allender associated the heroism of soldiers with her cause and its stalwart advocates.

Whereas Allender's representations of soldiers were various and contradictory, her construction of police was much less complex. On July 7, 1917, Paul reprinted a cartoon from the New York *Call* in which a brutishly huge policeman brandishes his billyclub at a much smaller suffragist and demands of her, "Don't You Know Better Than to Tell the Truth in Washington?" The cartoon is ironically entitled "Democracy." For November 16, 1918, Allender drew a similar cartoon, of the large policeman grabbing a banner as well as the woman holding it. The caption points to the Senate's unwillingness to pass the amendment in 1918 even after the president had at least nominally given it his support: "The Senate of the United States after Four Years Observation of Europe Still Believes This Is the Way to Stop the Demand for Democracy." In this cartoon, Allender tied the cruel behavior of the beat cop to the regime behind him—an authoritarian government abusing those citizens who lack basic rights. Allender believed that, unlike soldiers, large and gruesome policemen could effectively serve as frightening symbols of institutionalized violence toward women on the picket line.

As a small minority in the Senate continued to oppose suffrage in 1918, these men also became fair game for attack as antidemocratic fiends. For the October 12, 1918, issue, alluding to the use of mustard gas by the German

VOL. V, NO. 77
FIVE CENTS

OFFICIAL WEEKLY ORGAN OF
THE NATIONAL WOMAN'S PARTY

SATURDAY, JULY 14, 1917

SOLD BY THE
POLITICAL EQUALITY ASSOCIATION
146 EAST 41st STREET, NEW YORK

Drawn by Nina E. Allender

Celebrating Independence Day in the National Capital
in the Year of Our Lord, 1917

Suffragist cover for July 14, 1917. Cartoon by Nina Allender. Caption: "Celebrating Independence Day in the National Capital in the Year of Our Lord, 1917." The police are shown as being at least as threatening as the crowd.

army, Allender's cartoon shows the individual woman holding a handkerchief to her mouth as fumes sent by the Senate rise around her. The slogan is "Gassed!" In the January 18, 1919, cartoon, the Senate is represented as an overweight, balding, bespectacled, expensively dressed man—unconcerned about justice or positive action for the citizenry. He sits in a comfortable armchair wearing a crown reading "U.S. Senate Divine Right," and he bellows, "Democracy—Piffle!" Before him is the confident suffragist, carrying a banner that says, "American women demand a share in the new democracy." Such cartoons associated these senators with German aristocrats like Kaiser Wilhelm and his Reichstag: women are the soldiers who will fight these tyrants until true democracy is won.

Although Allender used pickets in her cartoons to point to Wilson's hypocrisies, the police's cruelty, and the Senate's inaction, she also used them to dramatically portray women's strength. As was always true in Paul's suffrage rhetoric, cartoons about picketing did not emphasize women as victims. In many of these cartoons, instead of being helped or hindered by soldiers, women were constructed as valiant warriors successfully waging their own campaign. These cartoons presented not the sole picket, but women in groups. A March 3, 1917, cartoon, for example, presents a long line of marching women, the first one carrying a banner with the single word "Liberty." The caption reads, "Through War Clouds to Victory." In Allender's June 14, 1919, cartoon a large group marches, and the slogan is "Banners Victorious."

Throughout the campaign, the *Suffragist's* cartoons showed the reader how to construct herself—as a working-class or middle-class woman protecting her children, surviving in wartime, managing her home, plowing fields, and ultimately standing her ground against police and mobs as she devotes herself to attaining the vote. Seen through Allender's eyes, this woman is beautiful and determined, and she has the insight and humor to recognize the hypocrisies and cruelties of men. Whatever else she accomplishes in her busy life, she is by definition "The Suffragist," committed to this cause and possessed of the intelligence and drive to prevail. As each reader finished looking at the cartoon and opened the magazine, she did so positioned as the strong and determined woman who would read further and become more fully involved.

On the Inside

As the reader opened the *Suffragist,* she immediately caught a sense of forward movement in the very positive "News Notes of the Week," also called "Review of the Week" or "Notes of the Week." These short news paragraphs covered recent progress: in the first issue on November 15, 1913, for example, paragraphs concern the CU's new offices, speakers in various cities, a visit in Washington by the New Jersey delegation, a reception to welcome Rheta Childe Dorr, and the progress of the suffrage amendment in the Senate. In many issues, these short paragraphs also considered women's advancements around the world, positing readers within a progressive international movement. During the war, this section even contained articles on German women who were doing war work and securing the vote, without any animosity shown toward them.

The Editorials

The third page of the *Suffragist* contained the masthead information, including the names of the executive committee of the CU and of the journal's editor and business manager. Below this information was a boxed rendition of the Susan B. Anthony Amendment and a boxed history of its recent progress in the legislature, a physical alignment of this amendment and political action concerning it with these CU officers. To the left of these boxes appeared one or more editorials, generally written by Alice Paul and Lucy Burns. Readers found on one page the names of the key sponsoring group, the amendment itself, the recent political action concerning it, and, in the editorials, not a summary of recent occurrences but a persuasive account of how readers should view them, how Alice Paul and, by extension, suffragists evaluated the amendment and all that was happening concerning it.

In these editorials, Paul had two goals. She attempted to convince readers that each individual event was planned well and each occurrence in Congress and across the country would eventually accrue in their favor. These editorials constructed specific moments, but they also created one grand text and impression: their repetition mattered as much as their specifics. Through this cohesive emphasis on the positive, Paul established a chain of logic and a belief in inevitable victory.

In the first issues, many pieces concerned suffrage as a federal issue, Paul's point of separation from NAWSA and the impetus of her campaign. In the spring of 1914, she marshalled her arguments for the Anthony Amendment to point out the futility of the Shafroth legislation. In September 1916, when Wilson voted for suffrage in his home state of New Jersey, an editorial made sure that adherents remember the primacy of a federal amendment, which the president still opposed: "In Congress, where the chances for the success of woman suffrage were good, he turned his whole party machine against it; in New Jersey, where defeat was sure, he cast a solitary vote in its favor"

("Wilson's Vote on Suffrage"). During that fall, many editorials also reviewed the logic of a boycott of the Democrats, portraying it as part of a chain of reason that the Democrats themselves had triggered by failing to support federal legislation: "First the Democrats treat women unjustly; then they paternally advise them, for the good of the cause, to remain 'non-partisan,' i.e., inactive. Women are as determined as the Democratic party could wish them to be to remain non-partisan in the genuine sense—to be uncontrolled by party—to act in the interest of woman suffrage primarily, and not primarily in the interest or for the advantage of any party but their own" ("Women Must Remain").

Toward the end of the campaign, after Wilson had publicly endorsed suffrage as a war measure, Paul used several editorials to make sure her group understood that he was still not doing all that he could for the amendment: "When the President of the United States demands the passage of the federal amendment it will no longer be obstructed in the United States Senate" ("President's Responsibility"); "The President has rendered lip-service to woman suffrage, but still refuses to jeopardize his strength in the South" ("Power of Women"); "If the President really means that the passage of this amendment is necessary as a spiritual weapon for the conduct of the war, he will put all the power of his high office into securing this weapon" ("Defeat in the Senate"). As these examples from different years demonstrate, Paul consistently used editorial space to make the case for this one amendment and encourage readers to look at every event through this one lens.

In the structure of the editorials, Paul tried to recreate the difficult rhetorical situation of her readers. Many editorials began with reference to some stereotypical criticism of the movement, alluded to as having appeared in a recent letter or unidentified newspaper article. Then Paul would refute that negative judgment, thus providing readers with answers to the critiques voiced in their own communities. "Woman Suffrage and the War Argument," for example, starts with the claim that women don't deserve the vote because they don't fight in wars, a contention also refuted in Allender's cartoons. To disprove this conclusion, the piece quotes senators—fine authoritative sources to include in speeches—who argue that women send their sons to war and that their war work is "just as much sinews of war at times as are ball cartridges." "War and the Suffrage Campaign" refutes the common view that picketing in wartime is unpatriotic, arguing that pickets had to act "to obtain for women the opportunity to give effective expression, through political power, to their ideals, whatever they may be." Paul also at times evoked a sense of righteous anger against the negative viewpoints that she refuted. In "Begging for Rights," she quotes the word *begging,* used to denigrate lobbying visits with members of the House Judiciary Committee, which controlled the introduction of amendments to the Congress. She offers an impassioned response: "It is very seldom that women pause to consider the abasement of their position when public officers can dare affront them so frankly . . . an injustice so crass as to be ludicrous." In Paul's view, this abasement should cause women to redouble their efforts for the one amendment that every editorial advocated.

While stressing the primacy of the Anthony Amendment, these editorials also concentrated on the sense of optimism and forward motion so essential to Paul's nonviolence. In November 1915, when state suffrage votes failed in New York, New Jersey, Pennsylvania, and Massachusetts, she argued that the fact that these votes had been held, that attention had thus been paid to suffrage, should be read as "an astonishing political event" ("New York, Massachusetts"). When pickets experienced the gruesome realities of imprisonment in workhouses, she maintained that their great sacrifice was producing an immediate positive effect: "Never have so many suffrage concessions been made to the women of the nation as the President has made during the last few months" ("Real Advance"). On March 22, 1919, after the amendment had once again been turned down by the Senate, an editorial called "The Year's Progress" claimed "This is no time for discouragement." If each suffragist would flood senators with letters and telegrams, she went further, the amendment would succeed through the strength of her efforts: "Women of America, this is your responsibility." Paul never wrote in a tone of exasperation or defeat: all is moving forward. As she sought to engage readers, she often used an all-encompassing "we" that stretched from her own small group to every reader, bringing all suffragists along with her. Editorials frequently began in the third person and switched to the first to include readers along with the writer in one strong group: "Once again *Suffragists* are appealing to the President to do his part in removing the ancient sex inequality that has so long endured in *our* political life. *We* are appealing to him as the head of the national government and as the leader of the party which is in control of Congress" [emphasis ours] ("President Wilson and Suffrage").

As the *Suffragist* reader began to look at the journal, she saw herself in the determined woman on the cover, she read positive news items of the week, she looked at the huge list of names surrounding the Anthony Amendment, and then she encountered Paul's construction of each step along the way. The first three pages of each issue packed a strong punch. In perhaps three or four minutes of casual perusal, any reader could see what was going on and what Paul wanted her to think and do.

The Middle Section

The *Suffragist*'s middle section covered the most recent campaign events, with articles filled with positive details and large photographs. In the April 4, 1914, issue, for example, articles discuss hectic preparations for a demonstration on May 9 and a suffrage ball. On April 17, 1915, they concern state conventions, the suffrage booth at the World's Fair in San Francisco, and the campaign throughout the country. On April 15, 1916, they feature a CU conference, suffrage's importance in the next election, the itinerary of a train tour, and the organizing done by women in Washington. These articles were always accompanied by photographs of smiling and moving women, at their parades and in their headquarters, clearly headed toward success. By reporting preparations for a suffrage event, Paul could create excitement for it and teach others how to arrange for such successes. After each event, glowing articles spotlighted the inevitable success and forward progress.

The middle section's articles, by varied authors within the movement, covered not just public events but every political choice that the group was making. Alva Belmont wrote about the policy of holding the Democratic Party responsible for the failure to pass the amendment. Ida Husted Harper compared the Shafroth-Palmer Amendment unfavorably with the Anthony Amendment ("National Suffrage Amendment"). Articles also covered key governmental processes, like how Congress considered an amendment and how lobbyists did their work.

Articles in this section also tied current events to the history of the women's movement, to legitimize these suffragists by placing them within a well-regarded historical line-up. Many articles concerned Susan B. Anthony, constructing her as an example of heroic suffrage activism and committed feminism—as a leader whose path Paul and her constituency were following, the predecessor of their activist values and their nonviolent campaign methods. Articles quoted Anthony as arguing that progress required women to first change their view of themselves. According to Anthony, as quoted in an article by Lucy Burns, women needed to be "on guard not only against political foes, but against the inherited subservience of women which so often makes them the unconscious mouthpiece of men's opinions and prejudices" ("Susan B. Anthony"). Other articles associated Anthony with aggressive approaches to the campaign to link her with the NWP instead of with NAWSA. In "Susan B. Anthony, Militant," Vivian Pierce says that Anthony merited the "militant" label "before this opprobrious term was invented"; she "did not realize her 'militancy.'" Other articles compared her *Revolution* to the *Suffragist,* her activism during the Civil War to Paul's wartime picketing, and her belief in a federal solution and her desire to hold the party in power responsible to similar NWP choices. On February 16, 1918, in "Susan B. Anthony, 1820–1918," the *Suffragist* further associated Anthony with not just the NWP but with Alice Paul herself. The article opens with this Paul-like quotation from Anthony: "I was born and reared a Quaker and am still one; . . . but today all sectarian creeds and political policies sink into utter insignificance compared with the essence of religion and the fundamental principle of government—equal rights. I have not allied myself and shall not ally myself with any party or any measure save the one of justice and equality to women." This article and others portrayed Paul as the ultimate inheritor of Anthony's values and the one who could bring her plans to fruition.

With Paul and her predecessor Anthony providing the moral framework, many other women entered these pieces as the campaigners necessary to fulfill their noble goals. Weekly articles featured the hard work in Washington, the travels of national organizers, the financial contributions of wealthy donors, the special stunts of women who took physical risks to create stirring events, and the participants at meetings and in parades. Articles include long lists of participants so readers regularly encountered the names of well-known women—and felt encouraged to have their own names placed there, too.

Along with these articles in the middle section, photographs added to the sense of involvement and heroism. Including shots of women in action as well as formal portraits of major participants, this visual rhetoric regularly filled two half pages, or several pages after a convention or parade. The emphasis was on making everything look thrilling through a variety of photographic techniques. To present suffragists as respectable women, the editors used cameo framing and double boxes with individual portraits, both techniques mimicking the look of studio portraits. To emphasize excitement in pictures of events, editors employed a variety of techniques: overlapping photographs at various angles; using panoramic pictures of large crowds spanning two pages; wrapping text around pictures; and accompanying pictures with labels to inform readers where these events occurred and what the key participants were doing. All was to be attractive and inviting, as an assistant editor wrote to a contributor: "and please don't send us any *homely* pictures unless they are of very important women" (Young). These layouts emulated the photogravures of Sunday papers and the lush style of monthlies like *Harpers,* making suffrage look attractive and stylish, as part of an accepted and admirable social scene.

In this middle section, at irregular intervals but generally once a month, there also appeared "Comments of the Press," another means of featuring the forward progress and inevitability of suffrage. Here, Paul did not print any of the very negative newspaper pieces that her decisions triggered. Instead, she only quoted paragraphs, along with headings written by her editors, that constructed the press and public as approving her actions. By regularly publishing just these positive responses, she reassured her readers about the public's response and the inevitability of success.

This section first appeared on January 31, 1914, reprinting a positive editorial on the CU by Judson Welliver in the *Washington Times*. On August 15, 1914, the regular inclusion of paragraphs from newspapers across the country began. Once a month these excerpts filled between one half and two pages, more when there was a substantial amount of good coverage, as for the large parades, and less when coverage turned negative, as during wartime picketing. These short excerpts did not dwell on facts, but on positive editorial judgments. Sometimes this section included excerpts from radical journals like the New York *Call,* but much more commonly from dailies across the country, as a more persuasive version of general opinion. The quotations were accurate, but carefully chosen and titled to reinforce the journal's arguments. As the *Suffragist* decried Wilson's claim that he could not support a federal amendment because he had to honor states' rights, an excerpt from the *San Diego Sun,* with the ironic label of "Excuse Him: He's Tied," asked questions that assailed this logic: "Why not leave the tariff question to the states? . . . Why not condemn Abraham Lincoln for his emancipation declaration because South Carolina didn't like it?" On the issue of picketing in wartime, the journal presented the few positive quotations. The prosuffrage *New York Tribune,* for example, was quoted on July 7, 1917, under the heading of "Honor Suffrage Soldiers": "All honor to Alice Paul and her associates! The men who deride, belittle and insult them in their efforts for real—not sham—democracy are not really men—only a semblance." In 1918 these sections appeared more frequently as Democratic senators who opposed the amendment began to seem obstructionist. During that period, Paul especially included quotations from southern papers to emphasize that this most problematic of regions had finally begun to support the amendment. *Suffragist* editors probably especially enjoyed quoting a *New Orleans Item* article from December 20 that labeled those senators as "a little minority of servants of whiskey, vice, child-laboring and kindred interests" ("America Last").

In these excerpts, as well as the articles and photographs, this middle section portrayed the group in action, enacting the principles that informed the cartoons, editorials, and the amendment itself. As a constant and determined force, this section argued, these women would succeed.

Ending with a Business Appearance

After the middle pages, the final business columns added to the sense of strength and forward progress. The treasurer's report listed every person's name and the amount of her contribution along with a grand total. Readers could see that Alva Belmont and other wealthy women had given one or two thousand dollars that week, while many others, also named, had contributed ten or twenty dollars to the always increasing bottom line. These last pages also listed the names of subscribers recruited by current members within the past week, with the repeated heading of "5,000 new subscribers" and often a short quotation from a subscriber about the magazine's glories. Under that heading on the last page of the April 15, 1916, edition, for example, appears the following encomium: "A woman voter from Los Angeles, in sending in her subscription to the *Suffragist*, writes: 'I hope I shall continue to take it until we have suffrage all over the United States. I do not let any copies I receive stop with me. I pass them on to other women voters after reading them.'"

These last pages also included boxed ads, from an inch to a quarter page in size, filling up to a page and a half. They certainly provided income for the journal, but they also constructed this campaign as natural for women, as part of their regular lifestyles and as supported by the business establishment. Even the first issue contained ads from a variety of Washington firms: a manufacturer of hair products, a grocer, a store selling trunks and leather goods, a tailor, an engraving company, a luncheonette, a hotel, and a real estate trust company. In 1914 the journal established a long-term relationship with S. Kann Sons & Co., a D.C. department store on Eighth and Pennsylvania Avenue, which advertised its ladies wear by the season: 350 new trimmed hats, for example, in October 1914; tailored skirts in April 1915; fur-trimming services in November 1915. Although ads for clothes, groceries, and beauty products appeared most commonly, some ads targeted the professional needs of working women. On April 4, 1914, ads for the French College of Dressmaking and L.C. Smith and Bros. Typewriter appeared. The Smith ad is headed "Do You Run a Typewriter or Does the Typewriter Run You?" Even as Paul's picketing became increasingly controversial during 1917, her advertisers stayed with her. Throughout the campaign, like the lists of subscribers and of donations, these ads testified to the movement's respectability and solvency, to the ability of these women to effectively pursue nonviolent activism within the confines of a modern city.

From the Suffragist to Press Bulletins

With this carefully constructed journal appearing each week, Paul had a solid basis of communication with her constituency. But the journal also served a second purpose: as a source of daily press bulletins. While setting up the *Suffragist,* Paul began a press department that kept suffrage news constantly before the American public—"to convert as much of the press as possible, so that it makes the cause its own, and as for the rest, to give it such compelling news that not even a European war or an attempted boycott by the government will keep it off the front page" (Bland 12). From this office, Paul sent out stories to wire services several times a week and to press galleries at the Senate and House and at the Washington Press Club each day. These pieces stemmed from the same research as articles in the *Suffragist,* and they often involved the same main points and supporting paragraphs.

Although Paul and Lucy Burns oversaw these efforts, as they did the *Suffragist,* the press department also involved many paid and volunteer employees. Press efforts began with preparation for the first parade, in March 1913, which was led by Paul and Elsie Hill, a daughter of Congressman Ebenezer J. Hill from Connecticut, who had graduated from Vassar and was then teaching French at a Washington high school. Each day, Paul wrote press bulletins and Hill came in after school to take them to the newspapers. Jessie Hardy Stubbs took over these responsibilities in 1914; Florence Brewer Boeckel took them over in 1915 and continued for the rest of the campaign. Boeckel built a press department in one room of the headquarters, working at first with two paid assistants. Later she added several stenographers, typists, and mimeograph workers as well as women who kept clipping books. Abby Scott Baker joined her in 1916 as national press chairman, circulating stories to every congressional district and publicizing every national event.

With the regular press contact provided by the bulletins, the *Suffragist* became part of a circle of publicity. As Paul wrote to all her field organizers on September 20, 1916, pieces from the *Suffragist* could be "put in the local papers almost intact by giving them a local lead or quoting them as coming from someone of your local partners if she is willing to stand sponsor for such a quotation" (Letter to Organizer). Then in the "Comments of the Press" section, the *Suffragist* included newspaper articles from around the nation that originated in these press bulletins, creating the impression that the entire country thought like Paul and the NWP.

Circular Letters

As Paul published the *Suffragist* and sent out press bulletins to reach a larger newspaper audience, she never discontinued the circular letters she had told NAWSA her journal would replace. Whereas newspapers reached the general public and the *Suffragist* reached her entire constituency, these letters could quickly get through to selected individuals and solicit changes in their thinking, speech, and action. In the fall of 1914, for example, Paul used the *Suffragist's* cartoons, editorials, and articles as well as press bulletins to explain to the public and to her constituency her policy of opposing Democrats, but circular letters to a select few enabled her to secure the volunteers needed to lead the effort in each state. In January 1916 letters from Paul and other officers recruited the women needed to plan conferences in each congressional district and to help the organizers coming to their states. In an April 1918 letter to party members in the western states, National Secretary Virginia Arnold wrote about a visit by the chair of the Republican National Committee to the West and the continuing opposition to Democrats: "Please see him and impress suffrage, that his party can be the one to carry it over and reap that benefit" (Letter to Maria Dean). Circular letters from staff members often quote Paul to emphasize the importance of the requested action, as in a December 1916 letter from Abby Scott Baker, the National Press Chairman, requesting funds for publicity work: "Miss Paul thinks that this year there is nothing more vitally important to our federal amendment than the press work. It is, as you know, the very life of any public movement" (Letter to Mrs. Rosenwald). Telegrams could also help direct the effort when Paul needed to solve problems in the field. In October 1918, after hearing that campaigners were endorsing Republicans, she telegrammed many field workers: "Do not advocate election of any Senators but make campaign purely anti-Democratic" (Telegram to Margaret Whittemore).

In these letters, Paul generally made her requests, many of which seemed to involve superhuman effort, in question form with no question mark. On March 10, 1914, for example, Paul wrote to Elsie Hill: "Could you not be a Suffrage organizer, beginning with the close of the school year. You could stop, of course, any time that you wanted to, and go back to teaching. You can teach and make money all your life, you know, but there will never come again this great need to helping in our movement. Could you not get rid of your apartment and such millstones about one's neck, and live on very little for at least one year as the rest of us do. You know, of course, what you ought to do but I hope you will consider this." Such requests appear in letters that she sent throughout the campaign: "Will you not have as many telegrams as possible sent to Colt urging him to vote. It would be well also to have every person who sends a telegram to Colt to telegraph Lippitt too"; "Will you not get us some articles and cartoons and illustrations for the paper if you can possibly do so"; "Will you not let us know if you can proceed in your state with this plan of congressional district organization, and send us full details concerning it for the Suffragist" (Letter to Emily K. Perry; to Dora Lewis; to Florence Bayard Hilles). Paul seems to have employed both the lack of question mark and the simple sound of the request to make a positive reply more likely.

Although these letters kept the group together and secured action throughout the campaign, they may have been most essential during 1917 and 1918 when newspapers and civic groups castigated the NWP for picketing in wartime. Lucy Burns wrote a circular letter headed "Dear Member of the Woman's Party" on November 9, 1917, for example, to tell the group that Paul and six others had been given a seven-month sentence for holding a banner at the White House gates, imprisoned for asking Wilson for political liberty at home while he advocated it abroad. Her letter stresses details—of Paul's being force-fed in prison and refused the rights accorded to common criminals— and it ends with a request for action, following Paul's form of questions: "Will you write President Commissioner Gardiner, and L. F. Zinkham warden of the jail and get 'every lover of fair play' to do the same." In this difficult time as in earlier years, suffragists needed the NWP's opinions and facts delivered to them in articles but also in specifically targeted letters.

* * *

Throughout the campaign, Paul relied on the *Suffragist,* press bulletins, circular letters, and personal letters and telegrams to provide ongoing persuasion for the amendment. This rhetoric created a powerful circle of influence. Campaigners could draw on the editorials to shape their own persuasive speeches and writing; they could envision themselves as "The Suffragist" and join in the many events discussed in the articles; once they joined in, circular letters could help shape their own events and help them stay involved with each moment of the action. As details of these activities also appeared in press bulletins, arguments went out from a group of activists to the nation. Excerpts of this coverage could then be placed in the *Suffragist* to legitimize the cause and spur further action. This ongoing combination reached those who already supported the amendment as well as a larger group—to stimulate a positive identity and a sense of ongoing action.

4. Parades and Other Events

Escalating the Nonviolent Pressure

Throughout the campaign for suffrage, Alice Paul felt that her combination of individual letters, circular letters, the *Suffragist,* and press bulletins provided the necessary written persuasion for her supporters and the larger public. But Paul also felt—as did Gandhi—that the successful nonviolent campaign could not be run with written appeals or speeches alone. Like other Quakers who had served as witnesses for social reform, Paul believed in the compelling power of the rhetorical scene or moment, the lasting impact of visual rhetoric.

Beginning in 1913 Paul created a changing panoply of visual events that brought the suffrage movement into the forefront of the nation's consciousness. The events involved large numbers of people as participants and spectators, and ultimately involved all Americans as readers of magazines and newspapers that covered these controversial choices. In a *LaFollette's Magazine* article from September 1917, which the *Suffragist* reprinted in October, Belle Case La Follette reminded readers that only five years earlier the capital had been "enjoying a veritable Rip Van Winkle sleep on the subject of suffrage," but that since then Paul's always vivid and often shocking events had served as a strong alarm and a catalyst for change.

The First Parade

When she started her campaign in January of 1913, Paul decided to employ a traditional political strategy—a parade—but to do so in the most controversial of manners. Paul knew from her experience in England that parading provided a symbolic announcement of unity, purpose, and strength—a message of "we are here, moving forward, in small groups melded into one." Parades by town militia and civic groups had a long tradition as "celebratory performance" in North America, the transformation of "ritualized aesthetics into symbolic action." But the parades of the suffrage movement reworked the ceremony's familiar trope of solidarity: what men had used to "proclaim their collective agency," women used as a "conscious transgression of the rules of social order" (Borda 25–28). As an advocate of nonviolence, Paul sought this transgression within spaces and during times that lacked a "stability of acceptance"(W. R. Miller 57). She staged parades in volatile situations and never repeated the same type of activity: she wanted nothing she did to seem safe.

As the campaign to secure federal legislation progressed, Paul sought new arenas for events, new circumstances that would increase the risk as well as involve more women from across the nation. She repeated activities from the Washington stage on the national stage, with a parade in the capital one week and in cities and towns across the country the next, so that her supporters as well as opponents encountered a growing national force. She also alternated between scenes involving the large group and scenes involving one or two individuals—to focus on both the tremendous numbers of women committed to a federal amendment and the strength of each individual woman. As she involved the city and the town, the national and the local, she worked on increasing the level of danger and surprise. Under her direction, women marched down Pennsylvania Avenue, maintained a booth at the 1915 San Francisco World's Fair, set out cross-country in cars and on trains, visited the president in the White House and later pursued him in hotels and from boats, picketed the White House, and then, during the war, labeled the president "Kaiser Wilson" and burned him in effigy. In these escalating situations, she exploited every possibility of displaying women who faced—through the strength of their nonviolent resolve—all types of physical, psychological, and political danger.

As soon as Paul arrived in Washington, she initiated her visual campaign. She wanted to announce her presence on a grand scale to immediately invigorate the lifeless campaign to seek a federal amendment. She decided to stage a parade. It would be the first women's parade in Washington, the first national suffrage parade, and the first organized mass march on Washington, the only other being a failed attempt by the five hundred men of Coxey's Army, who had terrified the citizenry as they entered the capital in 1894 to protest widespread unemployment. Paul decided to schedule her own threatening event on the day before Wilson's inauguration, to beat the new president to the capital and to put women's priorities before the people first, as a prior claim on their attention. In later articles, the Congressional Committee often repeated a story about Woodrow Wilson coming into town that day and finding the streets deserted. When he asked where all the spectators were, the story went, the driver told him that they had all gone to the suffrage parade. This oft-repeated anecdote reiterated the parade's themes: women's claims preceded those of any new and temporary male leader.

As soon as she envisioned this symbolically significant parade, Paul started forming the committees of women needed to plan it, women that she hoped would stay involved afterwards. She understood the difficulties of mounting such an event quickly, as she later recalled: "Between the second of January and the third of March wasn't very long to get up a procession in a city where you weren't known and where you had no workers and where you had about every obstacle that you could have" (Fry). When Paul began, the Congressional Committee of the National American Woman Suffrage Association (NAWSA) was defunct, its only purpose was for its chair to formally present the federal amendment to Congress each year. It was an active committee of only one—Elizabeth Kent, wife of a congressman from California, working with a ten-dollar annual budget that she didn't spend. As Pennsylvania suffragist Caroline Katzenstein later acknowledged, "There was no thought of putting the Amendment through Congress or of lobbying for it, no thought that it could be adopted," and thus there was no active group (174). NAWSA gave Paul a list of past members of the committee, but of the forty or fifty names, she soon found that none had taken any active role with Kent, and most had moved or died.

To prepare for the first parade and begin creating a national nonviolent campaign, Paul visited everyone she could discover who had a commitment to suffrage. Kent offered to help, as did Emma Gillette, dean and one of the founders of the Washington College of Law, instituted to train women for the legal profession. Belva Lockwood was also at Paul's first meeting. Lockwood was a lawyer who had run for the presidency on a prosuffrage platform in 1884, following the logic that "If women in the United States are not permitted to vote, there is no law against their being voted for" (Kerr 151, 153). They were joined by Helen Gardener and Elsie Hill.

Paul asked Helen Gardener to take charge of publicity for the parade. Although Gardener felt Paul was too young and inexperienced to head a Congressional Committee, she worked diligently on the parade, as Paul recalled: "She would arrive in the early morning and stay all day long and never budge and certainly she was 100% wonderful, I thought. Didn't see how anybody could have been better" (Fry). Gardener had gained notoriety by giving a series of talks in 1884 on free thinking and publishing them in 1885 as *Men, Women, and Gods, and Other Lectures.* A widely quoted remark from her lectures concerning Christianity is "The religion and the Bible require of women everything and give her nothing. They ask her love and support, and repay her with contempt and oppression" (*Plain Talk* 8, 10). Although many women heard her lectures, Gardener came to a wider notice among feminists when, in *Facts and Fictions of Life,* she published a carefully researched refutation to a neurologist's widely publicized claim that the female brain weighed less and thus was inferior to the male's. Gardener brought seriousness and prestige—and an added bit of danger—to the cause.

By the middle of January 1913, within a month of her arrival in Washington, Paul created subcommittees to plan the event that she had chosen. By January 8, her stationery listed officers of NAWSA and the Congressional Committee, members of the "Joint Inaugural Procession Committee," chairs of District of Columbia suffrage societies, and the names of several local judges and their wives, whose inclusion could help her to recruit other participants and financial sponsors. Paul knew that along with hard-working committees and significant personages, she needed individuals with professional skill to make a grand statement that would attract massive press attention. She brought in Hazel MacKaye, an actress and professional pageant coordinator who was a member of a prominent theatre family, to design parade floats and a tableau. As NAWSA's Annual Report for 1913 reported, what Paul was carefully but quickly planning was "the most elaborate pageant procession the country had ever known."

Having secured a hard-working local committee as well as supportive social luminaries, Paul immediately sent circular letters to suffrage organizations around the country so they would send marchers to the parade and begin a long-range commitment to a federal amendment. Letters solicited participants for various units within the parade: professional groups, such as dentists and nurses; religious groups, beginning with the Friends Equal Rights Section from the Philadelphia Yearly Meeting of Hicksites; college groups, beginning with women from Swarthmore College; and state and local suffrage societies. Paul also immediately initiated a committee that planned parlor and hall meetings in Washington "almost every day" to gain further participants and swell the audience, while also introducing Washington citizens to her long-range campaign goals. As Paul built an active planning group, she kept those at the NAWSA headquarters in New York informed of her progress. As she recalled, they were anxious to have the parade, but "they were always harping on the fact that they couldn't afford to pay anything toward it" (Fry).

As she worked with Gardener on the crucial positive publicity, Paul recognized that the impact of this "inaugural" event would depend on the route, on getting the most out of the symbolic potential of the nation's capital. The superintendent of the district police, Richard Sylvester, first told her that he would give her a permit for Sixteenth Street, a principally residential street where many embassies were located. Paul wanted a permit for Pennsylvania Avenue, from the Capitol to the White House, to access not just the primary symbols of government but also the crowds massing for the inauguration. The chief denied her request, Paul reported to her supporters, not because the route was too crowded with traffic or because it was being readied for the inaugural events, but because, in his words, "It's totally unsuitable for women to be marching down Pennsylvania Avenue," an indication that he agreed with her assessment of the street's symbolic power. At this impasse, Elsie Hill asked her mother—since her father was in Congress, and Congress allocated money for the District of Columbia police—to speak to the police chief. Together, mother and daughter secured the route Paul desired. This was perhaps Paul's first real victory, one secured by women over the objections of old-fashioned male authorities, just as the amendment itself would be. To explain his change to the press, Sylvester maintained that he had thought at first that these women intended to march at night, when they could not be adequately protected, but he had later realized that they intended an afternoon parade ("To Permit Women's Parade"). Paul, however, claimed that determined, influential women had caused him to change his mind.

Securing this day and this route for this parade was Paul's first assertion of nonviolent danger. Parades had gone down Fifth Avenue in New York and had occurred as part of state campaigns on main streets in other cities. But this was a national effort and this was Washington: these women would not be walking down a commercial or residential street, but would precede the president down the street of power. In her January 11 letter to Mary Ware Dennett, Paul argued that this route, along with the story of obtaining it, should be heavily featured in appeals to potential participants, because it symbolized women's assumption of their rightful "place." And she made sure that press bulletins featured the drama of the successful quest to get the "inappropriate" route. This publicity, in fact, enabled Paul to secure the cooperation of a local company that wanted to make money on what they recognized as a large and financially viable event. The firm managing the seating for the inauguration helped Paul and Gardener publicize the parade and sold seats in grandstands erected for the inaugural procession, giving Paul a percentage of the money from the sales, with which she paid the parade bills, as NAWSA required her to do.

With the route settled and publicity under way, Paul began concentrating on how the parade would look: on the symbolism of every inch. The theme she chose was not suffrage but "Ideals and Virtues of American Woman-hood"—to get women to celebrate themselves and develop the self-respect necessary for change. Paul wanted the women that marched to do so in the most reputable guise, as well-dressed middle- and upper-class women. If the women looked beautiful, like those in the *Suffragist*'s photographs, they would naturally symbolize morality and a correct vision of the future, and they would draw other participants. As Paul told an interviewer many years later, "It may be an instinct, it is with me anyway, when you're presenting something to the world, to make it as beautiful as you can" (Gallagher 23). When she discussed this preinaugural parade with Amelia Fry, she continued to develop that theme of exploiting the approved female form: "The only difference between the previous ones and the one on March 3 was that we concentrated especially on attempting to make ours extraordinarily beauti-ful and therefore introduced a great many beautiful costumes and pageant features, all of which made it of the type which is supposed to be particularly feminine." In her final phrase here, "supposed to be particularly feminine," Paul reveals her constant attention to rhetorical effectiveness for a specific audience. Viewers on the parade route, the crowd in town for the inaugura-tion, would find the women beautiful—and thus acceptable on this street and in their advocacy of suffrage. With this look for the parade, Paul was able to exploit the relationship between temporal notions of women's beauty and their social worth, which she had studied with Edward Westermarck at the London School of Economics.

To create the aura of beauty to which a crowd would respond, Paul asked each group of marchers to dress in one color and dress well. Marching to-gether, the groups would create a rainbow, representing women coming out of the dark of the past into a bright future. To bring order and beauty to the groupings, Paul chose complementary colors for participants walking next to each other. Social workers, business women, and librarians, for example, appeared in shades of blue; artists, actresses, and musicians wore shades of rose. In front of each group of marchers, women carried an elaborate ban-ner that listed the group's affiliation and combined its assigned color with Paul's new suffrage colors of purple for loyalty, white for purity, and gold for life—to visually meld the individual constituencies into one.

Even though she carefully planned for each marching group, Paul knew that more than women in rows would be required to keep a crowd involved and reach their emotions, to provide memorable moments and extensive press coverage. As William R. Miller argues, effective parades must be "imagi-natively staged with full use of vivid symbols of the movement's purpose and unity as well as devices to amplify the message and boost morale" (147). To achieve an imaginative staging, Paul recruited 26 floats, 6 golden chariots, 10 bands, 45 captains, 200 marshals, 120 pages, 6 mounted heralds, and 6 mounted brigades. These dramatic visual elements filled in spaces between the marching groups and created a grand spectacle, the details and symbolism of which were spelled out in a program given to spectators and the press.

A model of the liberty bell, brought from Philadelphia, started things off, accompanied by a banner making clear the purpose of this parade: "We demand an amendment to the Constitution of the United States enfranchising the women of the country" (Katzenstein 175–76). Following immediately behind the bell as herald was Inez Milholland, a beautiful labor lawyer from New York, who was dressed in white robes and riding a white horse named Gray Dawn. The *New York Times* described her with these details: "an imposing figure in a white broadcloth Cossack suit and long white-kid boots. From her shoulders hung a pale-blue cloak, adorned with a golden maltese cross" ("5000 Women March"). Intended to remind viewers of Joan of Arc, this costume evoked a combination of feminine beauty and willingness to sacrifice. With these introductory images—of religious, political, and historical power—Paul constructed suffrage as a social and moral imperative.

Because the event was occurring under its auspices, the national board of NAWSA led the paraders. President Anna Howard Shaw walked at the head of this group, with the rest of the board, including the national treasurer, Katharine Dexter McCormick, "the one who was always afraid of our sending the bills in." NAWSA members in their colors, white with yellow sashes, followed in great numbers. Then came the rest of Paul's well-coordinated marchers. Reports at the time varied, and certainly Paul repeated the largest figures, but there were at least five thousand participants, with some estimates reaching eight thousand ("Congressional Union for Woman Suffrage"; Katzenstein 175).

After the robed woman on horseback and rows of marchers from the nation's largest suffrage organization, Paul placed her most eye-catching marchers. "General" Rosalie Jones led the first group, followed by her Ambassadors of Justice, who were dressed in hooded brown cloaks and carried knapsacks and staffs. Jones had formed a walking pilgrimage of women from Baltimore to Washington to join the parade, gaining recruits as she went along. Their initial entry into the capital a few days earlier had been carefully noted by the *Washington Post* and other newspapers, so reporters and viewers were looking for them in the parade.

A series of floats with still and silent figures appeared behind these first marchers, the first indication to the crowd that they would be seeing much more than lines of walkers. In colorful costumes, the women on the floats

Inez Milholland on Gray Dawn, March 3, 1913. Milholland preparing to lead the preinaugural parade in Washington, D.C.

The first D.C. suffragist parade, March 3, 1913. Crowds converging on the head of the parade; the police did not clear a path.

represented the progress in women's rights since the first women's rights convention at Seneca Falls—and thus represented ideals and virtues of American womanhood. The first float depicted the suffrage movement in its pioneer stage, in the 1840s. It featured a single strong pioneer woman, dressed in a light purple cape. As the parade program informed viewers, the other women on the float represented the adversaries that she faced: three figures in black symbolized obstruction to her progress while four women in darker purple appeared as scorners of suffrage. The second and third historical floats, depicting 1870 and 1890, were similar, focusing on singular women enduring obstruction and scorn. Following the historical floats, a beautiful float represented the status of suffrage in 1913; it held many brightly dressed women and girls and no negative portrayals, making a strong rhetorical (and perhaps wishful) contrast to the earlier ones. Thus, the older women had inspired a younger group, and together they would secure women's complete involvement in government ("Order of Organizations"). These floats dramatized women's growing strength, placing the current bid for suffrage within their ongoing progress toward self-respect and equality.

Following these key floats were others that emphasized men and women working side by side and seeking suffrage together. During later years, Paul minimized the role of men in her campaign, but at this first big parade she featured the symbolism of their endorsement of women's rights, an appeal aimed directly at the largely male audience that was in Washington for the inauguration. One float depicted a man and woman on a farm, and was followed by a delegation of women farmers on foot, dressed in brown. Another held a soldier and nurse, and was followed by a group of nurses. After these two came men and women on floats and women in marching groups to signify education, law, medicine, and labor. As a contrast to these positive portrayals, the last float in this series was the government float, showing a man bearing the burden of state on his shoulders and a woman with her hands bound. This grouping of floats and marchers argued that women were cooperating with men in all the key occupations; it was only in government that women were being turned away and their potential wasted. These floats were followed by a separate delegation of men, placed not as leaders at the front of the parade, but as sympathizers who followed the many marchers and floats.

After the series of floats, bannered groups appeared, which the parade's viewers would find acceptable and even noble—groups that were presented to reorient viewers who looked at suffrage and suffrage parading as radical or inappropriate. These groups included homemakers and mothers as well as representatives of the General Federation of Women's Clubs (GFWC), which had formed in 1890 as a union of individual clubs of primarily older middle-class women, many with significant social standing in their communities. By 1910, the GFWC involved 45 state federations and 971 individual clubs (M. I. Wood 166–67; M. W. Wells 63).

After these representatives of traditional womanhood, Paul lined up women wearing banners of their occupations and organizations, again paying careful attention to their order. The first divisions featured the most "respectable" employments and activities. Exploiting the respect ceded to Civil War nurses, Paul led with representatives of the International Council of Nurses, Army Nurse Corps, Navy Nurse Corps, National Red Cross Nurses, and Red Cross Volunteers, along with other conservative, acceptable groups such as the Women's Christian Temperance Union and the PTA. Next came women representing an array of less traditional professions: dentists, lawyers, artists, "pen women," home economists, federal employees, and businesswomen as well as teachers and social service workers (Ford, *Iron-Jawed Angels* 50; "Order of Organizations"). This whole series of floats and marchers challenged the notion that women were staying in the home and thus did not need the protection or influence of the vote.

In her desire to include everyone, Paul also reserved a place for representatives of the National Association of Colored Women, which had been formed in 1896 by Mary Church Terrell. Ida Wells Barnett and Oswald Garrison Villard, the National Association of Colored People founder, led the group, whose plans to march near the end, by themselves, did not seem to create much fervor in the newspapers or among other marching groups. To one of her associates, Miss C. L. Hunt in Washington, Paul wrote in January of 1913 that even though some criticism had begun to swirl, "As to the colored women—I can see no reason why they should not be in the procession. We are expecting to include them and I have written to an official of the colored women's organization asking her to call at the office so that we could talk over plans for their disposition in the parade." These women joined in the procession as did, according to W. E. B. DuBois's *Crisis,* other "colored women [who] marched according to their State and occupation without let or hindrance" ("Politics").

A controversy did occur, however, when Elsie Hill, head of the college committee, recruited a group from Howard University to join the college section and march there with their own school sign next to other young women. When this intention became public, it was much noted and criticized in the local press. Because of this attention, Paul began to receive letters from supporters saying that they were not going to march in a procession with African Americans. As Paul recalled the issue, "It was quite a problem. It was extremely difficult because we had so many women saying, 'There will be nobody from our town, there will be nobody from our state to do this,' then lots coming forth in the newspapers inflaming everybody." To solve the problem, and stories vary on these facts, Paul seems to have separated the small group of Howard students, Marie Hardwick and five others, from the other college marchers and placed a group of Quaker men, led by one of her relatives, around them: "And so we put this men's group next to them, and the men's group were perfectly polite. Finally everybody calmed down and accepted it, so it was this men's group that really saved the day for us" (Fry).

In this incident, Paul revealed the kind of compromise she would continuously rely on to keep the focus on her one national issue. She certainly didn't want southern participants to refuse to join in: their departure would indicate that southerners opposed suffrage and that their Democratic legislators would block its passage. On the other hand, Paul didn't want to anger these African American women or make their exit from the parade into a news item that would take attention away from suffrage. Though she sought danger, she sought only danger that brought suffrage—not race, regionalism, or any other issue—to the forefront. By deciding to keep the group of marchers from Howard small and separate from other young women, she sought an acceptable middle ground that would enable suffrage to be the issue and would feature Quakers as enlightened purveyors of nonviolence.

After all the groups of educated and productive women came by in their parade divisions, Paul used another set of floats to emphasize America's divided and unjust government and to physically tie these well-respected mothers, nurses, and librarians to their arbitrary political status. The first float in this series represented the first Bill of Rights Congress and thereby drew attention to the essential rights of citizenship. The banner float then featured a huge map showing nine suffrage states—Arizona, California, Colorado, Idaho, Kansas, Oregon, Utah, Washington, and Wyoming—in light colors set among thirty-nine states in the dark. Then representatives from suffrage states marched, each group preceded by a chariot draped in the colors of the state's suffrage organizations. After the suffrage state organizations, the parade ended with another depiction of the political division in America: a woman in white, marching alone to represent the suffrage states and surrounded by women in black representing the thirty-nine states without suffrage. The banner carried before this group featured a quotation from Abraham Lincoln that, used in this context, depicted women without the vote as slaves and those men who opposed enfranchisement as slave owners: "No Country Can Exist Half Slave and Half Free" ("Order of Organizations").

Following the parade, Paul planned for a tableau on the steps of the Treasury Building to further focus on ideals of American womanhood and create a final positive association. For women to be out together marching for their own cause was certainly controversial—women in the streets might seem too aggressive or even sexual. Therefore, to create a conclusion to the event that would emphasize its moral rightness, planners relied on familiar Baroque and Romantic music and tropes of beauty, silence, and virtue presented in the guise of a traditional small-town event. Symbolic scenes or tableaux—in which actors representing historical personages or community values moved silently into formations—were a traditional part of civic pageants presented in many American towns on national holidays. Such an ending, as Paul envisioned it, would construct suffrage as part of this proud patriotic tradition.

Hazel MacKaye, an experienced pageant director, designed this tableau to create an allegory that was fully explained in programs handed out through the crowd, a "throng of many thousands" (MacKaye 683). Paul and MacKaye intended for the combination of the parade and tableau to create an artistic and rhetorical whole; the procession reviewed women's history in the United States and demonstrated their current strength and unity, and then the allegorical tableau displayed the ideals that had informed women's ongoing struggle for equality and would guide their coming victories. The columned Treasury Building, located right by the White House, and the classic, togalike costumes in which women appeared there suggested the possibility that full suffrage could engender a new Athens, a democracy incorporating the best of human values.

Percy MacKaye, Hazel's brother and America's premier pageant designer, who had planned many productions on patriotic topics, helped write the program given to spectators and later published a thorough description of the proceedings. As his program and article described, the first figures stressed the best traditions of American government that women strove to embrace. As the national anthem played, a figure robed in red, white, and blue, representing Columbia, a goddess of republican government, first came out from behind the building's columns. As trumpets continued to sound, a group joined her: Justice, in robes of violet and purple; Charity, proceeded by two small children strewing her path with petals; Liberty, a floating figure who paused for a second at the top of the steps and then swept down with her attendants; Peace, a figure in silvery white, carrying a dove that she released at the head of the steps; Plenty, carrying golden cornucopias laden with fruits; and Hope, appearing and disappearing between columns like a bright spirit, and then boldly leaving her hiding place followed by attendants in rainbow colors. As the group "in swaying gauzes" moved out from the building to its steps, they "danced with bodies nobly free in action," while the audience watched "like the audience of a cathedral ritual" (MacKaye 683). All here was

A tableau, March 3, 1913. Liberty and her attendants on the steps of the Treasury Building, following the first D.C. suffragist parade.

laudatory and traditional, like a church service or a Fourth of July pageant. Suffrage and the women striving to attain it, the event argued, should be lauded, not feared.

Hazel MacKaye had carefully planned the music to increase the pageant's emotional impact. By starting with "The Star Spangled Banner," Paul and MacKaye constructed the group as brave and self-sacrificing American patriots. The national anthem was followed by parlor pieces, each well known to the audience and each with a symbolic connection to a section of the tableau. Liberty, for example, came down to the brass fanfares and martial rhythms of the stirring "Triumphal March" from *Aida*, Verdi's grand ceremonial piece about the plight of an Ethiopian slave held in Egypt, a struggle for liberty. Hope first appeared to the dreamy sound of "Elsa's Dream" from Wagner's opera *Lohengrin,* a Romantic piece about a woman dreaming about help arriving to save her from false accusations of murder, just as women hoped to achieve justice through suffrage. Then, as the figure of Hope boldly left her hiding place followed by attendants, they moved to Dvorak's "Humoreske," a famous strong-rhythmed parlor song that could indicate the excitement of hope fulfilled.

Although Paul wanted this well-planned spectacle to delineate the ideals and virtues of American womanhood that led inexorably to suffrage, she also wanted to introduce the artistic visual rhetoric that she would be wielding throughout the campaign. This parade, Percy MacKaye argued, announced a new energy and national focus in the American suffrage movement as well as a new level of theatrical and rhetorical accomplishment: it was the "first convincing art expression of the woman's movement, and the first national expression of the new art of pageantry in America." He argued that Paul's stirring visual scenes—the "expert direction, with symbolic costumes, insignia and floats"—signaled her separation from the Pankhursts: "Thus at the capital of the British Empire, women have been smashing windows, scattering flames and acid: at the capital of the United States, women have been building pageants, scattering the creative fires of beauty and reason." This scene may have appeared magical but "it was attained scientifically—by applying expert imagination to a definite end." That end, a federal amendment, would be obtained by fully appropriating the best possibilities of nonviolent visual rhetoric (680, 683).

As the groups lined up that morning, with all their plans carefully made for the symbolic parade and tableau, Paul encountered a difficult situation that increased the danger of the event and that she skillfully manipulated to insure that a national audience paid attention. The grandstands were completely filled and so were the streets, primarily with tourists who had come to see the inauguration and had read in the newspapers about an unprecedented women's march. Paul and her committee had tried with little success to impress upon the police that a huge crowd would be attending, but the chief's attention was focused on the inauguration. The night before the parade, Elizabeth Selden Rogers took Paul to see her brother-in-law, Secretary of War Henry Lewis Stimson, and ask him to convince the police to plan for more of a presence on the route. Stimson told Rogers that if the police coverage was inadequate, she should get in touch with him and he would send the U.S. Cavalry.

When the marchers started out, they were immediately enveloped by the huge crowd—"we had this mass of people and we didn't know how to get through; we tried to get through and we just saw it couldn't be done" (Fry). Paul called Stimson, who did indeed send the cavalry as promised. As soon as the horsemen forced their way onto the route, they opened the way block by block by wheeling their horses into the crowds and forcing the viewers back, causing the parade to take many extra hours but allowing it to go forward and ultimately reach the tableau site.

Opinions varied on whether the surging crowd in the streets was antagonistic or supportive and on whether the police were just understaffed or actively unhelpful. Paul herself much later said that the police were "doing the best they could, having their leaders not providing enough policemen" (Fry). But, right after the parade, she knew that portraying the patrolmen as an active enemy would create a much more dramatic story. So she immediately stirred public opinion against authorities by asserting, in a *Washington Post* interview, that the top police and civilian officials had conspired to endanger the marchers: "There is no question that the police had the tip from some power higher up to let the rough characters in the city through the police lines try to break up our parade" ("Begin Police Grill"). The police had purposefully sent small numbers, she argued, to let the crowd overwhelm the participants and thus make these nonviolent suffragists vulnerable to violence.

The Parade's Rhetorical Aftermath

Almost immediately following the parade, Paul's supporters began to broadcast their own sense of outrage over police indifference and brutality. On the next day, Harriot Stanton Blatch sent Wilson the following remonstrative telegram and released copies to the newspapers: "As you ride today in comfort and safety to the Capitol to be inaugurated as President of the people of the United States, we beg that you will not be unmindful that yesterday the Government which is supposed to exist for the good of all, left women while passing in peaceful procession in their demand for political freedom at the mercy of a howling mob on the very streets which are being at this moment efficiently officered for the protection of men" (Blatch and Lutz 197). To gather specifics for the press and for an official complaint, Paul began collecting notarized depositions, which she asked individual marchers to provide before they left town or as soon as they got home. Marcher Leota E. Livingston from Franklin County, Ohio, for example, sent in under a notary's seal, written in this official's voice and referring to her as "Affiant," the kind of details that Paul could use to build a persuasive case against the police department:

> That during parade while marching she was stopped many times by ruffians who said insulting things to the marchers, that her banner was grabbed and pulled at a number of times by men who jeered and hooted at the marchers. That her daughter and the other two women who were marching by her side were called chickens, time and again, that on one avenue in said city the bystanders closed in on the marchers and impeded the march and caused great disorder. That there were plenty of policemen standing along the line of march but not one of them made any attempt to protect the women, and one policeman laughed and encouraged the ruffians in insulting and assaulting the women, that during said march the women were walking orderly and peaceably in the street.

In the days following the parade, Paul and Helen Gardener relied heavily on such specifics to create press bulletins distributed in Washington and in the hometowns of the participants while also seeking a response from Congress.

Newspapers that might have just reported the facts of a parade and then turned their attention to the inauguration responded with long sympathetic stories based on altercations that their reporters had witnessed, the stories provided by participants, and press bulletins sent to them immediately. The *Washington Post* on March 4, for example, chose dramatic verbs to describe the melee created by police inaction: "Five thousand women, marching in the woman suffrage pageant today, practically fought their way foot to foot up Pennsylvania Avenue, through a surging throng that completely defied Washington police, swamped the marchers, and broke their procession into little companies" ("Woman's Beauty"). Along with emphasizing the shocking details, the *Post* stressed the women's strength and their nonviolent response to this persecution: "They suffered insult and closed their ears to jibes and jeers. Few faltered, although several of the older women were forced to drop out from time to time." This last sentence appeared also in the *Baltimore Sun*'s story on that day, reflecting this paper's similar use of the press bulletins sent out immediately from Paul's headquarters ("Woman's March").

While stressing the women's bravery, many stories focused attention not just on the paraders but on the police. Oswald Garrison Villard, editor of the *New York Evening Post,* summarized the possible interpretations of their actions, saying that these officers were "either derelict or incompetent" (NAWSA Annual Report, 1913). In the *New York Times,* which opposed woman suffrage, the reporter admitted that even antisuffragists had viewed the police's conduct as an "insult to American womanhood and a disgrace to the Capitol City of the Nation"; the article argued not only that the officers could not control the crowd, but that they "even seemed to encourage the hoodlums" ("Parade Protest Arouses Senate").

All of these newspapers featured large headlines, as well as detailed and sympathetic texts. The *Washington Post,* for example, on March 4, the day of the inauguration, split the top half with two headlines—"Woman's Beauty, Grace, and Art Bewilder the Capital" and "Woodrow Wilson Arrives to Become Nation's Head Today"—beneath which were a picture of the tableau on the Treasury steps on the left side and pictures of Wilson and his vice president Thomas R. Marshall on the right, with the one suffrage picture taking up as much space as the other two. A subheading to the suffrage story pointed to the women's difficulties in completing their march—"Artistic Moving Spectacle Is at Times Marred by Scenes of Disorder Along the Line of March"—thus making the difficulties that the women faced a key element of the prominent story.

Although this press coverage was certainly gratifying, Paul knew that for the conflict to have its greatest effect, she needed more than an overwrought crowd and a bumbling police department: she needed proven police malfeasance. When Elizabeth Selden Rogers wrote to Paul from New York on March 5 to encourage her to continue exploiting the police's mistakes, she claimed that this very public demonstration of the "lack of respect of men for women" could provide a galvanizing moment. Indeed, Paul planned to use the occurrences as symbolic of ongoing government mistreatment of women, occurring because women lacked political equality. Washington police officials, she argued, were not willing to prepare adequately even for women to march down the street; instead, they placed these middle-class women in danger of attack from the worst (lower-class) elements of the crowd. Until women had the vote, they could not be assured of even the most basic right of the citizenry—physical safety. As an advocate of a new level of respect for women, Paul wanted to publicize not only the police's offenses but also her group's nonviolent response: they had continued to march on calmly in the face of danger, led by their inner strength and dedication to a noble cause.

As Paul was collecting (and shaping) affidavits, giving interviews, and helping Gardener with press bulletins, she also reached, as she seldom would later, for public support from prominent men. She asked several supporters of suffrage and the parade to arrange a protest meeting in the Columbia Theatre in Washington, without naming her as the instigator, thereby making the decision seem to be their own spontaneous and well-publicized response to the police's outrageous treatment of marchers. Writing to Louis Brandeis on March 8, 1913, Paul told him, "We shall be very glad if" he would agree to sit on the platform at this meeting "to protest against the management of the crowds on the occasion of the Suffrage Procession on March third."

A Harvard law graduate, Brandeis had initiated suits to protest the high rates charged by the Boston gas company, the monopolistic practices of the New Haven Railroad, and the low wages paid in the New York garment industry. His research on sweatshop labor had resulted in a book, *Women in Industry* (1908). Besides being a well-known advocate of justice for vulnerable citizens, he was also a desirable choice for the dais because of his influence with Wilson, who had consulted him on monopoly legislation during the 1912 campaign and considered him for attorney general. When Paul contacted him, Brandeis declared his willingness to join the group, as did Senator Moses Edwin Clapp of Minnesota, a progressive Republican who was closely allied with suffrage supporter Theodore Roosevelt (Pullen).

Besides creating a strong publicity opportunity, this meeting, seemingly convened by political dignitaries, gave Paul another group and committee chair who could receive affidavits about police violence and then comment on them to reporters. Many telegrams sent to these men before and after the Columbia Theatre meeting began with elaborate compliments that connected these influential politicians with hard-working suffragists: a letter from a New York suffrage organization, for example, stated that they wanted to honor "the public spirited men of Washington who are today voicing that indignation which is burning in the hearts of those party representatives from New York who marched in the parade." The letter urged these men to call for a congressional investigation to "deal drastically with the apparently studied official negligence which made this outrage possible" (Board of Directors).

As planning for this meeting of influential men went forward, Paul also began to press for a congressional investigation into the police's actions during the parade—to create a strong tie between the problems on the route and women's need for equal treatment under the law. As Sarah Colvin, a suffragist from Baltimore, commented in her autobiography, Paul's strong lobbying for a public accounting of the police's actions "soon had woman suffrage one of the most talked-about subjects in the United States" (130–31). To encourage press and governmental action, Paul accused the police not just of failing to control the crowd but of encouraging disorder. The police were to blame, not anonymous members of the crowd who could not be prosecuted. Using this approach, Paul could portray the largest part of the crowd as prosuffrage, as siding with the marchers, which is also how she constructed the American public. She was thus emphasizing a class-based view of "we" and "they," as Harriot Stanton Blatch expressed it: "the vast majority of the crowd watching the parade had a friendly attitude, and the rioters dominated only because the anti-suffragists in this particular instance were of the roughest element and were allowed by a grossly negligent police force to push their way to the front line of onlookers" (Blatch and Lutz 196–97).

Paul's protest and the Columbia Theatre meeting quickly led to an official investigation in Congress, which provided the funding for district police. She achieved this confrontation in part because of Chief Richard Sylvester's enemies on the force and in the city, a vulnerability that Paul was fully able to exploit. Personal notes, mostly anonymous, began arriving at her head-quarters almost immediately, including several on the next day claiming that Sylvester had kept his power by blackmailing prominent citizens and that, if this instance led to his ouster, she would have done the city a great service. Some men on the force viewed Sylvester as a politician, a wheeler dealer, and not a real policeman with a policeman's loyalty, as one note informed her: "Every man on the force fears his petty spite work and his admirers on the force are the incompetent fawners" (Letter to Dear Madam). To take full advantage of this opposition, Paul created a brochure entitled "Some Facts Regarding Sylvester," which she sent to members of the Senate and House.

With negative press and public discussion occurring, Congress appointed an investigative committee "to examine several persons to determine accu-rately the attitude of the police toward the suffrage marchers," to ascertain not whether events had gotten out of hand but why they did. These days of hearings, involving police, participants, and spectators, secured the exten-sive coverage that Paul sought. In his testimony, Sylvester defended himself by claiming that he had ordered his commanders to protect the marchers: "I did my duty. . . . My conscience is clear." His strategy was to blame not these police captains and certainly not himself, but individual officers who, he claimed, had acted "contrary to discipline, contrary to law, contrary to justice, contrary to my express orders" ("Senate Police Inquiry On").

During these highly publicized hearings, many women testified concern-ing their own experiences, but it was Paul who spoke for the group and secured press attention as Washington's new suffrage leader. Paul testified that Sylvester knew he would need a much larger force and, in choosing not to provide it, had caused harm intentionally. She also stressed that the failure in preparation was not her own: "We want to show that we did everything possible, took every possible step" and "We exhausted every possible means of getting protection on that day, and we made it known to every official the immense number of women that were coming, and that they must be prepared" (*Suffrage Parade* 134). In Congress and in the newspapers, Paul constructed herself as the well-organized and sensible leader doing everything she could to protect women marchers who faced danger bravely and nonviolently.

In the days of testimony, other witnesses joined the principal contestants. Secretary of War Stimson testified that Paul had immediately recognized the crowd was out of control and that she had requested his forces because the police were both undermanned and indifferent. Additionally, senators heard from police, members of the cavalry, participants, and bystanders, while also receiving written affidavits and viewing film footage and photographs. By March 15 the committee judged that it had heard enough and ultimately did not relieve Sylvester of his duties, but instead delivered a censure concerning the day's failures without commenting on the chief's motivation ("Will Quit Police Quiz").

The issue ultimately left newspapers in late March with little discussion of the final verdict, but by then Paul had reaped a huge publicity benefit, greatly increasing the duration of her parade's presence in leading newspapers and in the public consciousness. Later, Paul began claiming that this altercation had led to Sylvester's firing even though he did not lose his job that spring. He did retire, however, in March 1915 when Representative Frank Park of Georgia made charges against him. That month, even the *New York Times* admitted that one factor that led to Sylvester's downfall was his failure "to control the crowds along the route of the celebrated suffragette parade," a judgment Paul used as evidence that her accusations had been accurate and that the nation was beginning to recognize the rights of its women citizens ("Chief Sylvester Out").

Through the publicity opportunity of the parade, the men's meeting, and the investigation, Paul made clear to the public and to Congress that women had come to town first, that they could marshal crowds, that they could use a powerful visual rhetoric, and that they would not accept injustice from a government and its functionaries for whom they could not vote. In conducting an investigation, Paul believed, Congress had responded to her pressure, a forerunner of taking action on the amendment. As William L. O'Neill commented in *Everyone Was Brave: A History of Feminism in America*, "The upsurge of support and sympathy around the country proved Miss Paul was right in thinking that vivid techniques would bring new life to the constitutional amendment" (129). With this high visibility, Paul had brought her nonviolent campaign for a federal amendment to the capital's and the nation's attention. And she wanted to continue to keep suffrage before the capital and the nation. For Paul, such an event did not bear an exact repeating. It would become too safe. She did not want annual suffrage walks, like those used in the New York state campaign. Instead, she escalated and altered her visual events to keep the sense of danger and the publicity continuing.

After the inaugural parade, Paul began planning to expand beyond her Washington-based Congressional Committee. Because NAWSA focused on state work, she decided to develop a subsidiary organization, which she named the Congressional Union (CU), of women in each state who wanted to focus on federal work. The original Congressional Committee served as an executive committee for this quickly developing national organization.

Petitions and Automobiles

In June and July of 1913, relying on the new resources of a larger group, Paul began working on another rhetorical event—a combination of written political documents and a parade to the Capitol. After the inaugural parade, suffrage had been brought up on the floor of the Senate and referred to the Woman's Suffrage Committee. On June 13, this committee made the first favorable report on suffrage in twenty-one years, and the Senate placed it on the calendar. To support suffrage in the Senate and extend her publicity, Paul made plans for a demonstration in Washington. On June 28, she wrote to her colleague Mary Beard that this time petitions for the amendment from around the country would be the "focus of the affair." This time, Paul could make the connection between her new local groups and her Washington committee, emphasizing that local clubs and organizations could work assiduously for the federal amendment even if they were also pursuing state legislation. Committees formed in early June in every state with the gigantic task of circulating thousands of letters to women whose names were secured from women's colleges, women's clubs, suffrage associations, branches of NAWSA, and the Progressive and Socialist parties. These letters asked women to "sign for suffrage" (Perry). Using this method, CU members collected 250,000 signatures on petition sheets in less than five weeks. In each state, they chose representatives to bring the petition to Washington, some, like Jeannette Rankin from Montana, making well-publicized automobile pilgrimages from their home states.

As she did for the inaugural parade, Paul encouraged well-known women to join in this effort and made their names known to the press. Among those who lent support to the event were Elizabeth Kent; Anna Kelton Wiley, a consumer activist who was a prime mover behind her husband's passage of the Pure Food Act in 1906; Elsie May Bell Grosvenor, daughter of Alexander Graham Bell and wife of Gilbert Grosvenor, who headed the National Geographic Society; the Senator Robert and social activist Belle Case La Follette; Julia Lathrop, head of the federal Children's Bureau; Adele Steiner Burleson, wife of Albert Burleson, the postmaster general; Anne W. Lane, wife of Franklin Lane, secretary of the interior; and Helen Beall Houston, wife of David Houston, secretary of agriculture.

On July 31, 1913, Paul's big demonstration came to Washington. The group started at Hyattsville, Maryland, five miles to the northeast, where Paul spoke and the mayor greeted them. They then drove slowly to the Capitol, accompanied by members of the press who had been prepared for this event through daily press bulletins. After they arrived, delegates from suffrage organizations in each state met with members of the Senate's suffrage committee, legislators from their own states, and other groups, a "strong and effective ocular demonstration of the wide spread demand for woman suffrage through a National Constitutional Amendment" (Faber 130). Then they went to the White House to meet with Wilson, who repeated his customary comment that the matter of suffrage had not before been called to his attention. The day ended with a banquet for 250 at the Brighton Hotel.

With this grand event, Paul was exploiting the titillation, the danger, of women behind the wheels of cars. In 1913, when almost all automobiles were owned by men, a woman driving was a dangerous and usurping event in itself. Certainly their appearance in a long train of decorated cars—entering Washington and heading right up to the Capitol—gathered press attention. This event not only presented the nation with women's ability to move freely on their own, but it also demonstrated that they could create a legitimate and persuasive political document, brought to the legislature by their own representatives. The transgressive appropriation of freedom of movement was yoked with the very traditional step of petitioning Congress—except it was women who were petitioning their government for themselves. When the women left their cars and brought their 250,000 signatures into Senate offices, they caused a serious debate on suffrage on the Senate floor.

NAWSA Responds

In the fall of 1913, in response to all of this activity, officers of NAWSA, which had originally placed Paul in charge of the federal efforts, began to respond negatively because Paul's group was moving forward too quickly, without consultation, and was taking energy away from state campaigns. In a letter to Lucy Burns in November, President Anna Howard Shaw warned Paul's organization "to keep things steadily in hand . . . for there are certain laws of order that should be followed by everybody." Shaw felt that Paul's controversial events might lessen public respect for the movement and cause a long-term effort to falter: "It required a good deal more courage to work steadily and steadfastly for forty or fifty years to gain an end, than it does to do an impulsive rash thing and lose it." In response Burns denied claims that they were acting rashly and described Paul as possessing "a very calculating and cautious temperament" (Letter to Anna Howard Shaw). But this response did not stem the criticism.

In December of 1913 at the NAWSA convention, members praised the Congressional Committee's efforts at staging big events, but expressed dismay at so much independent action. The officers decided that her national organization, the Congressional Union, could remain affiliated with NAWSA only if Paul agreed that NAWSA's board would oversee her finances and decisions. Shaw decided on these ultimatums, as she wrote in a letter to a friend, M. M. Forrest, in January of 1914, because she had come to see both Paul and Burns as dangerous to the movement: "In all my experience in suffrage work I have never known such determination on the part of 2 or 3 women, who really wish to ruin the association, as has been manifested by the leaders of the Congressional union" (Kerfoot 39). She especially worried that Paul was siphoning energy and money away from state campaigns and was refashioning the movement through the force of her own personality. In response to her dicta, Paul wrote to Shaw on January 17 disingenuously declaring her ignorance of any conflict or problem since what they all sought was suffrage: "We are utterly at loss to understand what we have done of which you disapprove and hope that sometime you will be willing to give us an opportunity to clear up whatever misunderstanding exists. We . . . only wish that you were willing to let us work for you this year as we did last instead of compelling us to work apart."

When Paul proved unwilling to give up control as requested, Shaw's answer was to expel the CU from the NAWSA and demand that Paul give up her office and files to the Congressional Committee, which would continue to bring up a federal amendment in the Congress each year without any national organizing or appeals for funds. NAWSA officer Ruth Hanna McCormick took over as chair of this limited organization.

Combining the Local and National

At this point, in early 1914, Paul and Burns decided to set out on their own as heads of a separate Congressional Union, without the backing of NAW-SA's two million members. As Paul recalled in the Fry interview: "You can't imagine how unimportant, poor, without any reputation, any friends or any-thing—we wondered what we'd taken upon ourselves." As Paul continued planning events for that year, she had a new upstart organization as well as suffrage to fight for. In 1914, while her organizers built local affiliates of the CU, Paul felt that she needed to stage events across the nation, with full coverage by each city's local press, to involve more participants and define a national movement. To combine the local and national, she chose a two-part event, with demonstrations in cities across the country on May 2 and one in Washington on May 9, revealing the relationship between women in their own towns and clubs and the proposed federal legislation.

This dual parading, Paul claimed in the *Suffragist,* occurred in response to Wilson's repeated claims that he had not been informed about suffrage and that he was not aware of a large constituency supporting it. These parades also responded to developments in Congress during the spring of 1914. On March 2 Senator John Shafroth had introduced the Shafroth-Palmer Amendment, which Paul was determined to bury in a national wave of support for the Susan B. Anthony Amendment. Then on March 17, after a two-week debate, the Senate had voted on the Susan B. Anthony Amendment, the first time since 1887 that the Senate voted on suffrage. For the first time, it received a majority, but only by one vote, not the two-thirds majority required for pas-sage. On March 18 Senator Joseph Bristow reintroduced the amendment, and on April 7 the Woman Suffrage Committee again sent it to the Senate floor where it was placed on the Senate calendar, the second favorable report in one Congress (Irwin, *Story of Alice Paul* 55–57). In the House, suffrage had been bogged down in the Rules Committee, which was controlled by Democrats who had long refused to send the amendment to the floor. During the week between the local and the national parades, however, the Judiciary Commit-tee of the House, where amendments originated, along with the generally recalcitrant Rules Committee, reported the amendment to the House for the first time since 1890.

For both the local and the national parades, Paul worked on coverage of a large group united not for endless state campaigns or the Shafroth-Palmer Amendment but for the one rational choice facing the Congress, the Susan B. Anthony Amendment. The report in the *Suffragist* concerning May 2 had its thesis in its title, "The Greatest Suffrage Day." "Hardly a town or a city, from the Atlantic to the Pacific Ocean," the article claimed, "failed to do its part towards making an occasion the like of which has never been seen—a whole great country making a simultaneous demand for the complete reform of the electorate" (2). Five thousand women marched in white dresses and bonnets in Chicago, the coverage continued, grouped in ten divisions by their suffrage organizations and city wards. In more than sixty New York towns and cities, there were parades and open-air meetings. In Manchester, New Hampshire, local clubs chose an automobile parade; in New Orleans' City Park, the Woman Suffrage Party of Louisiana held a mass meeting, with participants coming from around the state; in Cheyenne, the state's women's clubs sponsored a large gathering ("Nation-Wide Demonstration" 3). With such widespread participation, the *Suffragist* claimed, "never again will it be possible in the United States for anyone to declare that the great mass of women do not want to vote" ("Greatest Suffrage Day" 2). The ultimate "anyone" of course, was Wilson.

As with the May 2 events, coverage of the May 9 parade in Washington filled the *Suffragist* and major newspapers throughout the country, especially those where local parades had occurred and from where women left for the national event. Women from every congressional district carried resolutions to Washington, not just as a parade of organizations but as a group of official representatives armed with political documents, showing the local moving to the national, figuratively and literally ("From Ocean to Ocean"). On May 9 throngs of people came out in the perfect weather. There was a big police showing all along the route because "the Police Department intended to give such protection to the procession that all bad memories of last year's bitter experience would forever perish." The 531 delegates from the congressional districts, separated according to whether they represented free states or unfree, marched in white gowns along with a chorus adorned with flowers. They were followed by an automobile procession three blocks long, attended by the "thousands on thousands" of spectators ("The Greatest Suffrage Day" 4). When the marchers reached the Capitol to present resolutions from the states, they were disappointed that only eleven senators and one representative came out to meet them. That denial of their political worth, however, would make good suffrage rhetoric. The event did lead to resolutions for the amendment being introduced on the floor of each house, marking the first time that suffrage had been up for debate on the floor of the House of Representatives.

Once again Paul took advantage of a public clash, this time not with the police, but with NAWSA. The organization had opposed the May 2 plans and asked its affiliates not to get involved because doing so would detract attention from state efforts. Then, in the May 9 procession, NAWSA contributed a float—not for the Susan B. Anthony Amendment but for their Shafroth-Palmer Amendment. In the *Suffragist,* as we have seen, Paul had vilified this newer choice: "It is a little difficult to treat with seriousness an equivocating, evasive, childish substitute for the simple and dignified suffrage amendment now before Congress" ("New Amendment Proposed"). Many of Paul's supporters had thought she would refuse to include a Shafroth float in the parade, but she encouraged this participation to create a dramatic visual demonstration of this contingency's smallness and its separation from the real effort moving forward. Marching along with their float, NAWSA leaders were thus, in Paul's construction, publicly labeling themselves as obstructionist and naïve. In letters, bulletins, and articles in the *Suffragist,* she used this point of friction and danger to elicit interest in the march and to spotlight, in the physical comparison between the one float and the many, the growing effort for the Susan B. Anthony Amendment as well as for the CU, the organization that was spurring that effort.

Exploiting a World's Fair

In 1915, with significant action in Congress not forthcoming, Paul felt that she needed to further vary her events, so that she would not just be repeating what could become formalistic protests. She decided on another two-part approach: by placing a booth at San Francisco's Panama Pacific International Exposition of 1915, the first time a suffrage group sponsored a booth at a world's fair, and then by commandeering not a group of automobiles going from the suburbs of Washington to the Capitol, but one lone car going from San Francisco to Washington. As she did with the inaugural parade, she was seeking to align her group and meetings with a positive social event, a world's fair, that would garner huge crowds and positive sentiment. As she had not done to this extent before, she was also seeking an event that would build over months and generate a level of ongoing publicity unattainable with a one-day or one-week affair. She would later remember this combination as "one of the very big things that we did" (Fry).

A world's fair offered the perfect symbolic background against which Paul could construct suffrage as part of a scientific, rational, and prosperous future. Beginning with the first world's fair in 1851, in London's Hyde Park at the specially built Crystal Palace, these fairs celebrated the progress possible through industrial capitalism and improved relations between nations. They also gave reverence to a new level of personal acquisition. Offering "cornucopias of status symbols," they "did not just cater to middle class taste, they helped form that taste" as they presented a sanitized view of a scientifically enhanced future in which the best people had all the best values and things (Benedict 2–3, 7). By positioning suffrage within this tradition, Paul sought its inclusion as part of all that an affluent middle class wanted and deserved.

To celebrate progress and especially the best of America, the fair featured sixty-eight buildings, eleven major exhibit halls, twenty-one national pavilions, and twenty-six state pavilions, as well as a 450–foot tall Tower of Jewels, an artificial Grand Canyon, a Yellowstone Park with working geysers, and a large amusement zone. During the eleven months it was open, 18.9 million people visited the 635–acre site (Benedict 23, 31). The large Palace of Education and Social Economy, which housed Paul's booth, greeted visitors as they entered the main gates. Here, Paul's troops held forth in a long hall-like area decorated with Susan B. Anthony's portrait, American and suffrage flags, copies of the *Suffragist,* photographs of campaign events, a framed history of the Sixty-Third Congress's voting record, and a large banner in party colors reading "We demand an amendment to the United States Constitution enfranchising women" (Ewald and Clute 72).

Each day, workers at the booth informed visitors about suffrage and asked them to sign a petition for a federal amendment. Supplementing this daily interaction were special days and speeches that insured larger crowds and more press attention. Helen Keller, on a lecture tour of the West, came to speak and left a large signed photograph that was hung in the booth. In a letter to Emmeline Pankhurst published in the *Manchester Advertiser* in March 1911, Keller had argued for the extension of the franchise to combat the cruel and selfish control of the working classes, and especially working women, by the wealthy few: "I am indignant at the treatment of the brave, patient women of England. I am indignant when the women cloakmakers of Chicago are abused by the police. I am filled with anguish when I think of the degradation, the enslavement and the industrial tyranny which crush millions, and drag down women and helpless children" (Keller 119–20). Keller wrote that by expanding the influence of the poor and ignored, suffrage would lead to socialism, the "ideal cause." When she toured the country, she generally spoke about the needs and abilities of Americans with handicaps; that she had come to the fair to advocate socialism and women's rights certainly guaranteed a large crowd.

Besides having dynamic speakers like Keller, Paul planned for special events. At the booth, the group held weekly CU meetings, involving members as well as large numbers of women visiting the fair for the day, meetings well documented in the local press. On Bunker Hill Day, Paul created a procession and brought in a memorial celebrating women's contributions to this Revolutionary War battle. That day, speakers Gail Laughlin and Elsie

Hill decried the general lack of knowledge of women's roles to American history and suggested increased study, especially of women's ongoing work for freedom ("Bunker Hill Day"). Suffragists also drew crowds through the spectacular. Californian Hazel Hunkins, for example, took an airplane ride over the fairgrounds and dropped thousands of leaflets advocating suffrage. She would have refused, she told reporters, to take this, her first airplane ride, but Alice Paul had urged her on.

In early September, Paul held a women's convention in the fair's Palace of Progress—a gathering of those women who could vote and who could thus advertise the progress of political equality. Each state where women held the franchise sent a large group of delegates; other states contributed observers. By sorting attendees in this manner, Paul could construct this meeting as "the first convention of women with political power in their hands." To secure as much press attention as possible, she arranged for special speakers, including Theodore Roosevelt, evangelist Billy Sunday, actress Mabel Talliaferro, Italian educator Maria Montessori, and Chinese doctor Yami Kim. Congressional Union officers also gave talks to highlight their work toward a federal amendment: Elizabeth Kent, for example, spoke on the history of the federal effort, and Sara Bard Field discussed the waste of women's, and thus the nation's, time caused by state-by-state efforts (Transcripts of Speeches).

Often relying on facts provided by Paul's press bulletins sent out each day, newspapers across the country gave the convention very positive treatment. The *Colorado Springs Gazette* on September 14 praised this "first national political gathering of women," as did the *Washington Post* on September 16, commenting on the solidarity of the three thousand representatives there speaking for the four hundred thousand women voters, numbers supplied in many of Paul's press bulletins ("Women's Convention"; "Assemble in Convention"). The *Arizona Republican* on September 27 asserted that the women who had "come together for a political purpose" demonstrated "that thrilling religious quality that marks the crux of any great movement" ("Big Lift for Suffrage").

Voyaging Coast to Coast—By Car

As the group prepared to close its booth at the fair's end, Paul carefully planned the visual rhetoric of the final day, September 16. In the central Court of Abundance, at a meeting with ten thousand attendees, a crowd of supporters formally resolved in favor of the Susan B. Anthony Amendment, recorded their opposition to any other suffrage amendment that might be furthered by scheming Democrats, and sent greetings to the four states where there would be fall decisions on state suffrage amendments. Then Paul spoke on the political situation in the Sixty-Fourth Congress. Next the large assembled group formally voted to send envoys to Washington—by automobile—bringing the petitions signed during the many months of the fair, a trip that had long been planned but was here formally suggested and approved. In choosing the term *envoys* for these travelers, Sara Bard Field of Oregon and Frances Jolliffe of California, Paul constructed them as public ministers sent by one sovereign government to another to transact diplomatic business, coming from the free states where women could vote to the national capital where the Congress and president were keeping other women from doing so.

The celebratory moment of the send-off involved people in native costumes from many countries. The assembled group sang "The Woman's Hymn," a Women's Missionary Union song for which Field had written special words to associate suffrage with the stalwart efforts of this group founded in 1888 to support missionary work of the Southern Baptists. By echoing words like the original's "Work with your courage high, / Sing of the daybreak nigh, / Your love outpour," Field pointed to the sanctity of this sacrifice that women around the world and the two women entering a lone car were making for suffrage (Heck). The huge group then went out "in a procession of dignity and beauty" for the send-off of the decorated car, dubbed the *Suffrage Flier*, that would carry its two drivers and Field—Jolliffe had to come later by train because of an illness in her family—from San Francisco to Washington. Out to the car women carried the petition that had been featured at the booth, the longest ever signed in one place: 18,333 feet with 500,000 names. In the front seat were drivers Ingeborg Kindstedt and Maria Kindberg of Providence, Rhode Island. Field, in a letter to headquarters, wrote that these "ladies of strong suffrage persuasion" had bought a new motor car when visiting at the fair and had already planned to drive it home, but press bulletins spoke of their decision to buy the car and drive cross-country as sacrifices for suffrage, a dangerous adventure taken on not for personal pleasure but for this cause. Their purchase and drive, which could have looked like frivolity, were thus reconstructed as sacrifice. Like the purchase of the car, all of the details of the send-off received dramatic attention from reporters who attended that day or whose papers received a stream of press bulletins about the cross-country plans ("Woman Voters' Convention"; "Farewell of the Woman Voters").

Certainly for women to be crossing the country in cars without male accompaniment seemed both physically dangerous and a bit titillating, just as women parading down Pennsylvania Avenue and driving to the capital from Maryland had been in 1913. It had only been a few years earlier that the first well-publicized cross-country trips by women had taken place, stunts for manufacturers who used the crossing's dangers to tout the dependability of their cars, even in a woman's hands. In 1909, Alice Ramsey, a twenty-two-year-old mother from Hackensack, New Jersey, became the first woman to drive across the country. She made the trip in a Maxwell touring car, along with three female friends, as a publicity stunt for the Maxwell-Briscoe Touring Company. Newspapers carefully followed her fifty-nine-day voyage. In 1910, Blanche Stuart Scott, accompanied by her maid and her maid's sister, Amy and Gertrude Phillips, drove a toilet-equipped Overland from New York City to San Francisco, a trip that the Willys-Overland Company advertised as the first cross-country trip by a woman, ignoring Ramsey's feat of the year before. Scott made the voyage in sixty-eight days, stopping at as many Overland dealerships as possible. After these manufacturers both had their firsts, Hollywood sought its own. Silent-screen star Anita King generated a great deal of publicity in her KisselKar when in 1915 she became the first woman to complete a solo transcontinental trip. She left on August 25, 1915, for a fifty-nine-day trip, driving from San Francisco to New York to promote Paramount Studio and her own career, with dramatic press releases attracting attention along the way. Newspapers reported that she shot a timber wolf, fought off a menacing hobo and a lovelorn Wyoming rancher, and dissuaded a star-struck girl from running off to Hollywood (McConnell 23, 61–65, 100–01). When Field left San Francisco on September 16, she was joining King on the road. Although Kindstedt and Kindberg drove her, Field was constructed as another sole voyager, facing physical risk to promote not a studio but suffrage.

During the almost three months that Field was on the road, until December 6, she stopped frequently for events arranged by Mabel Vernon, who went ahead by train and, along with Alice Paul, arranged everything in each city. The tight travel schedule and impressive list of visits situated Field as a visiting dignitary, risking her life to get to each town and conduct important business. In Kansas City, Kansas, the mayor and high school band introduced her speech at the public library. In Kansas City, Missouri, she rode in an automobile parade to the office of Senator James A. Reid, who had voted against suffrage in the last session ("From San Francisco"; "Woman Voters' Envoys"). In New York, she participated in an automobile parade down Fifth Avenue, accompanied by many local dignitaries in an "escort of honor" featuring a display of the "great petition" ("Plan Big Welcome").

The CU's press department used the national and local press along the route to keep readers appraised of Field's progress—and especially of the dangerous sacrifice she was making. Paul asked Field to regularly send in journal entries to the national headquarters so that specific anecdotes and facts could add life to the stories released from there. On September 28, Field wrote to Lucy Burns that she found the request for information difficult to fulfill at the end of long days of "this gasoline flight eastward" since she had hardly any free time "apart from my beloved machine which I think upon and through." But Paul had assured her, Field wrote to Burns, that her letters need not be "literature but just facts and leave it to the magic of your blue pencil to make azure skies of my drab material." The desert, Field continued, was "the most trying and perilous part of the journey," about which the press "eats up such news." In her letters, Field even discussed herself in the third person, using the dramatic tones fit for publicity: the woman's vote is "now trumpeting its message and sending this Envoy across 3000 miles bearing its demands."

Drawing from these details sent to them in press bulletins, newspapers dramatically depicted her as a woman alone, crossing mountains and deserts, finding her way in strange cities and towns. During the trip, as many newspapers reported, she got lost in the desert for a full day, fixed breakdowns, and fought rain, sleet, snow, and mud. Stories emphasizing such striking details, Paul realized, also provided space for discussions of meetings and of the amendment itself (Severn 150–51). For Paul this combination had the power of "getting it dramatized by going across the country so the whole world—the whole country would know about it—I think it was very effective and very useful." Here was one brave woman moving forward, representing the priorities of so many, and Paul was determined "to get all the drama out of it we could" (Fry).

When the car reached Washington on December 6, where Jolliffe had arrived by train, it was met at the edge of town by a parade meant to appear as a pageant, designed by California pageant director Mary Austin, a graduate of Blackburn University who had helped to originate the little theatre movement. The large crowd in Washington beheld a fantastic sight: first twelve young girls in suffrage colors held hands across the road; society leader Mrs. John Jay White of New York then appeared as a marshal on horseback followed by a cavalry brigade and women riders representing the thirteen suffrage states; then came the envoy auto with Field, Jolliffe, Vernon, Kindstedt, and Kindberg inside, a women's liberty bell from that fall's Pennsylvania campaign for state suffrage, the three hundred guests who would accompany the envoys to a reception at the White House, a hundred women with pennants, twenty bearers carrying the four-mile petition on huge spools, an automobile parade, another cavalry squadron, and a final band. When the entire group stopped in front of the Capitol, a double line formed to escort Field and Jolliffe as well as the petition bearers up the steps, with the petition unfurling behind them ("First National Convention").

When Field and her escorts arrived at the Capitol, their plan was to ask a welcoming group of legislators to allow them to speak from the floor of the House, having researched that others, including Louis Kossuth, the Hungarian revolutionary discussed in Mary Beard's article from 1913, had done so in what they viewed as similar circumstances ("Have Americans Lost"). But though Field's voyage was long and the procession grand, no large group came to meet them, and they could not gain access to the House floor. Then, at the White House reception, Wilson told them it was too late to urge the Anthony Amendment in Congress—he had already written his message for that session and sent it to the newspapers. In his charge to the legislators, he told these visitors, he had emphasized just one thing: war preparedness. He told the assembled women, in his usual vague, positive manner: "I can only say to you that nothing could be more impressive than the presentation of such a request in such numbers and backed by such influences as undoubtedly are behind you." And he promised to confer with his Senate colleagues "with regard to what is the right thing to do at this time concerning this great matter." About his own stance, his message was again vague: "I hope I shall always have an open mind, and I shall certainly take the greatest pleasure in conferring in the most serious way with my colleagues" (Porritt, "Woman Suffrage and Congress").

Although the envoys did not quite get what they wanted from their government, they were well celebrated and publicized when they arrived at Paul's headquarters. In the fall of 1915, while Field was on the road, Alice Paul had rented a home in front of the White House, on Lafayette Square, at 21 Madison Place, a site, in fact, that had long been known as the "Little White House." Using her family's money and donations, Paul had left her cramped quarters on F Street for this huge mansion where she and other campaigners could live and the whole group could work—and where they could visibly declare themselves as equal players in the national political scene. The house had been erected by agriculturist Benjamin Ogle Tayloe in 1828, who established there a meeting place for politicians. Henry Clay, Daniel Webster, and John C. Calhoun were frequent visitors as were presidents Van Buren, Harrison, Taylor, and Fillmore. From 1901 to 1902 when Senator Marcus Hanna of Ohio lived there, it became known as the "Little White House" because of frequent visits from McKinley and Roosevelt as well as many senators (Hutchinson 27–36). When Field left the Capitol, a large group escorted her to this locale to celebrate the voyage and demonstrate the CU's political power.

Although the parade and envoys did not get the response from Wilson and Congress that Paul had sought, Field's months on the road had secured a huge amount of publicity, the result of another nonviolent event in which women placed themselves in danger to prove their devotion to their cause. Field had brought suffrage from coast to coast through great personal risk, symbolically appropriating the breadth of the country to the cause, while demonstrating the strength of the one as a member of the many. By the day after her arrival, press releases also included the twin affronts of the House's and the president's inadequate responses to further argue that this government did not respect and did not represent women.

A Cross-Country Train Trip

In making plans for Field's trip, Paul recognized the impact of women traveling across the country without male escort, but of course she would not choose to repeat that particular event. In the spring of 1916, an election year in which Paul was considering a boycott of the Democrats for their lack of support for the amendment, she chose special cars of a train that went from coast to coast. In this move, for the first time, she sent a group from East to West to demonstrate the unity of women with and without the vote and to posit suffrage states as a locus of power, as a destination. This was not the single Field, but a large political deputation, a well-organized group of elected delegates meeting with women who voted and with their elected officials, in effect, a campaign swing.

In choosing the cross-country train trip, Paul was appropriating a male political staple, first used in a presidential campaign by Ulysses Grant, who went from Washington to Denver during his 1868 campaign, accompanied by Civil War generals. Wilson had also used a railway car, the Magnet, to cross the nation in 1912, stopping for frequent receptions and speeches, accompanied by sympathetic members of the press. In Indianapolis, the first stop, he had introduced his "New Freedom," the phrase he later used to label his domestic program (Heckscher 259–60). In starting out on the train in early 1916, these suffragists were quite self-consciously adopting an established political technique, one that Wilson would not begin using that year until October.

This time Paul wanted to demonstrate that fighters like Field were members of a resilient whole, one as powerful in an election year as male political parties, so she now chose a filled train, decorated as the "Suffrage Special" and carrying "envoys" to the West, three to seven representatives from each of ten eastern states. From New York, for example, the group included Lucy Burns, Alva Smith Belmont, Harriot Stanton Blatch, Elizabeth Selden Rogers, and Inez Milholland. The twenty-three representatives spent thirty-eight days touring the suffrage states. As a group that was being denied in Washington, specifically at the Field reception and generally in the drive for suffrage, they were physically leaving Washington to enter the real national power base, the entire country and especially the voting states.

When the women left after another of Paul's grand send-off processions, they did so with a fine public relations team to reinforce the symbolism of the occasion. The chartered train had ten sections and two drawing rooms, with offices equipped for Ella Riegel as business manager and Abby Scott Baker as press chair. Reporters came to the train at its stops—having been alerted in advance—and received daily facts and colorful stories. When time permitted, Baker and her assistant Caroline Katzenstein also called on newspaper editors, another technique that boosted their coverage, as Katzenstein recalled in her autobiography: "The campaign was so picturesque, its purpose so dynamic, it made a good story, and the newspapers of the country gave it abundant space" (190).

The organizers planned for the trip to be "more of a 'triumphal march' than a grueling campaign" (Katzenstein 190–91). From April 9 to May 16, the envoys covered principal cities in the suffrage states—Arizona, California, Colorado, Idaho, Kansas, Montana, Nevada, Oregon, Utah, Washington, and Wyoming, as well as Illinois, where women had presidential suffrage. The group stopped in some places for a half hour and in others for up to four days, with speeches at the train in small towns and with luncheons with suffrage groups, sessions with local dignitaries, parades, and street meetings in large cities. In Seattle, for example, one of the longer stops, "the station was gaily decorated in purple, white and gold bunting, great baskets of hanging flowers and American flags. At 9:30, a bugler called together a big group, including the mayor, who bade them welcome. The delegates then made speeches from the rear platform, and Harriot Stanton Blatch gave a 'most beautiful address.'" Next "prominent hostesses" took the delegates, in an escort of 150 decorated automobiles, around the city for an hour and a half, after which they split up to go to various luncheons, some with three hundred guests, at hotels and clubs. There followed a tea, a dinner "particularly unique in the fact it was served only for women," and a huge mass meeting with Blatch and other speakers. On the next day the envoys went to a university meeting and then a huge outdoor meeting in Bellingham (Whittemore). As the women attended these events, Burns flew in a small plane piloted by an officer of the Washington Naval Militia and dropped leaflets over the suburbs of Seattle announcing a convention planned for June. Though she was at first concerned about losing the banner that draped the plane, she confessed that she "forgot all about suffrage and votes for women in that wonderful experience" ("Washington Hears Message" 7).

Like Field's trip and the booth at the World's Fair, this train excursion served a rhetorical function that parades could not: it had a duration, and thus press coverage, of months, not just a day or two. In a string of positive articles, the *Suffragist* stressed the women's positive treatment as official delegates ("Itinerary of the Suffrage Special"). Press bulletins emphasized the women's political and moral purpose, and newspapers followed their lead. The *Seattle Post Intelligencer,* for example, adopted religious imagery in its account: "The wise men followed the star in the east. For the wise women gleams a ray of hope in the west and today comes out of the east a band of women to hitch their suffrage wagons to the western star. Woman suffrage throughout the nation is dependent upon western women" ("Western Star"). The *Oakland Tribune* reported that these women planned to "declare war on backsliding politicians and see that they climb on the bandwagon or get rolled under its wheels" ("Eastern Missionaries"). In discussing this assault on the Democratic Party, the *Chicago Examiner* also adopted military imagery: "the final movement on the citadel of nation-wide suffrage has begun" ("Suffrage Goal in Sight"). Many of the articles repeated the number of women voters as four hundred thousand and the terminology of "free states," both used in press bulletins.

A convention at Salt Lake City on May 11, 1916, was the last official meeting on the train's way back east. The convention passed resolutions asking Congress for favorable action on the amendment and elected three women voters to deliver these resolutions. The women then returned to Washington for a conference at headquarters on April 8 and 9, participating in another well-reported Paul ceremony that involved buglers, a large chorus of women in white who sang "America," and a meeting at the Capitol with senators and representatives.

A Martyr Celebrated

By 1916 Paul had employed women walking, driving cars, and riding on trains; she had sent the one and the many for short and long distances; and she had sought various forms of risk to prove that women were political personages who, in every American town and in the nation's capital, were insisting on their own rights. Then, at the end of 1916 came the apotheosis of these events, a public creation of a female hero, Inez Milholland, who became mortally ill in October as she traveled through the Western states on a speaking tour for suffrage. While Sara Bard Field had become a symbol of courage and dedication as she made her way East, here was a woman who could be lifted to the level of martyr.

Born in 1885, the daughter of a journalist, Milholland went to Vassar, where her work for suffrage first made the *New York Times* in June 1908: she had organized a suffrage meeting involving forty women in a graveyard adjoining the college after the president forbade her from holding a meeting on campus ("Vassar's Head Indignant"). Soon after graduation, she organized Vassar students to join in shirtwaist strikes in New York City, was arrested, and was a co-defendant with Alva Belmont in an action for damages. She then sought and was denied admission to Oxford, Cambridge, Harvard, and Yale on account of her sex and went to law school at New York University. By 1910 she was busy working for suffrage—giving street speeches, selling literature, and joining in parades—while offering legal advice to striking shirtwaist workers. Admitted to the New York bar in 1912, she made a specialty of criminal law in the interest of the poor. She then participated in the Pankhursts' campaign in England, where she married Frida Eugene Boissevain in a very publicized society wedding in 1913. When she came home, she found herself no longer an American citizen because of marital laws that converted a wife's citizenship to her husband's, an injustice that she immediately protested in the press. Her husband gave up his English citizenship so that she could continue to be an American, another well-publicized moment of an activist's life.

In the suffrage campaign, Milholland was frequently sought as a speaker because of her speaking skills and her record of activism as well as her beauty. In 1908, during a suffrage parade in New York, she stood in a Greek toga in a huge plate glass window on the second floor of a building on the route. In several other parades, she rode on horseback in a toga, as she did in Paul's 1913 preinaugural parade. In October of 1916 she left her law practice and went out on a speaking tour for Alice Paul, using her law school and citizenship experiences as evidence of a woman's need for political and legal equality, which could only be achieved through suffrage. At each stop, she wore lovely dresses and stood on stage while her sister Vida sang suffrage anthems ("Mrs. Inez Milholland Bouissevain"). In Montana, Utah, and Nevada, crowds showed great enthusiasm for her looks and for her stirring mixture of personal testimony and appeals for immediate action ("Women Voters Hear").

When Milholland was speaking in Los Angeles in October, she fell to the floor. She had pernicious anemia that she had not known about, and she had been weakened by overexertion. Her last words on the platform, as Paul publicized them, were "Mr. President, how long must women wait for liberty?" After Milholland collapsed, Harriot Stanton Blatch at once left for Kansas and Illinois to finish her tour (Blatch and Lutz 271). Milholland died on November 25 at age thirty-one.

Recognition of her new publicity value came while she was ill. On November 17, 1916, New York State advisory council member Ethel Adamson wrote to publicity chief Abby Scott Baker that they could take advantage of the illness to symbolize women's willingness to sacrifice: "If it did not seem indelicate to use such sad circumstances it would make the most wonderful publicity if the story of Inez's gallant work were known, and her willing sacrifice of her strength and health! And to think it is only what you all have done too. I am moved to a most ardent enthusiasm when I think of you women who have borne the brunt of the thing." This public declaration of martyrdom could be especially fortuitous, Adamson noted, because of difficulties in the campaign that fall, specifically their failure to keep Wilson and Democratic legislators from being re-elected. A national hero could improve their public rhetoric and reputation.

After Milholland's death, the *Suffragist* constructed her as a suffrage martyr. The December 23, 1916, cover presents her as a Joan of Arc figure astride a white horse. The slogan is "Forward into Light," which became a watchword for the discussion of her moral and religious import. The phrase came from a banner she had carried at the head of a 1911 New York suffrage parade—"Forward out of error, leave behind the night, forward through the darkness, forward into light!"—a line taken from an 1871 hymn by Henry Alford, "Forward! Be Our Watchword!" Both picture and slogan presented her as holy.

With continuous press bulletins stressing her sacrifice, stories about Milholland's life and death multiplied in the daily press. The *Philadelphia Ledger* wrote that "She spent herself without stint in the service of her cause. . . . Beautiful and courageous, she embodied more than any other American woman the ideals of that part of womankind whose eyes are on the future." The *New York Evening Post* effused: "She was of the stuff that changes history and makes civilization . . . a martyr to her devotion to the suffrage cause, despite her apparently superb physique." According to the *Los Angeles Evening Express*, "She gave all she had to the cause, and having given all else, at last gave her life" ("Daughter of Light").

As Paul made plans for a series of commemorations, Milholland's family stepped in, asking her to restrict her efforts to one memorial. To take full advantage of the possibilities for press coverage while avoiding a public conflict with the Milholland family, Paul planned for one memorial that would combine Christian and state religion: in the Statuary Hall of the Capitol on Christmas Day. In 1864 the Congress had converted the old House of Representatives Chamber into a hall where each state could place two statues of its home-grown leaders, primarily explorers, members of Congress, leaders of state government, and generals during the Revolutionary and Civil

Wars (Murdock 7). Texas, for example, contributed statues of Sam Houston and Sam Austin; Virginia, of Robert E. Lee and George Washington. Of the forty-six statues that had been placed there by Christmas of 1916, only one was of a woman: Frances Willard of Illinois, leader of the Woman's Christian Temperance Union (Murdock 31). Government policies stated that services could be held there only for those people whom the statues commemorated and no large group could meet in the space because rare books housed there might be stolen. Paul, however, overcame these objections to her reception, a power move, like getting Pennsylvania Avenue as the route for her original parade. With special permission, she had finally secured a site within the Capitol, instead of attempting once again to leave petitions on its steps. And she had placed Milholland within the territory of American heroes, visually inserting a woman, one who exemplified leadership and self-sacrifice, into a setting that was almost exclusively male.

For the Christmas Day memorial service, Paul carried the banner Milholland had held in the 1911 New York suffrage parade. Lucy Burns followed with a banner again making the association with religious sacrifice and holy causes—"As he died to make men holy, let us die to make men free"—from Julia Ward Howe's "Battle Hymn of the Republic." Then followed suffrage leaders, a boys' choir, and young girl attendants. They all came through the Capitol Rotunda to a purple curtain where the group heard speeches and read resolutions to Wilson and the legislature. As in all Paul ceremonies, music and visual rituals melded with the spoken and written words. A chorus furthered the religious theme, making the connection to Christ on Christmas Day by singing hymns like "Ave Maria" while stationed behind velvet curtains so that the sound "seemed to be coming from above." Standard bearers stood around the room during the entire ceremony. The great place "might have been a temple celebrating the triumphant but tragic return from some high quest" ("Nation Honors Inez Milholland").

The speeches stressed religious and mythic themes and even implied that Milholland knew what the price would be, that she knowingly gave her life for this holy cause. Expanding on the theme of *Suffragist* articles and press bulletins, Nevada organizer Anne Martin said that Milholland "poured out her precious strength until she had none left to give, and died." She "gave her life for the freedom of women and for the welfare of her country." Senator George Sutherland, a Republican from Utah, then said that her death was a "supreme self-sacrifice to God," one for which she deserved to be in the statuary room with the nation's other heroes. She didn't give her life deliberately, Sutherland said drawing a fine line, but she would have gone on even if she had known the cost ("National Memorial Service" 8).

In these speeches, the National Woman's Party sought not just to present Milholland as a martyr to the cause but also to focus on those who created the need for that sacrifice—thus, on those who killed her. In *Suffragist* articles, the killer was those leaders that opposed suffrage and made women continue to struggle for it: her death was caused by the "selfish interests of political groups, fearful of the gift of freedom to a class" ("Inez Milholland Boussevain"). The resolutions at the memorial service, however, pointed not just to the legislature's responsibility for this death but to Wilson's. He needed, one resolution declared, to "intercede to stop such waste of human life and effort." Another directly argued that more women might die if he did not act, thus also connecting this death to his inaction: "Women are exhausting their lives in waiting and appeal. . . . Will you not be moved to act so that her death shall have delivered from the sacrifice of life her countrymen?" ("To the President"). By the end of the memorial, Inez Milholland was firmly constructed—through the speeches, music, decoration, and crowd of spectators—as a martyr to the cause, burned at the stake by Woodrow Wilson.

* * *

In the four years that ended with this strong rhetoric in the Capitol, Paul had created an unprecedented panoply of nonviolent visual events, focusing on the individual woman and the larger group. To make suffrage—and especially a federal amendment—into a national issue that the American public and its leaders could not avoid, she courted many forms of nonviolent danger that gained press attention. Women marched down Pennsylvania Avenue before the president could get there, and they insisted on an investigation of the police who would not offer them safety. After that initial foray, they continued to put themselves in challenging, newsworthy sites: in front of the Capitol armed with resolutions and petitions, at a world's fair, on the roads and the rails, and in the Capitol and its Statuary Hall. When they gathered in the hall for the Milholland memorial, they were making one of their contemporaries, like the women in parades, cars, and trains, into an American hero. Through this continuing activity, these women developed and demonstrated their own self-respect, proving to themselves and then to the nation that their next move should be to the voting booth.

5. Lobbying and Deputations

As Alice Paul established her organization and began planning nonviolent events, she was aware that parades and tours might not by themselves accomplish her goals of educating a legislature, president, and nation. She knew that she had to find ways to go directly to leaders of the Democratic Party and to Woodrow Wilson, who in his first term initiated legislation on tariff reform, the Federal Reserve, monopolies and labor, and the Panama Canal but refused to take any action on suffrage.

From the beginning, Paul sought not just periodic public events but also regular meetings at the Capitol and in the White House. She created a full-time lobbying effort, sending women from across the country to meet with their legislators, not just for friendly chats but for frank discussions of congressional action. She also sent small and large groups to see Wilson at the White House for as long as he would allow them there. Later, after he began to refuse deputations, she combined visits to the White House, when some formal event gained her entrance, with encounters on the streets and at public meetings. These women went to see legislators and the president armed with data and arguments, and they expected rational and consistent responses. They also intended simply to be there, in the nonviolent tradition, with the rhetoric of their presence proving their ongoing commitment, as did Gandhi's lobbying and deputations in South Africa and India. Like Gandhi, Paul knew she needed to do more than publicly oppose the government: she also had to establish her group's right to *work within* the government through increasingly assertive—and thus dangerous—lobbying and deputations.

"The Snap and the Crackle around the House"

Although lobbying can be part of any political effort, Paul believed it had a special role in a nonviolent campaign. She wanted to influence legislators, but she also wanted to further extend women's physical presence. Whereas paid lobbyists often try to remain anonymous, working behind the scene, Paul wanted hers to be known, by legislators and the press, to prove the determination and organization of suffrage workers and their ability to work within the political arena, just as women would when they began voting. In the press, these lobbyists were frequently accused of blackmail, seeking out details about men and then threatening to expose those details to their constituents. As Paul recognized, such publicity was unjust and negative, but it was publicity, and it did feature women's ability to confidently enter and even conquer a new and difficult space—literally, the halls of power in Washington, D.C.

In the beginning, as with so many elements of the campaign, Paul and Burns took charge of the lobbying, at first with help from Jeannette Rankin of NAWSA, a paid organizer. From 1914 to 1915, Burns directed the lobbying, recruiting volunteers to begin meeting with legislators while also preparing printed materials to give to legislators, soliciting letters and telegrams from their constituents, and appearing at party conventions to chart their progress. By the time Burns handed the job to Anne Martin and Maud Younger in 1915, she had built "one of the best" lobbies in Congress and compiled the nucleus of a card catalogue that became famous before the campaign ended (Breckinridge 270–71; "Her Pressure on Congress").

The size and character of this large-scale effort marked an important difference between the CU and NAWSA. Maud Wood Park as a NAWSA lobbyist tried to make and keep friends, ingratiating herself with these powerful men. She restricted the number of lobbyists so they could form personal friendships. Lucy Burns described the CU's relationship to senators differently. These lobbyists wanted to challenge and educate, not ingratiate; they wanted to make these men consider the issues and redefine their thinking. As historians Eleanor Flexner and Ellen Fitzpatrick commented about NAWSA's number of lobbyists and their effect in comparison, "When it attempted to compete with the Congressional Union in lobbying in Congress, the results were pitiful; at one time the disparity in numbers ran as high as forty-one to three" (261).

Paul and Burns involved women in the lobbying effort who came to Washington for a parade or a conference or even on vacation. They also wrote to many women to invite them to the capital to meet their legislators. Since all of these women could not be housed at headquarters, they frequently stayed with Elizabeth Kent and other prominent Washingtonians. Mrs. John J. White, the Connecticut state CU chair, came frequently with two or three women, who might stay for days or weeks. Other nearby states where the CU had a large membership, like Pennsylvania, Maryland, and New Jersey, also sent groups of women regularly. Anita Pollitzer, who was teaching at the University of Virginia, came every weekend and went immediately to see her congressman. This large and varied staff allowed for a continuing presence, and it provided women with an opportunity to participate in government, building their own knowledge of the legislative process as well as their own sense of self-respect and worth.

As she did with the *Suffragist,* Paul quickly sought talented women to take over the lobbying, although she insisted on maintaining control. When Maud Younger, a labor activist from California who had campaigned there for a state suffrage amendment in 1911, began leading the lobbying in 1915, she consulted with Paul about how to approach senators, which women to involve, and when to press for a vote in the House or Senate. Paul and Younger had met when Younger came to the Convention of Women Voters at the San Francisco World's Fair. Paul asked her to come to Washington, which she did soon after, at first renting an apartment, but then moving into headquarters, where she lived through the rest of the campaign. Younger, like Paul, had lived in a college settlement house where she had come to a similar conclusion, that this sort of philanthropic effort could never lead to fundamental change: "Gradually I saw the absurdity of trying to order the lives of others, and learned that all they needed was an opportunity to develop their own lives—an opportunity denied these people of the tenements" ("Revelations of a Woman Lobbyist" Sept., 7). For women, only legal equality could provide increased opportunities, Younger felt, and legal equality could only be achieved through suffrage.

Once she set up her office in the headquarters, Younger had twenty or thirty temporary lobbyists working with her at all times, taking care of many key tasks. They visited with legislators as well as their staffs, constituencies, relatives, and business partners; they consulted with lobbyists in state capitals; they studied articles about these men in newspapers and magazines. This variety of work meant that everyone could be involved in lobbying: women who preferred to avoid direct visits could still be involved. Women who could not come to Washington or even their state capitals could contribute by sending in relevant periodicals and visiting relatives and constituents. Younger especially wanted to involve prominent people in lobbying. Senators might complain; they might delay; but they found it difficult to avoid well-known women from their own states, especially when those women had already informed hometown papers of their visit.

Younger and Paul carefully orchestrated these visits. Whenever lobbyists went out, they did so with detailed instructions concerning the information they should secure, relying on a card system that allowed women who might never meet each other to build the group's power over the years. When a lobbyist started out for the Capitol, she was given a set of twenty-two cards, with checks by those items on which Younger wanted her to concentrate. Each one covered an influence that might determine a legislator's opinion on suffrage, such as his ancestry, birthplace, education, family (especially the opinions of his mother, wife, and daughters), religion, military service, occupation, offices, hobbies and clubs, the newspapers he read, his greatest achievements, those people who had the most influence on him, previous votes and opinions on federal and state suffrage, and strengths and weaknesses of his state. Even daily habits rated a card and careful attention. When a reporter asked Maud Younger, "Why do you want to know the habits of the congressmen?" she replied, "For several reasons. If they get to their offices early, the one that comes at 7:30, this is often the best time during the day to see them. And if a member is a drinking man we want to know that. One of our lobbyists may go to him and not know what's the matter with him, or how to evaluate his answers" ("Her Pressure on Congress" 72).

Although each lobbyist might deal with just a few cards or questions, they were all asked to contribute to the card headed "Exact Statement and Remarks," on which they listed remarks made by the congressman during the visit, along with notes on the attitude conveyed by him. Katharine Rolston Fisher, for example, interviewing Representative Augustine Lonergan of Connecticut, in his office on April 4, 1917, quoted him as stating, "I am unqualifiedly opposed because I am a states rights Democrat. I have told a number of women in my district so." Fisher recorded also that Lonergan "was rather curt." When Sarah Grant saw Lonergan in his office on April 18, she wrote that he "thinks nothing but war legislation will come up now. . . . Seemed interested but very busy. 'Come and see me after the war legislation is through.' Not ready to make any statement." Armed with this data, a third lobbyist could mention his contradictory answers and seek clarification on the reasons for his antisuffrage stance (Lobbying Cards).

After each visit, the lobbyist created a detailed report so subsequent visitors could refer to promises made or excuses proffered, and Paul could judge the strength of support in Congress. The trail of answers also led to further means of persuasion. If visitors continued to receive varied responses, a press agent at headquarters might send an article to the legislator's local paper pointing to the discrepancies in his answers. At his speeches, questioners might quote his responses and ask him to clarify his position. If a senator claimed to a lobbyist that women in his district didn't support a federal suffrage amendment, Paul would immediately plan rallies in his home state; if he said that he needed more information, influential citizens from home would mail it to him.

As the lobbyists made constant visits, sought information, and offered ever more cogent arguments based on their growing files of data, they also used more traditional forms of communication between men and women, both to blunt the force of the ongoing visits and to present another face to the press while still emphasizing the amendment ("Birthdays and the Judiciary Committee"). Prominent residents of the home state sent birthday cakes, bearing a suffrage banner and an American flag, to members of the House Judiciary Committee, which had the power to request that the Rules Committee approve the amendment for a vote in the House. The inscriptions on these cakes, in purple, said, "May the coming year bring you joy, and the Susan B. Anthony amendment." On their birthdays, legislators received "a dainty purple basket filled with little blue flowers," forget-me-nots, with this message:

> "Forget me not" is the message
> I bring in my gladsome blue;
> Forget not the fifty-six years that have gone,
> And the work there is still to do;
> Forget not the suffrage amendment
> That waits in committee for you.

On Valentine's Days, organizers asked women to inundate congressmen with valentines that referred to the information gained about them. In 1916, for example, a valentine sent to New York's Democratic Senator James A. O'Gorman focused on his pretense of states' rights as a reason for opposing suffrage:

> You voted for the income tax amendment,
> Nor did direct elections find you slow,
> But when it comes to suffrage, "That's a matter
> Each state must settle for itself, you know!"

California's Senator James Phelan received valentines that focused on his polite but meaningless meetings with women—and the CU's vow to oppose him in the next election:

> You're flirting with me, darling,
> But leave me still in doubt,
> You'd better be my Valentine or

Look
A
Little
OUT!
("Valentines Pour in upon Congress")

To the president on May Day 1916, CU member Joy Young took a large basket of flowers in suffrage colors along with two notes, one asking for the immediate passage of the suffrage amendment and one declaring that four million women were then voting, a reminder of women's ability to successfully oppose recalcitrant Democrats during that election year. In giving such gifts, cakes, and birthday cards, suffragists might be acting more like traditional women visitors than when they showed up with their lobbying cards, but even in making these more traditional and acceptable choices they never took their focus off of political realities and suffrage.

As visitors continually sought an audience and asked well-planned questions, their assertiveness drew various reactions. At times, all of this attention seemed to flatter: many congressmen responded in great detail to lobbyists and corrected data from other sources. At other times, the repeated visits irritated or angered men who did not care to be thus interrogated by women. Often legislators "doubted their senses and lost their tempers" when "after years upon years of please politely phrased," they began encountering lobbyists wielding "words of political power" ("Hearing Before the House" 5). As Alice Duer Miller portrayed in a poem, written in a senator's voice for the *New York Tribune,* many legislators felt exasperated when short, polite visits would no longer placate the suffragists who came to Washington from their states:

> I put them on committees,
> I say they're bound to win,
> I send congratulations
> When another state comes in;
> And often on their birthdays
> I will write a little note.
> And yet in spite of all I do,
> They nag me for the vote.

The old-fashioned attention described here would placate a kind and natural woman, Miller's senator implies: it is the unnatural militant harpy who continues to "nag."

In response to this perceived inappropriateness, in the spring of 1916 several members of the House of Representatives called for an investigation of

Paul's lobbying finances, creating the impression that she was amassing funds for ominous purposes, though there was no offer of proof. The investigation never occurred.

With accusations coming from the legislature, articles appeared in the mainstream press and kept the furor going. The *New York Times* on March 2, 1919, reported in epic style that these lobbyists had started with just ten dollars, Elizabeth Kent's original budget, and had since raised $425,000 to pressure busy legislators every day. Their expenses in Washington for that year alone, the article continued, would be $100,000. Here, in response to a reporter's claim that "some of your opponents assert" that malfeasance had occurred, Maud Younger had the chance to argue that suffragists had used no improper tactics and certainly had not blackmailed anyone ("Her Pressure on Congress"). More sympathetic newspapers, like the *New York Tribune,* printed fuller versions of her denials and praised the card system, saying that Paul and her colleagues were outdoing Scotland Yard. A *Minneapolis Tribune* editorial, "Suffrage Lobbying a Science," complimented the twenty to thirty women constantly working at headquarters ("Lobbying and Political Work").

With fuel provided by the negative articles in the *New York Times,* several antisuffrage magazines reported vague claims that Paul's lobbyists had hired detectives to collect their information, implying that the women themselves were not capable of amassing this information. They also labeled the card system as the backbone of an ongoing form of blackmail: suffragists were using the information they gained about private lives to force congressmen into supporting suffrage. The *Woman Patriot* used the front-page headline "*New York Times* Reveals the Secret Card System Used by Suffragists to Control Congress" to introduce a three-page article on March 8, 1919, about secretive dealings through which these treacherous women were exercising inappropriate forms of pressure and control. A story in the next issue claimed that senators who supported suffrage had succumbed to this blackmail, could no longer be trusted by their constituents, and should be thrown out of office ("Card Index 'Converts'").

Even as such articles excoriated Paul, Younger, and this system, they recognized the power of the lobbying staff. In Paul's hands, lobbying was a well-planned rhetorical form, aimed not at establishing close friendships with legislators, but at educating and persuading them each day, with the card system creating a type of accountability that the women exploited to gain votes. These women worked for and expected solid answers. They assumed that they had the right to come to the Capitol not just as polite visitors but as serious interlocutors—they would not go away. Lobbying constructed these women as educated equals making political decisions based on their own research and analysis. For Paul, this effort fostered strength and self-respect, and it served in tandem with large public events to bring suffrage into each politician's mind and office.

Deputations in Drawing Rooms

Lobbying gave suffragists access to legislators at a level that women had not reached before: they expected to speak regularly to each Democrat or Republican who had declared his opposition. They also went to President Wilson personally, either to convince him to support the amendment or to create public recognition of the fact that he would not. Whatever he maintained, Paul felt that more than any other president, he controlled his party. His Democratic caucus, as Rheta Childe Dorr described it in her autobiography, was "the most complete machine Congress has ever known. . . . No Democrat dared act independently of the caucus or even question its decisions" (*Woman of Fifty* 289). Although at various times he told suffragists that he lacked information about the amendment, had to advocate states' rights, or had to center his attention on war, Paul believed that Wilson could always make suffrage happen, just as he had secured tariff legislation, the Panama Canal, and war. Rheta Childe Dorr spoke of deputations as "drops of water which we hoped would finally make an impression on the stone" (*Woman of Fifty* 288). That stone was Wilson.

Wilson first invited interaction by claiming to a deputation in March of 1913 that he did not know much about suffrage: Paul was ready to inform him. As she recalled in her interview with Amelia Fry, "By the time we got through all these deputations he certainly knew that there was a widespread interest in the country. What he had asked us to do—to concert public opinion—we were trying to do. That was our point." And she kept the women coming to make sure that he missed no fact about the amendment: "You know we kept these deputations with anybody we could think of that might be a new group" (Fry). Though Paul used visual and verbal rhetoric to reach women, male voters, and the legislature, her ultimate political target was always Wilson, just one man, a single target that made success seem possible and led to a righteous anger when he would not relent.

As Paul continuously sent deputations, a name she insisted on to stress that each visitor represented a large contingency of American women, she created a complex array of gendered rhetoric, working with social expectations to again foster an aura of danger. Especially at the beginning, Paul relied on the middle-class power inherent in the ceremony of well-connected ladies paying a polite social call. In the nineteenth century, middle- and upper-class women visited each other regularly in their parlors, leaving calling cards and following complex rules about days and durations of visits. As dictated by etiquette books, these visits were meant to be polite and restrained, not a place for difficult subjects or any breach of decorum (Plante 121–24). In this visiting structure, women would rarely meet with any men at all. They would only make an appointment with a professional, like a doctor or priest, or perhaps with a family friend to seek advice. Thus, Wilson expected that these women would be coming to the White House only to receive his considered opinions and advice—gratefully and quietly. Paul, however, seeking a site for strong rhetoric, had plans for reconstructing what occurred in the parlor.

By scheduling visits with Wilson "at home," Paul could emphasize the worthiness of her group: they had the right to enter his drawing room and speak there. They were not there to see the first lady or to ask for a simple piece of advice. They had come on a political mission, and they meant to speak firmly concerning that mission. This mixture of old and new, appropriate and inappropriate, got attention in the press and proved difficult for Wilson, who, at least for a while, was not prepared to turn well-connected ladies away. When he began to view these suffragists as an endless bane, he became unwilling to meet with them any longer, and they were moved back outside where they began to chase him down, a less acceptable behavior that worsened their image in the press but increased their visibility. In both iterations of the visit, inside and outside of approved space, Paul was creating a physical presence that exploited gendered traditions: women were allowed in, she stressed, only when they didn't ask for anything; they were removed when they violated that social understanding; they were vilified for continuing to make their demands from the street, for insisting on the chance for women to move from the political "outside" to the "inside," as equal participants in a democracy.

In these deputations, Paul's primary goal was to educate Wilson, but of course these meetings involved a mixture of education, conversion, and coercion that often exists in nonviolent appeals to the powerful. As proponents of nonviolence, as William R. Miller described such campaigners, they wanted to "show him that we are responsible persons seeking a change of conditions to which the opponent's social structure can adjust, and that we have adequate support for a course of action that will deepen and prolong the conflict" (146). Paul's own remarks make clear that the deputations were not based on animosity toward Wilson, even though as a Quaker she did not approve of America's entrance into World War I: "I had a great respect for Wilson, great respect for him. And he was a nice type of man to have as your adversary because you could be pretty certain of what he would do in a certain situation.

. . . I think he was a very great man, a very, very great man" (Fry). Although she admired him, as a nonviolent campaigner Paul felt she had to get him to look carefully at how he made his own judgments so he would resolve the contradictions in all the claims he made—and support suffrage.

At these various types of visits, women encountered in Wilson an opponent of great complexity. Behind his politeness and his arguments for states' rights, many critics believed, lay a profound lack of respect for women as thinkers and as citizens. For his first job, he had taught history and political science at Bryn Mawr, from when it opened in 1885 to 1888. There he very much annoyed graduate student Lucy Salmon, a future Vassar history professor and NWP advisor, by saying "a woman who had married an intellectual man was often better educated than a woman who had college training." Department chair and dean M. Carey Thomas never forgave him for going over her head to the president "whenever he wanted to discuss his status on the faculty." According to Thomas, Wilson's attitude toward women was "put your sweet hand in mine and trust in me." In Wilson's opinion, she claimed, "intellectual power, leadership and logical thinking" were male qualities (Dobkin 20). Many women found the same prejudices in his writing as in his teaching career. Rheta Childe Dorr, for example, wrote that "He had a lofty conception of human liberty, but he no more included women in his definition of 'all men' than did Thomas Jefferson when he drafted the Declaration of Independence. Search the Woodrow Wilson 'History of the United States' and you will not know that any woman was ever a patriot. Read his eloquent work, 'The New Freedom,' and you will not know that any woman in the United States ever dreamed of freedom" (*Woman of Fifty* 284).

These negative attitudes toward women were further demonstrated in his campaign for the presidency. Frank Stockbridge, who conducted Wilson's publicity campaign for the 1912 election, described Wilson's firm disapproval of woman suffrage and his desire to dodge reporters who wanted to discuss the issue:

> We had barely crossed the Colorado river before California newspaper reporters of both sexes boarded the train and sought the Governor's opinion on every conceivable subject, chief of which in local importance was woman suffrage, which was to be voted on at the next State election. This is the only topic on which I knew Mr. Wilson to take an attitude that could be interpreted as dodging the issue. He was definitely and irreconcilably opposed to woman suffrage; woman's place was in the home, and the type of woman who took an active part in the suffrage agitation was totally abhorrent to him. In private conversation he made no bones of his aversion to the "unsexed, masculanized woman," as he termed them; his ideal of womanhood was the perfectly feminine type. There

was something degrading to the sex in public activities of a political nature, he believed. (566–67)

In Denver, where women were already voters, Stockbridge asked Wilson "to pacify the Suffragists" by sitting with them at two or three dinners and luncheons, playing a game of seeming support while keeping the conversation off the vote (567). On a train from Barstow to San Francisco, a young woman journalist kept trying to corner him on the subject, but he stayed within his circle of supporters to avoid her. When he was asked in California about his position, Wilson replied that since "the suffrage question is a live issue in California, to be voted on at the next election, it would not be becoming for the Governor of another State to say anything which might influence the election one way or the other." This carefully planned dodge, used by Wilson and his aides, could be repeated in many states. As his biographer Arthur Link described his attitudes, Wilson believed in 1912, 1913, and 1914 "that the world would be a better place if women stayed in the home," but since he could not say this openly, especially in suffrage states, "he put his refusal to support woman suffrage on other grounds" (Link, *Wilson: The New Freedom* 257).

Immediately after the preinaugural parade, Paul started drawing room visits to this difficult opponent. On March 17, 1913, two weeks after the parade, the Congressional Committee sent its first delegation to the White House: Paul, NAWSA leader and historian Ida Husted Harper, and Genevieve Stone, a congressman's wife who had been assaulted during the parade. To this group's questions about his position on suffrage, Wilson made the fateful reply and evasion that provided the justification for so much subsequent action: that this matter had never been brought to his attention before and that therefore he had no opinion on it and needed additional information. He said further, as he also asserted subsequently, "You'll have to convert public opinion, get enough public opinion in the country back of this. At the present time there would be no use of trying to get Congress to do this" (Lunardini 32). Here was a rhetorical challenge that Paul was glad to accept: he was inviting an ongoing nonviolent attempt to educate him as well as the legislature and nation.

When Wilson first proved himself willing to meet with suffragists after the parade, Paul continued to send groups of traditional and powerful middle-class women, maintaining and escalating the pressure. In March Wilson met with the National Council of Women Voters, an organization representing women voters from the suffrage states. In November a delegation of seventy-three women from New Jersey, the president's home state, came to see him. Paul had asked them to Washington and invited them to stay at headquarters.

By this point, however, Wilson was already beginning to tire of these groups, who took up his time and expected answers. When he said he did not have time to see the New Jersey representatives, they went to the White House anyway, accompanied by reporters, to wait. Wilson met with them that day, perhaps due to his own sense of propriety as well as the problem of having them remain there.

By the end of 1913 Wilson was beginning to change his response when unavoidable visitors asked him about his position on suffrage. To say that he knew nothing about it was becoming an embarrassment, a self-criticism, because so many women had obviously sought to teach him. He changed to the states' rights theme, assuring visitors that he supported suffrage, but that he believed states had the right to make decisions concerning the electorate, as southern states had done through Jim Crow voting laws. He also claimed he could not force any Democrats to act, that he only worked for his party's stated priorities—and the Democratic platform did not mention woman's suffrage. This response involved at least a fair amount of self-effacement, something rare for Wilson. To a deputation of college women, led by Elsie Hill, he introduced his next rhetorical shift, one that continued during the war: suffrage, however worthy a concept, could not occupy the time of busy legislators who had so many more pressing matters on their agenda, first tariffs and then war in Europe.

By the end of 1913 these rhetorical dodges were getting press attention. In the *New Republic,* Charles A. Beard described Wilson's pretense of being only a party messenger as ludicrous: "Everybody knows that Mr. Wilson and the small group of men about him do assume full responsibility in the name of the party for what has been done and left undone in Washington" ("Woman Suffrage and Strategy" 22). Many writers felt drawn to the dramatic possibilities of the visits—of women repeatedly assailing the logic of the grand professorial president. When a committee of fifty-five NAWSA delegates met with Wilson on December 8, 1913, at the time of the annual conference, several newspapers, like the *New York Tribune,* reported Anna Howard Shaw's full response to Wilson's declaration that he could not advocate this amendment in Congress because his party had not asked him to do so:

> I inquired if I might ask him a question. He said I might. I said: "Mr. President, since you cannot present our case to Congress, and since we have no committee in the House, who is to speak for us there?" He returned laughingly that he had found us well able to speak for ourselves, whereupon I said: "But not

authoritatively. Have we any one, Mr. President, to present our case with authority to Congress?" He hesitated a moment, the muscles of his face twitched; I was dreadfully frightened myself, and I do believe he was as much frightened; but he didn't evade the question. He answered squarely, "No." And to my mind that "No" was the most important thing in the interview. ("President and the Suffragists" 1210)

This well-circulated story emphasized women's lack of representation as well as their ability to make their case to Wilson, to corner him rhetorically, the feature of deputations that made Wilson loath to continue them. Newspapers might report such confrontations to support suffrage—or to exploit the entertainment value of a pompous president bested by women.

During 1914, as Wilson continued to alter his responses and to weather negative press coverage, he found that "each meeting was more embarrassing than the last" (Link, *Wilson: The New Freedom* 258). He was finally prepared to be not at home for these "parlor visits." Paul might have agreed that this method had gone about as far as it could go—she would not keep repeating the same technique when it no longer seemed dangerous, newsworthy, or effective. Instead, in 1914, in response to his denial of access, she organized two new extremes of deputations that he could not avoid, both highly publicized events.

To draw more members into her own ranks and to indicate her group's size to Wilson, Paul began planning for a deputation of working-class women, a more controversial group to bring to the president's home. The February 2 deputation involved four hundred working women from several states, representing eight million nonprofessional women workers whose political presence had been demonstrated by frequent strikes in 1911 and 1912, especially in the clothing industry. Once she secured permission for the visit, permission that was perhaps granted because of Wilson's desire to avoid further labor disputes and his recognition that these workers would matter in wartime, Paul carefully planned this deputation to present the perspective of a group that she had not publicly featured before. A letter Mary Beard wrote to Lucy Burns on January 18, 1914, described the careful use of these women to create an effect of danger, of a large group of disgruntled workers entering the streets and the president's house: "We will try to take working women with us on this occasion to make it seem that it is a spontaneous uprising of the proletariat." As Nina Allender's cartoons from 1914 also indicate, Paul was genuinely concerned about these women's plight—about their need for political power, not philanthropy—but she was also aware that their appearance at the White House could provide a new level of controversy.

To stress the significance of this deputation, Paul chose women of promi-
nence as its leaders. Margaret Hinchley, a well-respected officer of the Laun-
dry-Worker's Union of New York, spoke for the group, as did Rose Schneider-
man, a Polish immigrant and factory worker who was then vice president of
the Woman's Trade Union League, and Rose Winslow, a mill worker whose
life was often used to portray the hideous situation of working women. Ads
for Winslow's speeches said she "gave the best of her young life to industry,
and came out wounded." As ads and articles noted, Winslow spent eight
years, starting at age eleven, in silk mills in Pennsylvania, where she con-
tracted tuberculosis, becoming too ill to make a living. She then went to
night school to improve herself, the oft-told story continued, and became a
labor organizer. In her speeches at many labor events and during this visit
to the White House, she argued against the older style of philanthropic help,
the type that Paul had also rejected: working women didn't want charity, she
argued, but higher wages and the political power to secure them ("Working
Women's Deputation").

In addition to finding well-known speakers for the February 2 deputation,
Paul also sought press attention by sending a much larger group than Wilson
had expected when he agreed to the meeting. The large number demonstrated
the potential danger of these women, on the loose or on strike, as well as their
potential positive impact as dedicated hard-working citizens. After a mass
meeting outside the White House, at which these leaders and others spoke,
the four hundred moved toward the White House with a band playing the
"Marseillaise." To their great disappointment, in reply to their request for
the vote, Wilson again stressed his own inability, as his party's spokesman,
to speak and act freely: "I am not at liberty to speak as an individual" (Link,
Wilson: The New Freedom 258).

Although Wilson repeatedly said he lacked the power to help suffragists,
Paul still felt that he certainly possessed that power, and that additional
deputations might convince him to act. As she wrote to Alva Smith Belmont
in June 16, 1914, "We are going to the President again because he is, of course,
the principal factor in determining what legislation shall go through Congress this session." After the large group of working women, Paul chose the
contrary extreme of the most respectable of women's groups—representatives
of American women's clubs, whom she had also placed near the beginning of
the 1913 inaugural parade (Mary Beard, Letter to Alice Paul, 24 June 1914).

In 1912, at its annual meeting, the General Federation of Women's Clubs
(GFWC) had ruled that a resolution in support of suffrage was out of order.
The group then appointed a political science study committee to consider the
amendment and report back. At a national convention in 1914, representatives

voted to support a resolution for a federal suffrage amendment, recording, as the official history of the federation asserts, the members' "earnest belief in the principles of political equality regardless of sex" (M. W. Wells 204–05). As soon as this decision was announced, Paul sought the federation's aid, recognizing the sizeable clout of a group representing a million of America's well-regarded women, capable of reaching a president tired of facing more radical and less influential contingencies. Engaging these GFWC representatives for a deputation could also cement their relationship with the CU, not just with state or local suffrage organizations or with NAWSA. When the GFWC decided to send a deputation, Beard wrote to Paul to compliment her on the brilliant stroke of securing their participation: "I knew you would go after them, immediately, when they endorsed suffrage" (24 June 1914).

In concert with GFWC leaders, Paul chose Zona Gale to lead the group. Gale, who had graduated from the University of Wisconsin in 1895 where she absorbed Robert La Follette's vision of progressive civic reform, was an influential women's club leader in Wisconsin. She had written in 1909 in *La Follette's Weekly Magazine* about the clubs' social reform role—manifested in their advocacy of child labor laws, better schools and civic governments, better conditions for women factory workers, and suffrage ("Civic Problems"). She thus signified an activist view of club life, one that Paul wanted to exploit. In addition, her highly popular tales presenting a nostalgic view of the small town—*Friendship Village* (1908), *Friendship Village Love Stories* (1909), *When I Was a Little Girl* (1913), and *Neighborhood Stories* (1914)—made her seem like an advocate of old-fashioned American values. In a letter to Paul, Mary Beard commented that "Zona Gale is the woman to influence them, if any one can" (24 June 1914). Paul agreed.

Paul thought that with this safe and influential group Wilson might move beyond his earlier rhetorical gambits and truly speak about suffrage. When she wrote to Alva Smith Belmont on June 16, 1914, Paul reminded her that, with the labor group in February, Wilson had repeated his dodge about party platforms. Paul told Belmont he could not use that excuse again because of his strong personal advocacy of legislation not in the Democratic platform, an idea she repeated in letters to other colleagues: "His anti-trust and conservation bills now are both being treated as privileged because of his support as was the Panama tolls repeal." With his most recent tactic of evasion no longer available, she wrote, the women at headquarters felt encouraged to go to him again, with a group that was framed as sincere homemakers and philanthropists to whom he owed a sincere response.

With limited access to the president and with the involvement of this influential group, Paul and Burns planned for each moment of the June 30 deputation. Gale's involvement would help to insure large participation. In addition, Paul secured Anna Kelton Wiley to present the resolution to the president. They also planned for Rheta Childe Dorr, who had stopped editing the *Suffragist* in April but was still listed as editor on its masthead in June, to accompany Gale and Wiley as the club women's assured and informed voice. Dorr was an aggressive rhetor who would insure that the meeting would not dwindle into what Wilson would prefer, a polite tea party. Burns, Paul, and Dorr carefully planned what each of the women would say.

On June 30, Gale, Wiley, and Dorr led the deputation of five hundred white-clad GFWC delegates to present a resolution on the amendment to the president. After polite introductions and compliments, Dorr immediately addressed Wilson's repeated claim that he could only advocate what his party had approved: he had put through the Panama Canal tolls act, she reminded him, even though it had not been part of his party's platform. When she began citing evidence to contradict his claims, as she wrote in her autobiography, Wilson immediately reacted: "A peculiar change took place in President Wilson. His gray eyes turned to cold steel, a rigidity of his whole body replaced his former easy and graceful pose, and his jaws became set in a hard and dangerous line. I well understood then the terror he inspired in the bravest men of his party. So did the women who stood behind me. They actually swayed in alarm, pressing closer to my streaming back" (*Woman of Fifty* 293).

Although Wilson seemed to expect the arguments to end with his use of the stern glare, Dorr escalated the conversation by voicing a threat: suffrage states controlled one sixth of the electoral vote, she argued, "enough to work havoc in any presidential election"; women could end his presidency if he continued to avoid suffrage legislation through a string of dodges. In reply, "in a voice razor-edged," Wilson abandoned his party-representative argument and went back to his states-rights argument: suffrage should be considered only in state legislatures. Dorr pointed out a comparison that she intended as a counter to both of his stated principles: the amendment providing for direct election of United States senators had been advocated and approved at the federal level, resulting in the Seventeenth Amendment being added to the Constitution in 1913, with strong support from Democrat leaders but no advocacy for it in any official party documents or in any state legislature. Wilson shifted ground and began again, vaguely, on the primacy of the current Constitution, and then said that these women's clubs representatives should not have come to him at all. Dorr persisted, pointing out that, if the federal amendment passed, the states would get their opportunity during the ratification process to weigh in on suffrage. Seemingly exasperated and out of arguments, Wilson next said that "I think that it is not proper for me to stand here and be cross-examined by you" and turned and left the room (*Woman of Fifty* 291–96).

Because of the social status of the women's clubs, the presence of many reporters, and the press bulletins that Paul immediately released, newspapers widely reported this altercation. Although coverage varied in tone, the articles agreed that Wilson suddenly cut the visit short. The *New York Times* reported the event with a headline depicting the women's visit and manner as inappropriate and Wilson's power as sure: "Wilson Won't Let Women Heckle Him." This article claimed that his withdrawal signaled his own wily control: he was right in refusing to let these inappropriate interlocutors continue. Other newspapers were more critical. Rochester's *Democrat and Chronicle* commented ironically about obfuscations as a supposed political strength: "If adroitness in dodging awkward questions is proof of political ability, then Woodrow Wilson is one of the ablest politicians the country ever produced." An article in the *Indianapolis Progressive Star* noted that "the president 'wabbled,' not to say quibbled, in his talk to the women." The *New York American* on July 2 commented at length on Wilson's treachery concerning the Panama Canal tolls law: "When confronted by a group of ladies with this evidence of insincerity and equivocation the President lost his temper and retired—indeed, there was no other retort available to him" ("President and Suffrage").

After the double confrontation of working women and then women's club members, two hard-to-refuse groups that Wilson had met with reluctantly, he was no longer willing to meet with deputations, for which he had to provide much publicized evasions when the plain truth was that he preferred not to give women the vote. By January of 1915, after women from the Democratic Party came to the White House, he began claiming that war preparedness was taking up his time and that he would be unable to meet with any more groups.

When Paul realized that visitations had ended, she felt that this termination itself could become a powerful story, that the press could be encouraged to focus on Wilson's unwillingness to see well-meaning and influential women. In a May 17, 1915, letter to Lucy Burns, written in her usual positive tone, Paul discussed the relationship between Wilson's inaction and a new type of publicity, emphasizing his avoidance of women and his lack of sympathy with their plight: "It seems to me that we want to convict him before the country of evading us. It is certainly fortunate that he has ceased seeing us. We ought to be able to get publicity for a considerable time out of his refusing to see us and when we have exhausted the possibilities in that line and he has gotten the reputation of refusing to see Suffragists, I should think we might then go further and try to make him see us." In this avoidance, Paul argued, he was silencing individual women, just as his party was silencing all women and casting them as political outsiders by denying them the vote.

To create a demonstration of Wilson's denial of these Americans, Paul chose a more public and controversial form of visual rhetoric, a White House sit-in, and then responded vociferously to the public critique this decision engendered. In early May of 1915, when a Pennsylvania group attempted to see him, Wilson refused. Paul encouraged these women to remain at the White House; they waited there for three days. The *Washington Star* responded with an editorial on May 7 against this pestering of a busy president. Taking advantage of this rhetorical situation, Lucy Burns responded immediately with an editorial letter to the *Star*, published on May 8. This editorial, parts of which were later quoted in circular letters, gave Burns and Paul a chance to defend their nonviolent approach to social reform at a time when their conflict with Wilson was escalating and war in Europe seemed imminent.

In this editorial, Burns first stressed Wilson's agency. He had caused the women to wait. He had asked them to put their request to see him in writing, thus making these polite and dutiful American women return each day to seek a response. Next she objected to the newspaper's use of the label of "militancy" to typify these days of waiting. Burns used this opportunity to elucidate the difference between violence and nonviolence, specifically between war and her group's own nonviolent choices: "It is a little far-fetched to blame so innocent a series of actions, especially at a time like this when acts of most extraordinary violence are being committed all over the world, in the war escalating in Europe and in Mexico in the name of national independence." As every American well knew, on the Franco, Belgian, Russian, and Serbian fronts, soldiers and civilians were dying. Between January 15 and March 31, 1915, the French First Army suffered 27,026 casualties and the British suffered 33,678 (Mosier 131). In Mexico, American forces were occupying the port city of Veracruz to oppose President Victoriano Huerto, who had executed President Francisco Madero in February of 1913. Wilson hoped that American involvement in Mexico would force Huerto to hold elections and end a civil war that, within the previous year, had resulted in the death of two hundred thousand people. The contrast between these conflicts and the campaign for suffrage, Burns made clear in this editorial, was in the methodology, not in the seriousness of the conflict: like Mexicans and Europeans controlled by dictators, women of America were suffering "from the very real injustice of disenfranchisement," but they insisted on nonviolent means, such as deputations to Wilson, to fight for freedom.

Burns argued that instead of being portrayed as Wilson's enemies, these suffragists should be seen as his compatriots, as fellow advocates of democracy. In Mexico and Europe, Burns reminded readers, Wilson himself was attempting nonviolent means of opposition: he was blockading a port to force change in Mexico; he was, at least publicly, maintaining neutrality as he pursued diplomatic answers to Europe's conflicts. Yet, Burns noted, Wilson felt no allegiance or sympathy with these women: "We have found it possible to be patient with militant Mexicans, Germans, and English who have seriously interfered not only with official etiquette but with the life and liberty of American men and women. Some of the same forbearance might be expected for the women of America who are so patiently working for independence" (Letter to the Editor, *Washington Star*).

Although Wilson's refusal to meet with suffragists and the resultant sit-in offered Paul and Burns a chance for publicity for their cause and against the president, they knew that, with a world at war, the press would give only so much space to a lack of deputations. Once newspapers reported that Wilson was refusing to see these women, the story was essentially dead. In response to his curtailment of access, then, Paul decided that she had to initiate new attempts to contact him, moving from visits at the White House to confrontations in the streets, an escalating pattern of nonviolence, as William R. Miller described it: "The general pattern moves by stages from moderate to extreme forms of conventional action and then from moderate to extreme forms of nonviolent action. This movement carries with it a quickening of pace and tempo. As it goes toward the extreme it becomes riskier, harder to sustain. Greater demands are placed upon morale, courage, physical energy and discipline" (70). For most Americans and for the nation's press, forcing interactions with Wilson as he toured the country seemed disrespectful and inappropriate. Paul's group was taking on a new level of aggression and of public reaction, but she realized that the status quo would no longer further her cause.

Deputations in the Streets

Paul's first foray outside the capital immediately became notorious. On May 17, 1915, when Wilson went to New York on the U.S. yacht *Mayflower* to formally review five thousand sailors in the Atlantic Fleet, a group of women, including Mabel Florence, Secretary of the Political Equity League of New York, and Mabel Scofield, formerly of the staff of the Woman's Political Union of Brooklyn, went into the lobby of a New York Biltmore Hotel, where Wilson was having lunch, to request that Wilson meet with a deputation of New York women. When they asked to send a note to him in the dining room, they were refused. When Wilson was walking through the lobby to leave the hotel, they stood on a couch and called out to him, but he did not acknowledge their presence. As he went out to the harbor to board the *Mayflower,* the women tried to get a small boat to take them out to him, but none was willing to go near the ship holding the president.

This rhetorical moment had many complications of gender, which the activists knew would catch the attention of the press. They had increased the level of danger by pursuing the president, sending him notes, yelling out to him, and following him. Because they had pressed their cause physically, although they were still just asking for a meeting without offering any kind of violence, Paul knew that she would need to make her next rhetorical moves carefully. Her group wanted public attention, but did not want to seem like traitors or irrational harpies. Because of the sinking of the *Lusitania* on May 7, an "attack" on the president, especially one that involved his presence on a U.S. ship, would cause strong emotional responses. When these women decided to accost Wilson in New York, they planned to hold a protest meeting in a large hall if he refused to see them. After the *Lusitania* firing, Paul felt that such a public demonstration would be taking their aggression too far. From New York, she wrote to Lucy Burns that her group could not follow through with "the little performance we had planned without that also taking the form of militancy owing to the increased care that would be given to the protection of the President and to the quelling of any disturbance." Repeating the word "militancy," Paul further stated that she didn't want her own nonviolent action to be linked rhetorically with violence against the president and the country: "Militancy is not something to be started lightly and without much consideration, it seems to me, and I did not feel that we ought to start it then" (Letter to Lucy Burns).

Even with this curtailment of their plans, however, this altercation caused an immediate negative response. Under the headline "Bad Campaign Tactics," the *New York Times* employed an argument about polite and impolite behavior—good girls and bad girls—to belittle as well as criticize. These suffragists "are probably simple illustrations of the bromidic proverb that it takes all sorts of people to make a world." Talking of "taste and manners and decency," the article continued, would be a waste of words with such people. Their affronts—"the rowdy actions of unmannered individuals"—could only hurt the suffrage effort and harm "soberer suffrage associations."

Although Paul could not control the initial coverage in the *Times* and elsewhere, she wanted to quickly put a positive spin on what happened—to emphasize that women had been forced to pursue Wilson because he would no longer speak to them. She did not want her group to suddenly seem like English suffragettes, involved in some form of violence. About Mabel Scofield, a participant in the night's events, Paul even wrote to Burns, who was in Washington editing the *Suffragist*, "Please do not say she is English" (Letter to Lucy Burns).

Although Paul did not want to seem violent or unpatriotic, she also did not want to appear cowed by Wilson or by the prospect of war. Her expanding audience of working women, like those in the February 1914 deputation to the White House, might not mind seeing Wilson a bit pursued and was not eager for world war. These women might react negatively if she began to apologize or make excuses. In her letter to Burns on May 17, Paul urged her: "Do, I beg, put some righteous indignation into the account!" When Carrie Chapman Catt wrote to Paul saying that she needed to apologize in the press for this assault on Wilson, and then wrote to NAWSA members encouraging them to oppose Paul's actions, Paul's colleague Lavinia Dock replied by claiming that affluent men opposed suffrage anyway and would simply go on from this "offense" to something else, regardless of whether there was an apology. Dock argued emphatically: "Dear Mrs. Catt, the upper classes of men, whom you chiefly see, never will let women vote if they can help it." The labor vote, Dock asserted, would be needed for suffrage, and this contingency "is not at all disturbed by the heckling of a President." For Paul, the true "gist of the New York affair" was the continued aggressive nonviolent pursuit of this leader who controlled his party and the Congress—to demonstrate that suffragists had a right to question their leader, even if, or perhaps especially if, he tried to avoid them ("Can the President"). To keep the best possible construction of these actions before the public and her own constituents, Paul immediately sent out a flood of circular letters and press releases that stressed the rights of all citizens to question their president, that argued, in fact, that this nonviolent act proved they were patriotic Americans.

Having been turned away in New York and having little access to the White House except at what Wilson judged to be unavoidable occasions, Paul's troops continued to confront him in crowds, using tactics similar to those Paul had participated in with the Pankhursts. After accosting him in the relative privacy of a hotel lobby, Paul moved into a public space, during an official presentation. On July 4 Mabel Vernon publicly questioned the president at the dedication and cornerstone laying of the Labor Temple of the American Federation of Labor in Washington. While he was proclaiming his firm belief in liberty and justice, she loudly interrupted from her place on the platform as a labor representative: "Mr. President, if you sincerely desire to forward the interests of all the people, why do you oppose the national enfranchisement of women?" Wilson answered curtly and vaguely, "That is one of the things which we will have to take counsel over later" (Stevens, *Jailed for Freedom* 49–50). Paul carefully chose this temple dedication to question Wilson, an event where she could secure the attention of labor leaders and the labor press.

As the press and the public registered protests against such aggression, Paul and Burns found opportunities to defend these actions and argue further for suffrage. When suffrage supporter Julian T. Carr wrote to Paul to protest Vernon's act, she wrote back on July 11, 1916, in her regularly respectful but firm manner: "It is most helpful of course to have the view of people in different parts of the country. It seems to me, however, that Miss Vernon's question put to the President was an excellent thing." In this letter and others, Paul argued that Wilson and the public must be made to see that women would not abandon the cause of suffrage. In response to a negative editorial in the *Chicago Post*, Lucy Burns wrote to the editor, defending Vernon's action by asking readers to posit a switching of the genders involved: "If the great bulk of men in this country were disenfranchised and the President were personally responsible for it; and if he rose before a large assembly of men and announced that he served the interests of all classes, do you think that not one word would be uttered?" She further defended Vernon in language that echoed the Declaration of Independence: "The suffrage movement is a demand for justice. Any man or set of men who denies justice should suffer rebuke at the hands of the people. Any people or class of people which dares not rebuke a representative who denies them justice will certainly never be free."

For a final aggressive confrontation with Wilson, on December 4, 1916, Paul chose the Capitol and the silence of a written banner—a precursor to the next year's picketing. Elizabeth Selden Rogers' husband, a doctor who had saved the life of a congressman's wife, provided them with tickets for a congressional session, very difficult to get when the president was giving a formal annual address. A group of five—Caroline Spencer, Mabel Vernon, Florence Bayard Hilles, Elizabeth Rogers, and Lucy Burns—with a banner concealed in Mabel Vernon's coat, went to their seats in the front row of the visitor's gallery. Here was a formidable group: Hilles's brother was the fifth-generation Bayard in the Senate, Spencer was a prominent physician from Colorado, and Rogers was related to Secretary of War Henry Lewis Stimson. When Wilson was speaking of freedom for Puerto Ricans, these women unfurled their large banner over the balcony. It said, "Mr. President, What Will You Do for Woman Suffrage?" The *Suffragist* reported that the sudden appearance of this large banner, with its message directed to the president, stopped all sound for a few minutes, but then the president proceeded, continuing to enunciate what the *Suffragist* called "men's needs and men's business" although "it was hard for people to keep listening to him after that." Guards immediately came into the balcony and asked the women to leave; then a tall guard on the main floor jerked the banner down. Although the proceedings continued, this rhetorical strategy "was all the talk after" ("Mr. President, What Will You Do"). Of this incident, from a different perspective, Edith Bolling Wilson wrote in her memoir: "The audience did not appear even to see it, most of them being too intent on the President's words to observe the incident. A guard quietly removed the banner, not a word being said by anyone" (122). Although she dismissed it, it is interesting to note that she remembered this moment and wrote about it in 1938.

Although Wilson had not been willing to schedule White House visits for over a year and these public confrontations made future visits unlikely, the memorial service for Inez Milholland on Christmas 1916 provided one more entrance into the White House, a chance of addressing Wilson from within the drawing room after a long absence. When Paul received permission to hold the memorial service in the Capitol, Wilson felt pressured to approve their request for a deputation to meet with him, although he delayed them until January 9. Paul felt that a polite meeting with sympathies expressed by all would make no impact on the suffrage movement. She was looking for strong rhetoric, for danger, to take advantage of the rare opportunity to appear before him. Sara Bard Field led the group of three hundred women, and Elizabeth Kent read the resolution from the memorial service that asked that he "intercede to stop such waste of human life and effort" because "women are exhausting their lives in waiting and appeal." And then followed the line that especially infuriated Wilson: "Will you not be moved to act so that by her death Inez Milholland Boussevain shall have delivered from the sacrifice of life her countrymen?" Here Paul was quite close to saying that his party's failure to support suffrage—his own failure—had caused Milholland's death and would soon lead to more unnecessary sacrifice. Wilson, visibly angered, responded curtly with one of his regular responses: "I can't as the leader of my party do anything that my party doesn't want me to do or take any stand that my party doesn't want me to take" ("To the President"). After this impasse, the visit soon ended, and Wilson declared that he would accept no more deputations, not even the rare ceremonial visit, because of his involvement in international events.

* * *

From the day that she entered Washington, Paul sought not just public events like parades, conferences, and car trips, but regular interaction with members of government. She did this both to accustom women to viewing themselves as naturally involved in this sphere, as political agents who would soon be seated on the other side of these desks, and to convince male politicians that they must speak logically and act fairly. As part of ongoing congressional lobbying efforts, large numbers of women charted each answer to each question. They worked together to make legislators explain their positions and respond to their constituencies. To achieve ongoing presidential deputations, women continued their efforts to enter Wilson's drawing room and then trailed him in several cities. They questioned his answers, pursued him after he refused to answer, and finally used a memorial service to make the worst of accusations—of murder. Well-planned lobbying and deputations, Paul believed, would ultimately make American leaders and the public see that no excuse or evasion would lead to the women's giving up and going home. They were constantly on Capitol Hill and at the White House, a continuing visual presence in powerful sites where, Paul intended to demonstrate, these women were meant to be.

6. The Political Boycott

As Alice Paul pursued legislators and the president with the twin goals of educating them about suffrage and publicizing their repeated denials of women's rights, she was also trying to bring pressure on them during elections, to make use of the power women already had as voters in the West. Along with staging parades and other events, lobbying, and sending deputations, Paul initiated a more aggressive political effort, a nonviolent women's boycott in all states where women could vote: nine states in 1914 and eleven in 1916. Ultimately, she wanted to assert that women could turn the men in power out of office if they would not act justly. In the East, women were pursuing Wilson and asking him to defend his positions or change his mind, but in the West, in states where women already could vote, they opposed him and his party at the ballot box. This political choice required a nationwide structure, involving an executive committee, advisory council, state organizers, and local groups, all focused on securing a federal amendment and opposing politicians who would not support it. It was a structure and methodology that NAWSA opposed and that the press and public judged as a particularly disturbing form of activism.

In deciding to boycott all Democrats, including those who supported suffrage, Paul was holding the party in power responsible for the failure to give women the vote. She was not asking women to vote for Republicans or Progressives; she was not asking them to support any particular party, but simply to vote against those men who controlled the Senate and House of Representatives and who had used their power to block passage of a federal suffrage amendment. Through this controversial decision, Paul and her followers were attempting to educate and coerce not just an individual man but an entire political party, to teach a lesson about the results of ignoring the priorities of half the voters in suffrage states. She was also asking western women to consider themselves united with those who were still dispossessed: women all deserved to be equal under the law; none were free until all were free.

This choice, much more than the suffragists' parades and meetings, intimidated the nation's government and press, invoking a new level of danger by suggesting that women's voting power could be wielded against ruling men. In England the Pankhursts had employed similar boycotts, so this American decision seemed especially English and, hence, militant. The decision also engendered controversy because it required suffragists to vote against the supporters they had within the Democratic Party. To many, that opposition seemed illogical. But, Paul argued, every man that they opposed, even those who had publicly declared their support for suffrage, stood by his party caucus in its opposition to a federal amendment. Individual legislators might be supporting suffrage within their states, but at the federal level, they voted in a bloc against it.

In many circular and individual letters, Paul reviewed the reasons for opposing even Democrats who supported state suffrage. In a September 16, 1914, letter to Mrs. Malcolm McBride in Cleveland, who had written to protest this campaign, Paul recognized that almost all senators in the suffrage states were formally declared for suffrage, even for a federal amendment. At the state level, then, to vote for any one individual would make little difference "because as far as the individual goes there would be no choice whatever between candidates, as all of them would pledge themselves to support the suffrage measure." Instead of using their votes to endorse individuals, women should use them to oppose the party in power and its caucus control: "the party leaders can prevent the amendment from being passed, or even being considered in spite of the individual backing given by members of the party. When it comes to the test these members always subordinate suffrage to the will of the party as a whole, so that our only hope seems to be to bring the party into line." These senators needed to feel that their political future depended on their keeping promises of support: "the way to make them feel that it is expedient is, of course, to show them that failure to take it up means loss of votes." Whatever criticisms might greet this aggressive tactic, Paul argued further, women would be exercising the same right of choice that voters always did: "We cannot see any reason why the women voters should not use their vote to further the suffrage question just as many of them use their votes to further their views on the tariff or the currency and other subjects."

For the 1914 Elections

By the end of 1913, Paul knew that a national organization and an effective publicity mechanism would be especially important for this part of her nonviolent campaign plans. To create a boycott of candidates, suffragists would have to be well-organized and unified, ready for political action and its consequences. This effort would require not just the relatively few people involved in organizing a parade or in lobbying, but large numbers of women voters who would be willing to forgo other priorities to advance the rights of their sex.

In 1913 Paul's organizers all over the country had started state chapters of the Congressional Committee, chapters that were then functioning as auxiliary groups within NAWSA and were working toward a federal amendment. Their priorities were gathering the signatures on the petition presented at the Capitol in July 1913, holding meetings and demonstrations, and setting up local and state committees to work for the amendment. After the 1914 break with NAWSA, Paul's organizers worked to convince women to stay in their local groups and to expand them. She wanted them to maintain their focus on a federal amendment and to be prepared to embark on a boycott. In early 1914 Mabel Vernon went out to the suffrage states as Paul's first full-time organizer outside of Washington. She left a job teaching German in Philadelphia to take on this challenge, planning meetings through, in Paul's words, "this great, great gift of speaking" (Fry). The group paid her two hundred dollars a month, and she lived at the Washington headquarters when she was not on the road. Then in May 1914, Burns set up shop in San Francisco as a salaried organizer earning seventy dollars a month. For two months she and Rose Winslow canvassed the state. Then with Burns's and Vernon's help, Paul began recruiting organizers for all the suffrage states; they also traveled in nonsuffrage states to help with organizing there and to inform women of the boycott plans. As she established this structure of state, congressional district, and local organizations, Paul insisted that all key personnel be women. The result of this organizing gave her a full slate of leaders with the political knowledge and confidence to take on the reigning political party.

As organizers began establishing state and local groups, Paul also extended her executive structure. Her experienced executive committee included Lucy Burns, Crystal Eastman, Mary Beard, and Dora Lewis. Eastman, a friend of Burns from Vassar, had gone to Columbia for a master's degree in sociology and then to New York University for a law degree. She had worked on the Pittsburgh Survey, concerning the effects of industrialization on work-ers, and had served as a governmental investigator of industrial accidents. Beard, a historian, had joined the Women's Trade Union League and helped organize shirtwaist strikes in 1909. She had also worked with the Pankhursts in England. Lewis, a wealthy widow from Philadelphia and member of a prominent family, had been a member of the Philadelphia Equal Franchise Society when Paul was in graduate school there.

By the fall of 1914, as Paul and Burns came to preside over a newly inde-pendent Congressional Union (CU) undertaking a boycott, Paul enlarged this executive group to include Elizabeth Kent, Matilda Hall Gardner, Edith Houghton Hooker, Alva Belmont, and Elsie Hill: all were experienced and affluent. Hooker, a graduate of Bryn Mawr pursuing a career in social work, had led a failed attempt in Maryland to secure state suffrage. While continu-ing to campaign within her state and edit *Maryland Suffrage News,* she also worked for a federal amendment. Gardner, a Progressive party backer, was the wife of Gilson Gardner, an influential Washington journalist and chief correspondent for the E. W. Scripps chain. Paul needed this strong group to provide legitimacy for the controversial tactic of boycotting a party as well as for the funds to go forward.

To secure legitimacy for her new organization and its controversial tactic of a boycott, Paul also enlisted influential supporters for an advisory council, members of which she immediately began to list down the left side of her CU stationery, a strong visual symbol of support that would later take up two columns and leave little room for writing. Unlike the executive committee, women involved regularly in CU events, advisory council members met only a few times a year to review the campaign's progress and make plans. Paul began by seeking the upper class and the well known, those who could supply monetary support and create a positive public response. The chair of the advisory council was Elizabeth Rogers of New York, the prominent activist and social leader with whom Paul had gone to see Secretary Stimson to secure her preferred route for the inaugural parade. Paul and Rogers felt that placement on the advisory council was best for prominent women who might not have the time or inclination for regular active participation, but whose names would help the effort. Participation of these women gave all CU members a new standing, not just as revolutionary outsiders, but as part of an established and respectable group.

Early choices for the council, consisting only of women, included activ-ists with standing in the suffrage community, such as May Wright Sewall and Bertha Fowler, associates of Susan B. Anthony. Well-known luminaries, such as Helen Keller, Charlotte Perkins Gilman, and Julia Marlow, a stage actress, added their names. Paul also sought out academics, such as Emma Gillette, dean and founder of the Western College of Law, and Clara Louise Thompson, a Latin professor at Rockford College, as well as labor activists, like Florence Kelley and Mary Beard. Paul also recognized the power of socialites, such as Gertrude H. Cuthbert, who had a "wide social influence in Denver" and wealthy widow Alva Smith Belmont, who transferred her allegiance from NAWSA and became Paul's major financial supporter ("New Members"). Paul also encouraged the creation of state advisory councils to involve women with local standing.

For some supporters, especially those with labor connections, this reliance on the affluent remained problematic. Mary Beard, in fact, wrote to Paul concerning their first meeting in August 1914 at Belmont's home, Marble House in Newport: "I can't do the Newport stunt. I shall probably be the only one who, for labor attachments, feels the participation in the Newport plans is inadvisable. I do feel that way and that I would lose more than I would help by coming myself." Paul, however, knew the power of these women's money and influence—and the increase in notoriety when grand dames participated in potentially dangerous acts.

At this meeting in Newport, many members of the advisory council spoke, affirming the conclusion that only the federal amendment, which had to be sought through aggressive means, would change women's position in the United States. Harriot Stanton Blatch argued vehemently against wasting their efforts in individual states, where even newly arrived immigrant men could decide the future of American women. The group also confirmed that in seeking federal action they would be advocating only the Anthony Amendment, not the Shafroth-Palmer Amendment ("Newport Conference").

It was at this first meeting of the advisory council that Paul centered the group's attention on not just suffrage or a federal amendment, but on plans for a boycott of Democrats. Lucy Burns asserted that they couldn't support individual Democratic candidates, even those who advocated suffrage, because the Democrats had caucused against them as a whole body. Paul asked the members of the press to leave and then argued further for holding Democrats responsible. She did not concentrate on the current caucus as Burns did, but focused on the larger meaning of the boycott in the nonviolent campaign. Her first argument was that by refusing to vote for one party women could in fact influence the outcome of elections: "When once the political parties are made to realize that opposition to suffrage means their defeat, when once it is shown that suffragists can actually affect the results of a national election, our fight will be won." She also argued that this fight would create and demonstrate the solidarity of women: "We are always hearing of the immense power of the Catholic vote, the Jewish vote, the Mormon vote. There is the same power in the woman's vote." This demonstration of power would allow women to "form a stronger organization than has ever before existed" and thus achieve national suffrage and a full array of rights (Report of the Congressional Union 24, 36–37; "Newport Conference" 6). In the fervor of the moment, the group voted unanimously for a boycott. Later, however, some individuals withdrew their support. Helen Ring Robinson, a Colorado state senator, believed it unfair and unwise: in a time of international tensions, she argued that Americans needed to support their president and his party (Zimmerman 146). She resigned from the advisory council over this disagreement.

The newspapers and journals Paul contacted about this meeting and bombarded with press bulletins considered this event as the beginning of a new suffrage agenda. The *New York Tribune* noted that the meeting at Marble House "marked the entrance of women into the arena of practical politics. . . . At Newport, for the first time was launched a national movement of women armed to fight with political weapons for their rights" (Report of the Congressional Union, 36–37). Even though his wife had chosen not to attend, Charles Beard applauded these women in the *New Republic* and argued that their political action would lead to political power ("Woman Suffrage and Strategy"). But many newspapers viewed the attempt as overly aggressive and divisive. NAWSA opposed the boycott as destructive to their bid to gain suffrage state by state because many of their key supporters came from the Democratic Party (Ford, *Iron-Jawed Angels* 68).

On September 14, 1914, after Paul made her campaign policy public, two organizers for each suffrage state left for the West in a special railroad car decorated with purple, white, and gold banners. There they met furious opposition, both from women who did not want to oppose those Democrats who supported suffrage and from men who resented this invasion of the political process. Meeting spots were hard to find, and organizers were threatened. In "The Invader," a short story by Oreola Haskell, the main character Leslie Draycote is one of these young organizers. In a small town, when a young man describes her activities as a bit of fun, she makes the real work clear to him:

> "I can imagine many pleasanter ways to have a frolic," she said, "than to visit, one stupid little town after another, expend much energy afternoon and evening speaking with all the love and eloquence one has for justice to inane, indifferent, and sometimes hostile, people; to be ridiculed more often than praised in the country papers by men who never understand anything abstract or spiritual, who don't know the first principles of our cause; to work through hot and en-

ervating weather when one is tired and even sick; to get choked with dust on endless roads; to meet strangers all the time; to put up at a succession of homely and uncomfortable hotels where the food is always poor; to be criticized by women or pitied by them, and to be joked about by men; to be homesick six evenings a week, especially on moonlight nights; in fact to live anything but a pleasurable existence and to form anything but a triumphal procession." (8)

In this story, though, the state organizer does not give up. Instead, she uses all the techniques that Paul emphasized: when she cannot secure a local hall for a meeting, she finds a field outside of town; she enlists local socialites to help her; she plans a public meeting involving national and local speakers; she even speaks loudly enough to be heard over a band hired to drown her out.

In each suffrage state, as one organizer, like Leslie Draycote, toured the state, and another set up a central office, members worked feverishly to convince women voters to oppose Democrats. The effort did seem to bear fruit. Twenty-three of forty-three Democrats running for office were defeated, and many more were "thoroughly frightened," in Paul's analysis. Although she recognized that defeats had also been caused by the Progressives' return to the Republican Party, she claimed credit for reducing the margins of victory of three Democratic congressmen and for causing six Democrats to lose elections they were expected to win: Kansas Representative George A. Neeley; Colorado Representative Harry Seldomridge; Utah senatorial candidate James H. Moyle; Idaho senatorial candidate James H. Hawley; Oregon House of Representatives candidate Austin F. Flegel; and Washington House of Representatives candidate Roscoe Drumheller (Report of the Congressional Union).

In letters sent to campaigners and other supporters to shape their view of the results, Paul portrayed the CU as the ecstatic victor (Letter to Mary Beard, 9 Nov. 1914). "Our campaign," she indicated in her circular letters, "succeeded far beyond my fondest hopes" (Letter to Crystal Eastman Benedict). As she wrote to Mabel Vernon in Nashville on November 12, 1914, as well as to other women, this opposition to Democrats "made suffrage an issue in the suffrage states and has aroused the Congressmen from those states to a realization of the importance of this measure which they had never had before." To provide a more specific analysis, she noted that Democrats' margins were decreased even where citizens supported tariff legislation, and that Seldomridge's defeat was "really the loveliest of all" because his plurality in the last election had been a large one.

As she told Amelia Fry, Paul considered this boycott campaign to be the strongest suffrage event up to that time because it helped her to organize her troops and it made politicians and the public aware of the CU's growing power: "Well, I think it accomplished everything we wanted. It was one of the big outstanding things I think that we did." As she recalled, "One fifth of the Senate, one seventh of the House, and one sixth of the electoral votes came from the suffrage states, and it really was a question of making the two political parties aware of the political power of women" (Gallagher 23).

As results came in and Paul claimed responsibility for them, newspapers responded with full coverage. Many Republican papers, such as the *Cheyenne Tribune* and the *Jewel City* (Kansas) *Republican,* motivated by the damage that the boycott could do to Democrats, discussed it at length during and after the campaign. After the election, some papers gave the boycott credit for causing losses and close races. A headline in a Denver paper, for example, pointed to the suffragists' role in lowering a margin of victory: "Man Who Betrayed Colorado Interests and Double-Crossed Woman Suffrage Retains Job by Less Than One Thousand Votes" (Report of the Congressional Union, 51–52). Charles Beard wrote in the *New Republic* about the fear that Paul had created: "Without organization and money at that time, the [Congressional] Union thoroughly frightened Democratic politicians from the West, as thousands of letters and clippings in the Union office prove" ("Woman's Party" 329).

For the 1916 Elections

When the election was over and the influence recognized, Paul immediately tried to shift the organization's rhetorical focus away from that victory. Certainly she hoped the election results had taught these politicians the power of her organization, but she would have to work with them to continue moving forward. When she wrote to Mabel Vernon in Nashville on November 12, 1914, to discuss their success, she stressed that, with the boycott ended, "we need not press the point of its wisdom any further . . . it is simply a matter of the past." The group needed to establish new positive initiatives and reunite with women who had opposed the boycott. Paul also wanted to back away from this technique because it would be two more years before they could make use of it again, and, as always, she wanted ongoing action. To turn attention away from boycotting and toward the future, she immediately began organizing additional state and district branches and planning events like Sara Bard Field's cross-country trip.

In early 1916, however, Paul saw that a second boycott would be necessary because Democrats in Congress were still caucusing against suffrage. As she planned this campaign, she first sought to change the name of her group so that it would have a rhetorical status equal to her opposition's. In April of

1916, she renamed the Congressional Union the National Woman's Party, calling it a "party" to assert its equality with the Democratic and Republican parties. In this decision to create the National Woman's Party (NWP), with its own constitution, representatives, conventions, and platform, she was asking women to join in making suffrage their one political priority.

Paul unveiled the idea for an independent political party at meetings on April 8 and 9, 1916, at the Little White House. The party's members would be from suffrage states, where women could cast votes to further the status of their sex, with auxiliaries or associates from the nonsuffrage states. At this meeting, Anne Martin asserted that this new party would be "ready to undertake its most portentous election campaign." Paul also spoke about the wonderful power coming out of the suffrage states, enabling her "to form a stronger organization than has ever before existed." She planned a party conference in Chicago on June 5 to 7, shortly before the Republican and Progressive conventions in that city, another incidence of her careful attention to the impact of her rhetorical act within a specific scene. At this meeting of a new and equal party, the NWP elected Anne Martin as chair and Paul as one of two vice-chairs. The speakers included Crystal Eastman, Rheta Childe Dorr, Helen Keller, Mary Ritter Beard, Inez Milholland, Charlotte Perkins Gilman, Anna Kelton Wiley, Alice Chipman Dewey (John Dewey's wife and first principal of the Laboratory School at the University of Chicago), Florence Kelley (founder of the National Consumer's League and advocate of minimum wage and child labor laws), and Lucy Salmon (Vassar history professor). The group decided to carry the anti-Democratic campaign in the coming election into all states where women were voting, operating on a much bigger scale than in 1914 because they had grown stronger through national and local organizing ("Woman's Party Organizes"). When Ida Tarbell reported on the convention for the *New York World*, she admitted to admiring this "earnestly confident body of women" even though she was not a suffrage supporter: "Let there be no underestimating by women or men of that newest of political organizations—the Woman's Party. It sailed into port here last night, the purple, white, and yellow banners standing straight out to the wind, and such a landing as it made. In all this frantic uncertainty it is the one clean, orderly, definite piece of work I have seen done. It knows exactly what it wants. Moreover, it knows its power." Tarbell especially commented, as did other reporters, on the party's superior modes of planning, which would enable it to pursue a second boycott: "Last night they crystallized into a permanent organization all their planning and their thought. It was as clean and complete a bit of organization as I ever saw carried out" ("Woman's Party Is Made Up").

During this well-publicized conference in Chicago, representatives from each political party came to advocate for their candidates, another indication of respect for these women's growing political power. The convention's chair, Anne Martin, said to each of these representatives, using a parallel construction that John F. Kennedy would echo in his inaugural speech, "We do not ask you here to tell us what we can do for your parties, but what your parties can do for us." These meetings between Republican, Democratic, and Progressive party representatives and Woman's Party representatives, which all occurred on one night, garnered attention by reporters awaiting the Republican and Progressive conventions, just as Paul's initial parade attracted coverage on the day before the 1913 inauguration.

In a second article, Tarbell described the meetings with party representatives: "Never have I seen gentlemen pass so quickly from amused and interested confidence to puzzled and irritated humility—or plain scare—as at the meeting on Tuesday night." Dudley Field Malone came for the Democrats, Tarbell reported, angered that Paul was considering another boycott, but unable to make any pledge concerning the president's support for the amendment. When John Hays Hammond of the Republicans said that his party would protect women, they declared that they were their own protectors. Allan Benson of the Socialists told the group, in a condescending tone, that they lacked the education to vote well, as did many men. "Nevertheless," he said, "if you have nothing but ignorance you have a right to contribute that." In their measured responses, Tarbell concluded, the women proved their own confidence: Benson and the others could think what they liked without influencing the women's plans ("Organized Women Dramatic Phase").

Journalists like Tarbell felt that this convention would not just shock the parties but would also cause them to act. And it did. At their convention, the Progressives endorsed the federal amendment, the first national party to do so. They had adopted suffrage as a general principle in 1912, but had not considered federal legislation at that time. In 1916, the Republicans endorsed suffrage as a general principle, but recognized "the right of each State to settle this question for itself." It was the first time either major party had endorsed suffrage at all. Then, on August 1, Republican candidate Charles Hughes, under great pressure from suffragists and especially Alice Paul, endorsed the federal amendment. At the Democratic convention that summer, the Democrats also endorsed suffrage—to be attained "by the States." Unlike Hughes, Wilson did not change his policy choice as the campaign proceeded (Irwin, *Story of Alice Paul* 163–65).

By August, after Democrats at their convention advocated suffrage but not a federal amendment, Paul's strong and organized troops recognized that they would have to plan another boycott. The Democrats' tightly controlled caucus system was still keeping individual Democratic senators and representatives from siding with Republicans for the amendment. To pursue a second boycott, Paul called an NWP meeting for August 10 to 12 in Colorado Springs, using circular letters to assemble the group. She chose this date and this locale because of automobile races scheduled there to celebrate the opening of a new road up Pike's Peak, thus to take advantage of another large crowd but also to associate her gathering with an adventurous and brave future and with the power of the West (Letter to Mrs. Robert Morton). Here women from the twelve suffrage states, along with associate members from nonsuffrage states, decided on that fall's election strategy (Letter to Edith Goode). After the Pike's Peak meeting, Paul started a circular letter campaign to secure support for a boycott. In these letters and in the *Suffragist*, she congratulated Republicans, Progressives, and Socialists for their commitment to suffrage. She insisted, however, that her group was not endorsing any particular candidate—no group could subsume the NWP—but was instead opposing the party in power, which continued to advocate other priorities and to hide behind states' rights as a means of avoiding action ("Opposing Democrats").

Paul stayed involved in the minutiae of the campaign from a headquarters in Chicago while also raising money to cover expenses of workers in the field. As in 1914, she secured national organizers and local residents to speak at all kinds of venues—at luncheons, banquets, union and factory meetings, and county fairs—even though they faced opposition in many towns (Letter to Vivian Pierce). At rallies, she planned for them to mock Wilson's campaign banners proclaiming "He Kept Us out of the War" by raising placards declaring "He Kept Us out of Suffrage." In October, Paul asked Gail Laughlin to leave California and give talks at Ely and McGill, Nevada, because Harriot Stanton Blatch was not willing to speak in small towns to small groups. Paul also made sure that no local speaker appeared with Inez Milholland: she didn't like to be on a platform with another speaker because she was afraid her own words might seem inferior. In addition, Paul dealt with the strong response from Democrats and antisuffragists, who were much better organized to oppose a boycott than they had been in 1914. In Arizona, for example, Iris Calderhead reported that the Democrats were attempting to ban their street meetings. Paul helped her oppose local injunctions and plan meetings in private homes (Lunardini 95).

As Paul worked diligently on campaigns throughout the suffrage states, she recognized that different sorts of efforts were necessary for different locales. In places where a Republican or Democratic victory was assured by a large margin, she wrote on September 19 to Vivian Pierce, an organizer in Phoenix, the goal was to "demonstrate an active campaign" and "not the actual turning of votes, since we are not hoping in such cases to change the election results." She did not spend money on individual letters to voters in such places because those votes would not change the outcome. But wherever a change in the election result seemed possible, Paul's troops actively sought that goal, with individual letters, visits, and events that focused on the women's unity and the perfidy of Democrats.

More than in 1914, perhaps because a presidential election was involved, many groups objected to the boycott. Disagreement even came from within Paul's family. As she made plans for the boycott in the summer, she received the following letter from her mother:

> Dear Alice
> I wish to make a protest against the methods you are adopting in annoying the President. Surely the Cong. Union will not gain converts by such undignified actions.
>   I hope thee will call it off.
>   Aff Mother (T. P. Paul)

Her uncle Mickle Paul, president of the Democratic Club of Pennsylvania and one of the few members of her family who wasn't a staunch Republican, also wrote to criticize this negative campaign focus: "Stop, think and decide: Is it an advance or a retreat to destroy instead of building up a force to aid in the battle for justice to women."

NAWSA was also opposed, as it had been in 1914. Carrie Chapman Catt wrote to Anne Martin, describing anti-Democratic campaigners: "They are creative of publicity and agitation which may seem good to those who do not look deeply into the situation, but in the long run they antagonize more than they win." In a NAWSA pamphlet titled "The Aims and Policies of the National American Woman Suffrage Association As Contrasted with Those of the Congressional Union," Anna Howard Shaw spoke out strongly against this alienation of Democratic supporters: "These candidates were opposed by the Congressional Union quite irrespective of their services to the suffrage cause in Congress, all of them being, indeed, among the most powerful friends we have, and notably Senator Thomas, of Colorado, Chairman of the Woman Suffrage Committee in the Senate, the committee to which all suffrage legislation must be referred before action of the Senate can be had." The 1914 boycott, Shaw declared, had made lobbying work in Washington much more difficult, and the 1916 campaign would injure suffrage efforts further. Paul had, Shaw claimed, a primary goal not of furthering suffrage but of disrupting traditional allegiances and dividing suffragists: Paul was attempting the boycott to alienate NAWSA's suffrage supporters in the legislature, thus "smashing the National" and taking over the entire movement. Helen Ring Robinson, the Colorado state senator who had resigned from Paul's advisory council over this decision in 1914 and shifted her allegiance to NAWSA, spoke out strongly against this boycott in a letter sent to Alice Paul and to many suffrage supporters. She reasoned that to get a two-thirds majority in the legislature suffragists would need Democratic support, and the boycott might eliminate Democratic votes: "Would they be there? Chastened by the anti-party forces but eager to oblige? . . . There are those who think it might be too exciting to ask a corpse to oblige with a jig at its own wake—just to please the man who made him a corpse."

That fall, in the face of many cogently argued objections, Paul worked hard to keep the rationale for the policy before supporters. She wrote frequent exhortatory letters headed "Dear Organizer" to state workers. As she often did, she recognized in these letters that this difficult nonviolent choice would cause some supporters to leave the organization. And as usual, she preferred going forward with the smaller group of those who were willing to make difficult choices: "We will, of course, arouse more antagonism by this course than we would by vague generalizations, and the result undoubtedly will be that people will resign. However, a direct and vigorous attack will achieve much greater results in the election than will a more conciliatory policy."

As always, Paul hoped that controversial efforts would bring publicity to suffrage. Given the partisan nature of newspapers, she knew that coverage would vary, but even negative pieces would cause readers to focus on suffrage, a goal that was becoming increasingly harder to achieve with war imminent. She discussed the complications of this press attention, throughout all the suffrage states, in a lengthy letter to organizers: "If we are consistently aggressive in our attack it will probably result in the Democratic papers beginning to criticize and attack us, in return, on the suffrage issue. If we can only get the matter taken up by the Democratic and Republican papers as one of the burning issues of the campaign in the suffrage states, we will have achieved one of the main objects of our campaign. What we want to do, of course, above all other things is to make the National Suffrage Amendment one of the election issues. We can help attain this, I think, only by a positive and aggressive stand in our speaking and in our press work."

As Paul foresaw, press coverage of the women's boycott was mixed, with Democratic papers ignoring or vilifying it, and Republican papers co-opting it. But newspapers of all types recognized that these women were exploiting the traditionally male political game. The *Helena* (Montana) *Record,* for example, reported on April 8, 1916, that "The women are playing the political game as the politicians of the male sex have been playing it since the founda-tion of the republic, and the organization of parties. Their motto appears to be: 'If you are not for us we are against you, no matter what your politics'" ("Women and Politicians"). The *New York Evening Mail,* on June 7, 1916, reported that "The women have learned the lesson which has been driven into the consciousness of men through centuries of struggle. That lesson is that no political right can be obtained without insistent efforts to obtain it. . . . The movement is one which no party can afford to ignore" ("Demand of the Women'). In a July 1916 *New Republic,* Charles Beard discussed the party's unwavering, well-planned campaign: "Thus armed, it does not beg, it does not wheedle, it does not whine. It wages a trench warfare with exactly the kinds of weapons that men use. It knows that no other kind is effective. It speaks a language which the most seasoned and cynical politician can understand. It has money and organization and will and *votes*" ("Woman's Party" 329). Woman's Party members, Beard argued further, believed in noth-ing but Realpolitick, a pragmatic approach to governmental change.

Although Paul's political effort involved great numbers of women, Wilson was reelected, with 277 electoral votes to Hughes's 254. Many newspapers and peace groups immediately attributed this victory to women voters who believed that Hughes was more likely to involve the United States in world war. Democratic and Republican leaders in Kansas, for example, estimated that 70,000 Republican women in the state, out of 625,000 voters, had aban-doned their party to vote for Wilson on the peace issue, a bloc that helped elect him. In Washington state, 90,000 out of 155,000 registered women voters chose Wilson—in that state his plurality was only 16,594—and women also helped him to carry California, Idaho, Utah, and Arizona (Link, *Wood-row Wilson and the Progressive Era, 1910–1917,* 249–50). Antisuffrage media made the most of these results. The *New York Times* wrote that the "dream of solidifying woman as a sex and swinging her vote this way and that is shattered forever." Under the heading "Woman's Party Failed Utterly," the *Times* claimed that the boycott in fact helped Wilson to win because of the antagonism it engendered in both men and women ("Votes of Women").

In the legislative elections, Paul again had no clear victory. In the eleven suffrage states, final results were even: in Utah and California, Democrats gained seats; in Kansas and Montana, they lost them. Across the country, the Democrats' majority in the Senate slipped from sixteen to four, but the only change in the suffrage states was the election of Utah Democrat William Henry King over Republican George Sutherland, an active suffrage sup-porter. The Montana election, though, was especially exciting since Jeannette Rankin was elected as the first woman representative ("Democrats Lose 12 Senate Seats").

When the hard-fought 1916 campaign seemed so futile, women immediately turned to Paul to recast it rhetorically. Ethel Adamson, from the New York branch of the CU, wrote to Abby Scott Baker on November 6, 1916, that the NWP needed to "gather in the straggled strings for the winter's work," to bring together both the women who had supported and those who had opposed this policy and start moving forward again. Adamson wrote to Baker again on November 11, 1916, that women needed positive news because the election work had been so disappointing: "women have failed so utterly and ignominiously to respond to the appeal of liberty." Too many people felt, Adamson wrote, that this loss proved that women could not work together and would not sacrifice for freedom. That NWP members had no news from Paul, she continued, made them think there was no good news to give and no reason to stay united: "This sentiment in our ranks here is about to disintegrate the work." Having received no response, on November 17, Adamson wrote to Baker to plead for Paul's immediate rhetorical restructuring of the boycott: "Miss Paul with her wonderful optimism seems to be able to glean a victory out of the results which our women here have felt were so discouraging."

When these appeals for rhetorical action came in, Paul carefully shaped her response to declare her forces victorious. In letters sent to supporters, she reminded her group that their real goal had been to make suffrage a national issue, a goal at which they had succeeded, as the huge amount of press coverage made clear: "The whole power that we had was in the effort, whether we took away one vote or a thousand votes, to diminish the success in the campaign of the party we were opposing" (Letter to Kate S. Brading). In a press bulletin about the election, Paul claimed that "the National Woman's Party has attained its object in the campaign which has just closed. It made the national enfranchisement of women one of the most prominent issues on which the presidential campaign was fought in the suffrage states. It put the Democrats on the defensive. It forced them to declare greater and greater enthusiasm for national woman suffrage" (Press Bulletin, Nov. 1916). What the group did, she argued, was to successfully "organize a protest vote by women against Mr. Wilson's attitude toward suffrage. . . . Thousands of women pledged themselves at our meetings and in response to our canvassing." In letters and interviews, she frequently stated that "We were not concerned with the result of the election," though of course influencing that result had been her initial goal.

Besides making these general statements, Paul gave the best possible spin to the numerical data. In Illinois, the only state where the women's vote was counted separately, over 70,000 more women voted against Wilson than for him (Flexner and Fitzpatrick 270; Link, *Woodrow Wilson and the Progressive*

Era, 1910–1917, 249–50). There, Paul claimed in press bulletins and letters, the majority of women for Hughes ran ahead of his overall majority in the state. In ten other states where Wilson was victorious, she argued further, it was not the women's vote that insured the victory but instead male factory workers and farmers. His majority over the whole twelve states where women could vote was just 22,171 out of a popular vote of 4,810,000. In each one of these western states, men outnumbered women, in some states by two to one, so women's votes could not have elected Wilson. Harriot Stanton Blatch joined Paul in constructing the results as positive. In her autobiography, she remembered the arguments that she made: "In spite of the election of President Wilson, we felt that we had taken tremendous strides toward victory. We had made woman suffrage an important issue. We put Democrats on the defensive. We held the women's vote in line. We trimmed down Democratic majorities. We now looked forward to the next session of Congress, believing that the protest of women voters in this election would bring about the passage of the Woman Suffrage Amendment" (Blatch and Lutz 272). Inundated with NWP press bulletins, some newspapers accepted Paul's reordering of these results. The *San Francisco Examiner,* for example, reported that this campaign "has shown the country the sincerity of women in the suffrage fight, it has proven to politicians the hard work that women can do and the intelligence they can show, and it has practically ended any campaign of sneers against the cause of suffrage" ("Comments of the Press," 4 Nov. 1916).

* * *

Although Paul gave the best accounting of the results that she could to keep her members moving ahead, she recognized that the complicated situation of the 1916 election, with war in Europe, had limited her success. In pursuing the boycotts of 1914 and 1916, however, she had indicated to the American public, and especially to American women, the power that women could exercise as voters. The political parties had sent representatives to placate the new NWP; they had altered their platforms to include suffrage; Charles Hughes had endorsed a federal amendment. Also, Paul had formed a national organization that mirrored her dual parading in May 1914: women in their own hometowns were working with organizers from Washington to fight for federal legislation and thereby change their lives at home. As nonviolent campaigners, they had together planned a national boycott, asking women with the vote to use it for the good of other women. They had not achieved all that they attempted, but they had taken on a controversial nonviolent choice and seen it through, and with their leader there to construct the results as positively as possible, they were poised for further action.

7. Picketing Wilson

At the end of 1916, Paul felt that new techniques would be necessary to make a further impact on Wilson and his Democratic Party. Suffragists had lobbied assiduously. They had met with Wilson within the White House and without. They had held parades, mounted tableaux, and traveled cross-country. They had boycotted the Democratic Party and Wilson himself. But after he was reelected and after anger was his only response to the Milholland deputation, Paul and her followers knew they were at a dead end. Though many adherents and a great deal of publicity had been gained at each step along the way, the NWP still had not secured the action needed in the White House and in the Capitol, and no technique they had tried before seemed likely to alter that impasse.

In this disheartening period at the end of the year, Paul felt she needed to instigate a new nonviolent technique to rally her troops and keep them from exhaustion and depression. As William R. Miller comments, when participants experience such wrenching traumas, they may be "tired and the conflict will disintegrate into chaos or apathy." If they don't have a new positive direction presented to them, "their enthusiasm will wane and the movement will coast to a halt" (150). Paul wanted something new and dramatic, something that would prove that these women would not go away, that they did not have to follow Wilson's mandates or kowtow to his power, and that they had the strength to persevere and achieve victory.

The time had come, Paul believed, for a dramatic public demonstration of women's plight, one that would secure the press attention that lagged for their meetings and marches after Wilson's reelection, after the Milholland memorial, and as war filled the headlines. Paul recalled that the logic of that January was based on this question: "We had had speeches, meetings, parades, campaigns, what new method could we devise?" What she decided on was a nonviolent visual rhetoric—using women's bodies day after day to literally stand up to the president and for the cause. She decided to picket the White House, the first time a citizen group had done so. As Maud Younger wrote, these women decided to begin "visualizing to the world the long waiting of women for justice" ("Revelations" Oct., 12).

Paul's turning to this form of nonviolence again reflected her deep awareness of and allegiance to the Quaker tradition of witnessing, of church members investing their own time and their own well-being for change. When Helen Paul wrote to her sister on October 8, 1917, she acknowledged that their religion's dictates about standing in opposition to evil were at the heart of this effort: "All our sympathy and love is with thee—Principle is sure to win—injustice and evil have no power back of them for power belongs to good and the knowledge of this destroys their seeming power." Instead of arguing or trying to gain further entrance to the White House or Capitol, her members would simply stand on the outside of government, demonstrating through days and months their devotion to this right cause. Because of its possible strong effect, Paul believed, this picketing would result in "the saving of many years of women's energy, when it is so greatly needed" (Stevens, *Jailed for Freedom* 89).

These sentinels, appearing usually in four groups of three, hardly ever more than twelve total, were to affect President Wilson, and thus the campaign, more than any mass protests. Even deeper than the power of movement and of speech lies the power of presence, and it was that power Paul came to draw on for this new and potent escalation of the struggle. In an article about this decision, "The Indomitable Picket Line," Lucy Burns argued that NWP members had to create this continuous symbolic event to keep their momentum: "We can only express ourselves by action."

Convincing Her Advisory Board

At a January 1917 meeting of the advisory board, Paul first presented the idea of picketing the White House. Through this new method, as Paul and Burns explained to the assembled group, suffragists could stay physically in front of the president, the head of the majority party who controlled the amendment's future. In the seventy years since Lucretia Mott and Elizabeth Cady Stanton had convened a women's rights convention at Seneca Falls, mass meetings, petitions, educational campaigns, and processions had not delivered; they needed a more aggressive, insistent campaign, one centered on an all-powerful president of the United States.

To convince the advisory council to endorse this extreme step, Paul needed a very persuasive argument. Though she had been considering this campaign strategy since the fall, she wanted the suggestion to appear spontaneous—as though the entire united group were reaching this decision together. After planning carefully, Paul and Harriot Stanton Blatch addressed the board as though they were following a chain of logic that was occurring to them at that moment, one that led inexorably to the one choice of picketing. Blatch began with their current crisis: "We can't organize bigger and more influential deputations. We can't organize bigger processions. We can't, women, do anything more in that line. We have got to take a new departure. We have got to keep the question before him all the time" (Blatch and Lutz 275).

At this point, Paul took the next step by suggesting that the NWP consider picketing the White House, acting as though the idea had just come to her. Committed suffragists had appealed to President Wilson intermittently, she claimed, and had been repulsed; now they would appeal to him every day. This method, she continued, would involve holding banners and standing silently where Wilson would have to pass each day as he came in and out of the front gates. Their themes would be clearly stated and incontrovertible; Wilson would not be able to avoid the rhetoric—as expressed by the words or by the bodies of the standing women. He would not be asked for any temporary, polite answer, such as he might give to deputations; he would be asked to create action in Congress that would end this daily public display at each entrance to his house. Press coverage, Paul argued further, would thus come to suffragists, even with war in Europe, for they would no longer be infrequently entering the drawing room or walking in the streets, but they would instead be regularly posted at the site of governmental power and inaction. Though the fall of 1916 had been difficult, Paul argued, NWP members still possessed the inner strength to put themselves on the line, outside of the drawing room in the cold and in rain, remaining there until they became political insiders, until their amendment became law.

Persuaded by these arguments that were seemingly occurring spontaneously, the advisory council agreed to institute the daily picketing that Paul requested, which the group described as a delegation of "silent sentinels." For Paul, this term would become a key synonym for pickets, because it focused on their status as a well-organized troop, like town or army sentinels, keeping guard at the White House, providing a silent but highly visible conscience for the president and the nation.

The reporters who attended this advisory council meeting accepted it as a place where the entire group was vetting new ideas and making decisions. Even the *New York Times* reported the group logic as well as the name chosen

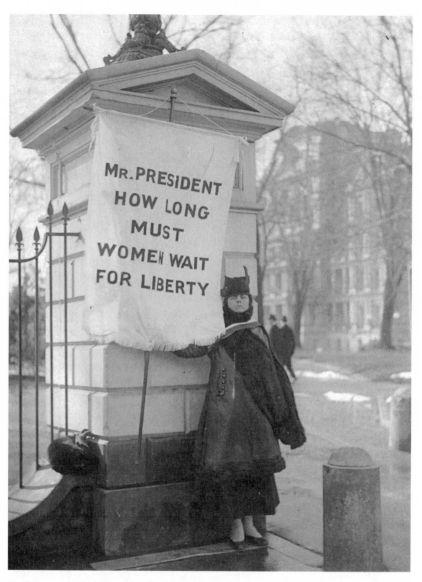

A silent sentinel. Alison Turnbull Hopkins holding the banner: "Mr. President how long must women wait for liberty." Photograph printed in the *Suffragist*, Feb. 7, 1917.

for the pickets: "Women suffragists, representing all parts of the country, disappointed over the result of an appeal which they made this afternoon to President Wilson in the East Room of the White House, held an indignation meeting and decided to adopt a new plan of campaign. They intend to post women pickets hereafter about the White House grounds. Their purpose is to make it impossible for the President to enter or leave the White House without encountering a picket bearing some device pleading the suffrage cause. The pickets will be known as "silent sentinels" ("Suffragists Will Picket").

After this meeting, Paul wrote letters to advisory council members to reinforce arguments for nonviolent picketing. To further define her reasoning, she also took advantage of an opportunity provided by Harriot Stanton Blatch, who had joined her Women's Political Union with the NWP. Blatch supported picketing, but she thought that American women should also consider the violent tactics being used in England. In the *Women's Political World,* she recognized that her own advocacy of violence separated her from Quakers like Paul: "I am not a Quaker, not a non-resistant. Both on my father's side, as well as my mother's, I inherit plenty of the spirit of '76.' My great-grandmother—so the story goes—loaded guns, and if she did not kill anyone in Revolutionary days it was because she was the proverbial bad shot. She aimed to kill her country's enemy. My grandmother, not being a Quaker or non-resistant, taught me to admire the courage, the devotion, the patriotism of my maternal ancestor" (Blatch and Lutz 200).

In addition to disagreeing on violence, Blatch and Paul also publicly disagreed on the reasons for and scope of the picketing. Blatch felt that, along with employing various types of violence, American women should concentrate on demonstrating their power through traditional political means; she thought of silent standing as a last resort of the powerless. Because women could vote in the western states, she argued, they had no need to participate in picketing, and in fact would denigrate themselves by doing so. This method instead should be left only to eastern women, who—without the vote—would be picketing to demonstrate not their strength but their weakness. In a letter to Paul on January 14, 1917, Blatch thus described picket lines as a "method of attack . . . adopted by weaponless disenfranchised women." In contrast to these silent standers, western women have power that "should be mobilized, it should use ballots not hairpins." In a letter to Anne Martin on February 14, 1917, Blatch continued with this same theme of picketing as an unbecoming and inaccurate show of weakness for those women who possessed the ballot: "To me it seems worse than foolish for a person with a battleaxe in her possession to use a toothpick as a weapon. Do you feel that such utterly non-political action becomes the voting woman at this juncture?"

In Alice Paul's view, even though picketing didn't occur in a voting booth, to label it as "non-political" was naïve. This standing up, she believed, provided a powerful witness each day at the site of the adversary, something even voting could not do. These silent sentinels, as an editorial in the *Suffragist* claimed, would "visualize the movement to the man and woman on the street" and then become "part of the vocabulary of the nation" ("Seventh Week"). Blatch's reasoning, Paul felt, also denied the strength inherent not just in each woman standing, but in women standing together. Whether they lived in the East or West, they were all free or not free. Paul argued that picketing was a highly powerful form of persuasion that demonstrated collective goals and might. In countering Blatch publicly, Paul argued persuasively for this daily, nonviolent, visual rhetoric.

The Picketing Begins

Amid a flurry of rhetorical clarification and defense, the first pickets appeared, the first group of American citizens to dramatize a political injustice by picketing the White House. On January 10, 1917, the "silent sentinels," twelve women in white dresses with Alice Paul in the lead, left the headquarters at 10:00 a.m. and walked to the east and west entrances of the White House, six for each entrance, standing three on each side, "demure and unsmiling and silent," as the *Suffragist* described the scene ("Suffragists Wait"). Just as she had done with paraders, Paul wanted to use their appearance as "demure," vulnerable, and respectable middle-class women as part of the effect. With different shifts coming out, women stood silently from 10:00 to 5:30, all holding banners in their suffrage colors. They did not speak unless they answered a question; then they replied quickly and returned to their silent standing. As Paul knew from her Quaker upbringing, such silence could demonstrate the moral force necessary to enact change. As Cheryl Glenn indicated, this silence could serve as "a rhetorical art for resisting discipline(s)," in this case, resisting Wilson's demand that their activism end ("Silence: A Rhetorical Art").

From the very beginning, President Wilson found the presence of these ladies both inappropriate and unnerving. Soon after the picketing began, as Edith Bolling Wilson recalled in her autobiography, the Wilsons were driving into the White House for lunch on a bitterly cold day, and Wilson asked the head usher to invite the pickets in for coffee or hot tea, thinking that they would happily leave the cold weather and reenter his drawing room. The usher returned to the president quickly, saying, "Excuse me, Mr. President, but they indignantly refused" (125). When the White House guards repeated his offer on subsequent days, especially when it was snowing or raining, the pickets continued where they were. Their dogged appearance outside his door was an embarrassment for Wilson, an endless reminder as he came and went, an ongoing rhetorical barrage.

To provide as much reportable news as possible and to demonstrate the diversity of suffrage's support, Paul orchestrated special picketing days. Maryland Day came first, followed by days on which pickets came exclusively from other states. College Day involved women from thirteen schools. There were also professional days such as Teachers' Day and theme days such as Patriotic Day, Labor Day, and Lincoln Day ("Silent Watch").

Along with these groupings, Paul incorporated special demonstrations within the lines. From March 1 to 4, 1917, she held a convention in Washington at which the CU, still representing women from the nonsuffrage states, melded with the NWP, representing women from the suffrage states. Using one clear appellation, Paul believed, would further unite women from across the country and would place "the emphasis more than does the Congressional Union on the political powers of women" (Minutes of the National Convention; Blatch and Lutz 277–78). On March 4, the day of Wilson's second inauguration, a thousand women attending this convention marched around the White House holding suffrage banners and then stood as one long picket line. For Paul, this event had a very special symbolism. Women no longer needed to march down city streets as they had before Wilson's first inauguration because the public had come to accept that women had the right to vote. The country's political parties had endorsed this right, if perfunctorily, at their national conventions in 1916. Women now needed to encircle just this president who was keeping women from what they merited as citizens. A year later, Eleanor Booth Simmons wrote in the *New York Sun* about the publicity that was gained through this special day of picketing: "I supposed no one undertaking captured quite so much advertising as did the picketing of the White House by the national Woman's Party. Their press agent told me that one day's picketing—it was the Sunday of Woodrow Wilson's inauguration, the day that a thousand pickets marched round and round the White House in the pouring rain, calling on the walls of Jericho to fall—well, 1,000 dailies opened their pages to that stunt to the amount of on average half a column in a paper. At least 500 tri-weeklies and semi-weeklies gave a column each, and the picture syndicates gave much space." Both the picketing itself and the various special days, Simmons noted, were keeping suffrage on the front page: "Before Alice Paul and the pickets came, days would pass when the word suffrage didn't appear in the dispatches. Since their activities, no word occurs more frequently than this."

During those first months, Paul's silent sentinels carried an array of banners, seeking to influence the president and passersby while also reaching a much larger audience by appearing in newspaper photographs. The words on the banners, carefully chosen quotations that could not be altered or taken out of context, created a highly persuasive form of nonviolent persuasion. A *Suffragist* article argued that American women might have chosen to "take up arms" to achieve equality, as Harriot Stanton Blatch might urge. In fact, the article listed the bayonets, machine guns, and other weapons that men had used to fight for liberty and then contrasted this violence with their own nonviolent choice: "We could and would not fight with such weapons." Instead, "Our simple, peaceful, almost quaint device was a BANNER!" (Stevens, "Militant Campaign" 9).

The sentences and short paragraphs printed on banners received continuous attention from the press and the public, as Paul had known they would. In the summer, after arrests and jail sentences began, Paul realized that their choices of slogans were even determining the amount of jail time. A judge indicated that, although the formal charge was obstructing traffic, the specific words on the banner had influenced his sentencing decision: "I am giving you only thirty days because your banners were so harmless. If any suffragists attempt to carry objectionable banners, the sentence will be longer." The public, as well as the judges, read these signs carefully.

From the first day, pickets held banners as large as four feet by six feet, decorated in suffrage colors, with long sashes and fringes adorning them. These banners were attached to poles, some on long sticks that caused the banners to wave above the women's heads and some on shorter sticks that made the banners furl out by their sides. The first banners read "Mr. President, what will you do for woman suffrage?" and "How long must women wait for liberty?" These phrases associated picketing with earlier heroic moments of suffrage campaigning. The question "Mr. President, what will you do for woman suffrage?" had appeared on the banner unfurled from front-row seats at the congressional session in December 1916. "How long must women wait for liberty?" came from Milholland's speech in California; they were the words that she uttered before she fell. In the next few days, pickets also began carrying banners with well-known sayings from Susan B. Anthony, including "The right of self-government for half of its people is of far more vital consequence to the nation than any or all other questions" as well as "Resistance to tyranny is obedience to God," a quotation Anthony had used in federal court in 1873 when she was tried for voting: she labeled it an "old Revolutionary maxim." On Anthony's birthday, special messages, such as "In our hands is the power to bring to a triumphant conclusion the work for the national suffrage amendment which Miss Anthony began" were also displayed to further associate the current picketing with her life-long campaign.

Other banners that winter dealt with legislation that Democrats were sponsoring instead of suffrage. These banners revealed the women's close attention to politics, demonstrating their readiness for the vote, while also playing on American racial prejudices. One of the banners used then and throughout the year said "Democracy should begin at home," a line challenging Wilson's movement into world leadership and echoing a well-known aphorism by Phillips Brooks, an Episcopal bishop and hymn writer who had given the sermon at Abraham Lincoln's funeral. This echo of his phrase "Charity should begin at home, but should not stay there" pointed to Wilson's lack of charity as he denied women the right to full participation in government even as he went to Mexico and Europe insisting on democracy for other peoples.

That winter, pickets often carried this paraphrase of Brooks, along with "What about the Filipinos?" a question that pointed to provisions of the 1917 Immigration Act, which became law on February 5. The act allowed Philippinos to immigrate to the United States, thereby allowing male Philippino immigrants to become voting citizens. Another large banner used in February and March, one that was carried between two pickets, said that women had waited after the Civil War to attain the full citizenship ceded to male slaves—and were still waiting. This banner ended with, "Will you, Mr. President, tell them to wait—That this is the Porto Rican's hour?" This coda compared the extension of the vote to male Puerto Ricans through the Jones Act, which Wilson signed into law on March 2, to the Fifteenth Amendment that had secured the vote for male slaves. Here was another group having its "hour," and this time the group was from an island far away. In crafting these signs, Paul was taking advantage of prejudices that many Americans held: these Phillipinos and Puerto Ricans should not be placed before well-educated, middle-class American women.

During that winter, as Paul's sentinels stood outside the White House, the nation reacted strongly to the unprecedented rhetorical choice of daily banners. Not all suffragists agreed with Paul's choices. The conservative suffrage journal *New American Woman,* for example, used direct address to harangue the pickets for their inappropriate, unwomanly behavior: "And, good ladies, why all this rudeness? Of what avail is all this bombast? Of what combination of gray matter is that which leads gently bred women to violate all conventional rules of polite assemblages? Women of no class nor of any party can ever be excused for thus disporting themselves" ("President of the United States").

Many newspapers also found the picketing inappropriate, too aggressive, and insulting to a busy president. They frequently quoted NAWSA officials, who opposed this unprecedented daily assault and portrayed Paul as the dangerous Other of suffrage, as an associate of the most radical of strike leaders and socialists, ever since she had brought four hundred working women to the White House in February of 1914. On the day after the picketing began, the antisuffrage *New York Times* compared the women unfavorably to Socialists. Even that group would not embark on anything so hideous: "one could not even imagine the I.W.W. [International Workers of the World] attempting it." The difference, the *Times* asserted, was that even male radicals had a better sense of rational judgment: "There is something in the masculine mind that would shrink from a thing so compounded of pettiness and monstrosity." The article went on to argue that such an action proved that women should never vote: "That the female mind is inferior to the male mind need not be assumed: that there is something about it essentially different, and that this difference is of a kind and degree that with votes women would constitute a political danger is or ought to be plain to everybody" ("Silent, Silly, and Offensive"). In a letter sent to the editor of the *Chattanooga Times* and other papers, Ida Harper of NAWSA, perhaps exaggerating somewhat, estimated that over seven hundred editors had taken a similarly critical stance (Letter to the Editor).

But even as picketing met with criticism, it garnered interest and even some admiration from the press; that respect, however, was often conveyed in gendered terms (Ford, *Iron-Jawed Angels* 156). Some papers grudgingly admired the women's tenacity. The *Washington Star*, for example, commented on March 10: "Feminine superiority is again demonstrated. The President of the United States took cold during a few hours' exposure to conditions the White House pickets had weathered for weeks" ("Comments of the Press," 17 Mar. 1917). NWP supporter Gilson Gardner, chief Washington correspondent for Scripps, frequently created sympathetic portraits (Ponder), as in this depiction of the March inaugural picketing, which focuses on the unprecedented public demonstration of women's physical stamina:

> During the eighteen years I have been a newspaper correspondent in Washington I have seen no more impressive sight than the spectacle of the pickets surrounding the White House on the afternoon of March fourth. The weather gave this affair its character. Had there been fifteen hundred women carrying banners on a fair day the sight would have been a pretty one. But to see a thousand women—young women, middle-aged women, and old women—and there were women in the line who had passed their three score years and ten—marching in a rain that almost froze as it fell; to see them standing and marching and holding their heavy banners, momentarily growing heavier—holding them

against a wind that was half a gale—hour after hour, until their gloves were wet and their clothes soaked through . . . was a sight to impress even the jaded senses of one who has seen much. (Blatch and Lutz 279)

An avid supporter of the pickets, Rheta Childe Dorr on February 7 asked readers of the *Chicago News* to engage in gender-switching by comparing the women's disciplined nonviolent behavior with actions men might take if they were disenfranchised: "You may disapprove of the 'silent sentinels.' You may really believe—in spite of the child labor law, which was forced on the southern senators, in spite of the Adamson law, in spite of many other instances—that President Wilson is powerless to induce Congress to pass a suffrage amendment. You may even believe that the women in Washington are hurting the cause. But does any one suppose that a large masculine class barred from citizenship, absolutely discountenanced by the president, would do anything half as mild as stand at the gates of the White House carrying a banner?" ("What Would Men Do?").

As the spring went by and expressions of respect continued to appear in newspapers, Wilson became anxious about the rhetorical impact of this picketing. At his request, his secretary and political aide Joseph Tumulty began planning for a partial press blackout. Wilson first suggested a total blackout by Washington newspapers, but Tumulty warned him, relying on a false comparison to the Pankhursts, that if these women were totally ignored, they might get violent: "[Total press] silence might provoke the less sane of these women to violent action." Instead, Tumulty and Wilson asked Washington editors to agree to keep the daily news of the women's picketing to a minimum (Ford, *Iron-Jawed Angels* 156). In response, Arthur Brisbane of the *Washington Times* consulted with editors of the *Washington Star* to propose that they "by a pact and agreement, refrain from giving the suffragette ladies any publicity." They decided to use the slightest of notices, nothing "to feed their vanity." When Brisbane then met with the president, the editor agreed that "a bare, colorless chronicle of what they do should be all that was printed. That constitutes part of the news, but it need not be made interesting reading" (Lunardini 127). But such a quiet agreement between the president and supportive newspapers proved hard to maintain as picketing continued. Washingtonians wanted to know what was going on, and the public's interest in articles in the *Washington Post,* which refused to enter into a pact, proved hard to ignore.

The Choice to Picket during War

Though some positive attention had been paid to the pickets through the winter, more than Wilson wanted, and they had been ceded a grudging respect, that situation would change drastically as the country headed into war. During the spring of 1917, and certainly after Wilson asked Congress to declare war on April 2, Paul had a decision to make and then to defend. During the Civil War, most suffragists discontinued their efforts, as Paul had chronicled in her dissertation. Similarly, NAWSA began devoting itself to the war effort, even though many of its leaders and members opposed it. By 1916 most NAWSA activists had joined the preparedness campaign and were praising America's entry into the conflict: whether they supported the war or not, they believed that their participation in volunteer organizations and in the armed services would lead to suffrage as a reward for their patriotism. Both Catt and Shaw, neither of them war supporters, accepted appointments on the Women's Committee of the Council on National Defense. In England, even the Pankhursts abandoned activism and turned their attention to war work; Emmeline Pankhurst suggested to Paul that the NWP follow her example and suspend suffrage activity. During the war, the *Woman's Journal,* which had been renamed the *Woman's Citizen* to emphasize women's full participation in the nation in its time of crisis, published not suffrage updates but positive news about working for the Red Cross and in factories. The September 28, 1918, issue, for example, discussed the suspension of the suffrage campaign for the Fourth Liberty Loan campaign. The first article, "Our—Not The," described women's involvement in their government, even without the vote, because of their work for the war. Article titles included "Selling the War to the People" (Thomson), "War Roster of Suffrage Officials," and "Suffrage and the Liberty Loan." Many NWP members thought of NAWSA members who opposed the war as hypocrites for suddenly taking on war work. In a letter to Alice Paul, NWP member Edna B. Kearns declared that "That 'Look at us, we don't picket—we help the country—please give us the vote' attitude disgusts me." But Paul refrained from such commentary; her one focus was suffrage.

As the nation prepared for war and as other suffragists at least publicly abandoned their cause, Paul recognized that a decision to continue picketing would be by far her most controversial act and would alienate many supporters. Well before war was declared in April 1917, Paul had begun preparing her arguments. A *Suffragist* article on May 22, 1915, for example, responded to negative coverage for accosting the president at the Biltmore Hotel in New York by claiming that women should not back off because war was imminent, that they had the responsibility especially then to fight for their inclusion in the political process. Looking back at the Civil War, the article commented that "We marvel at their lack of intuition and spirit"—at the poor decision to withdraw during such an essential time in the country's history. Such a policy involved "abasement," a "strategic error of getting 'out of the way' at high national moments" ("'Heckling' the President"). Paul carefully chose the word *abasement* to suggest that this decision had lowered women's prestige, that as they put aside their own noble priorities, they had proven not their patriotism but their unwillingness to fight for their right to contribute to decisions about their country's future. The goal of picketing was not to criticize this decision that men had made but "to remind constantly the President and the people of the country that American women are not enfranchised and that we cannot have a true democracy until they are." Besides indicating their desire to do their patriotic duty, working for suffrage was crucial during wartime because otherwise women would lose all the momentum of the previous years. They would have to begin again as women had following the Civil War and Reconstruction. Controversial techniques like picketing, she argued, were especially necessary during wartime to secure public attention for their campaign and keep the effort moving forward. In 1918, when Paul was asked whether her group could have worked for suffrage in a less striking and divisive way, she answered that, "In war time a mild conventional appeal for justice will not be heard" ("Pickets at the White House Gates").

At the national NWP convention in Washington from March 1 to 4, 1917, a month before war was declared, Paul's group first publicly stated its determination to continue fighting for suffrage during war (Resolution Passed by the Convention). From the convention, she sent a delegation to the president "to place before him our insistent demand that no action on war or another measure be taken without the consent of women," thus to indicate the importance of their campaign (Paul, Letter to State Chairmen). To emphasize reasons for the decision, she also sent out a spate of press releases to describe why patriotic women had to continue pressing for suffrage.

As Paul began to announce and defend her decision to the president and the public, she also used the *Suffragist* and circular letters to further her own participants' commitment to this decision and to prepare them to withstand the coming storm. In circular letters, through which NWP executive committee members tried to maintain the allegiance of their membership, they continued speaking in patriotic terms: "we must stand now for the establishment of a true democracy in this land"; "we are showing our highest patriotism." Florence Brewer Boeckel argued in the March 3, 1917, issue of the *Suffragist* that picketing symbolized a positive change in women's ethos, enabling them to take their own needs seriously instead of just adhering to the priorities of a male-governed nation: picketing was the "last protest against the tradition that women can be counted upon to give all and demand nothing" ("Reflections of a Picket"). On April 21, an article titled "Mutual

Responsibility" reminded readers that this country, which expected so much of women during wartime, was not willing to treat them as citizens. On June 9, 1917, in "The Indomitable Picket Line," Lucy Burns wrote that lowering the banners would be an abandonment of women's claim to liberty. She insisted that continuing to picket would have been the choice of Susan B. Anthony, the movement's hero. Anthony had worked hard as an abolitionist, giving speeches around New York state with Elizabeth Cady Stanton, Lucretia Mott, and Frederick Douglass. She and Stanton had formed the Women's National Loyalty League to petition Congress for the Thirteenth Amendment. But she had also continued to press for woman's suffrage during the war and after, persisting even though reformers like William Lloyd Garrison and Wendell Phillips insisted that women's rights should no longer be a key political issue (Lutz 113). In this 1917 article written during another war, Burns was evoking Susan B. Anthony's name and her lone record of continuing activism to remind readers that the earlier generation's widespread abandonment of the cause had not led to suffrage after the Civil War and to argue that the NWP possessed the group strength to enact what Anthony had failed at alone.

In the many articles in the *Suffragist* that lauded Anthony's choices and protested the tradition of women doing Red Cross work, entering factories, and proffering their sons without any choice in the matter, Paul was careful not to criticize the war itself. As a Quaker and believer in nonviolence, she opposed American entrance into this conflict, but she did not allude to that judgment. Instead, she concentrated on the right of all citizens to be involved in choosing the legislators and president who made the decision. The *Suffragist's* "War and the Suffrage Campaign" argued that her group had banded together to achieve political freedom for women—and women could do what they would with it "to give effective expression, through political power, to their ideals, whatever they may be." She knew that her choice of continuing to picket the White House would be controversial enough without its being associated with the controversial antiwar protest being mounted by Robert La Follette and other activists. NWP leaders thus publicly described their policy and membership: "Some of us, as individuals, are militarists, some are pacifists. We are united on but one ground—our fealty to political liberty for women" (Vernon, Letter from the National Secretary). To maintain this definition, Paul avoided discussing her own views even with close associates. On July 24, 1917, Crystal Eastman, then Executive Secretary of the American Union Against Militarism, wrote to Paul as though she had gotten inside information: "Miss Young tells me you are getting to be quite a pacifist in your sympathies." She had mailed Paul literature concerning pacifism along with her letter. That this colleague thought Paul might be "getting to be" a pacifist and would need literature on the choice shows Paul's restraint in discussing this matter that could rend her group.

Paul, however, was less reticent concerning her view of women's long-term role in ending warfare. Although she did not join the peace societies then forming, she did publicly endorse the belief that in the future women's fundamental, essentialist belief in peace could help lead the world away from war. Her viewpoint, in fact, echoed Gandhi's: "It is given to her [to woman] to teach the art of peace to the warring world thirsting for that nectar" (Gandhi, *Woman's Role in Society* 5). On June 9, 1917, in the *Suffragist*, Lavinia Dock spoke for Paul when she argued that women as natural advocates of peace had to protect each other and ultimately the human race: "Women must protect women, and with political voice and power they will learn to do it, because they will gradually come to see that only so can men be saved from their age-old self-destructive systems of competitive warfare" ("Urgent Need"). In one of her last interviews, Paul still argued that "Indeed, if we had universal suffrage throughout the world, we might not even have wars" (Gallagher 24).

Although Paul worked diligently to maintain her membership during wartime picketing, not all NWP members remained with her. Through the press and a round-robin letter, Harriot Stanton Blatch urged that the NWP stop its picketing during the war. Blatch mirrored the thinking of many suffragists who wrote Paul to withdraw their support. On June 22, 1917, for example, Myrtle E. Price of Kansas wrote to Paul in response to a fund-raising letter that drew many critical responses. Price argued that picketing had become "little less than criminal," as the most outrageous of the "foolish, childish methods you have used trying to harass our overburdened president." She aligned picketing with a lack of patriotism: "At a time like this, when there is so much that women can do to help, it seems incredible that there are any in the whole world who would try to hinder our government and its representatives in their efforts to bring peace to this war-mad world." Other resignations had less to do with support for the president than with an evaluation of the best means of achieving suffrage. Massachusetts suffragist and Progressive Party organizer Alice Carpenter, for example, wrote to Alice Paul on June 6— "I shall have to confess quite frankly that I think Mrs. Catt is playing a more intelligent game at the present moment than is the National Woman's Party"—thus expressing her belief that suffrage would come as a reward for hard work in wartime and would not follow any type of opposition to the government.

Throughout the year, NAWSA leaders publicly labeled the picketing as too combative, too insulting to the man whom they were attempting to sway. Anna Howard Shaw wrote to Dora Lewis on November 28, 1917, accusing the

NWP of treasonous activity in their continued action, of doing more to block progress toward the amendment than did antisuffragists. She even accused Paul's pickets of causing, through their dissension and lack of commitment to war work, the deaths of men in Europe. Opposing the government, she wrote, is "proving their disloyalty and doing their utmost to expose thousands of our young men to horrible deaths and the Allies to terrible loss of life and property." Carrie Chapman Catt also criticized the pickets, circulating pamphlets and posting signs against them during the New York suffrage campaign. Catt realized, however, that Paul's activism was keeping attention on suffrage—and creating a space for Catt herself as the acceptable advocate of the vote. In a letter to Mabel Vernon in June 1917, Katharine Rolston Fisher said that Catt was "quite like the parent who feels obliged to reprieve the naughty truth-telling child, but who is rather pleased to have the child say what she could not say herself."

A Changing Group of Adherents

As Paul moved further away from NAWSA policy, she faced changes in the NWP membership. At a conference at the end of July, Paul reported that only a few members had resigned compared to the thousand women who had joined that summer. Although she never admitted to any negative impact, her internal records show she may have lost as many as ten thousand members from her total of sixty or seventy thousand (Annual Report of Membership Department, 1916–1917). Although she spoke positively of her membership tallies and about her ongoing reliance on a devoted group, Paul also claimed that picketing brought in huge donations, six times the normal amount, but she frequently used financial records rhetorically, just as she did membership roles (Zimmerman 241, 244).

Although the membership and contribution numbers may be less than exact, this more controversial, more radical act of picketing the White House during wartime did bring in new followers. This picketing, this "standing up" to Wilson, to the white, male, upper-class president, was attractive to many working women, especially socialists and eastern Europeans who opposed the war. Paul's resulting new mixture of middle-class and working-class suffragists would remain on the line until the end, just the kind of smaller group that she envisioned as having the determination to make real change occur. From 1914 to 1916, Paul had seemed to prefer women of the "better classes," women of status in the community, who could lend respectability to and provide funding for a new movement. Throughout the campaign, she continued to cultivate relationships with women like Alva Belmont, who could pay for so much. But by 1917, as some older and more established suffragists quit the group, a greater percentage came to be women who were single and self-supporting, both college-educated professionals and more recently recruited blue-collar workers. As Paul wrote in a letter in September to Mrs. P. Pendergrast, a middle-class supporter, picketing was bringing "the laboring people of the state" into the suffrage effort, providing the momentum to keep the effort going. Mary Beard acknowledged this shift in support in a letter from May 2, 1917: "To keep up our fight we must now appeal almost entirely to the more radical elements in our society for the conservatives will give us no money since their funds all must go for war" (Letter to Mr. and Mrs. Phelps Stokes).

The picketing thus led to a changing membership in the NWP. By 1917, 87 percent of the organizers sent out to work in the states and encourage women to come into Washington for the picketing were between nineteen and twenty-nine, a significant decrease in age from earlier years. All earned their own living. Elsie Hill, daughter of a twenty-two-year Connecticut congressman, was a Vassar graduate and French teacher. Doris Stevens had attended Oberlin and then had gone into teaching and social work. The group also included labor organizers with little formal education: Rose Winslow was a socialist leader, a former factory worker and union organizer; Mary Gertrude Fendall was a member of the Farmer-Labor Party. In the summer and fall of 1917, of the 168 suffrage militants who were imprisoned as Wilson and the District Police began to react harshly to their presence in front of the White House, 70 percent were from WASP northeastern backgrounds, but only 40 percent were from the upper classes: 47 percent were from the middle class, and 13 percent from the working classes. Ernestine Hara Kettler, a woman who was born in Romania, whose mother worked in a sweatshop, and who was writing short stories and working with Eugene O'Neill, Louise Bryant, and Jack Reed in the Provincetown Players, described the group with whom she picketed: "One of them was Peggy Johns from New York. Another, whose name I do not remember, was an organizer in the needle trades in New York. The fourth was a lawyer from one of the Western states, either Wyoming or Arizona. They were all between twenty-five and thirty-five. I was the youngest in the group, twenty-one" (248, 254).

In the *Suffragist*, some articles reframed suffrage so as to reach this newer, more diverse group. At a dinner for pickets, as a *Suffragist* article attested, Katharine Rolston Fisher argued that disenfranchisement was the real prison, and thus that women of all classes were equally disserved by their government—and thus all needed to work together to improve their status. Both Wilson and the prison wardens were autocrats, she continued, making and changing rules at whim—authorities that women could only overcome by their militant camaraderie ("Prisoners of Freedom"). A March 3, 1917, *Suffragist* article described the active group that could defeat these authorities as "comrades" and "fellow-crusaders," borrowing language from socialist journals like the New York *Call* ("Seventh Week").

As union officials and socialist leaders joined the movement, it gained attention in the radical press, often in confrontational terminology that Paul herself would not use because it might detract from the one goal of suffrage. In "The Silent Sentinels," A. Sussman, a labor editor at the *Philadelphia Jewish World,* labeled the pickets as royal guards of the great army of women who were finally forsaking their harem, fighting to abandon the life of subjection and prostitution in which men held them. At a dinner for pickets who had served jail terms, John Reed spoke, contending that America's coercive government existed to serve the capitalistic goals of the rich—which did not include enfranchising any new groups ("Prison—and the Reaction"). On September 8, 1917, the New York *Call* labeled picketing and titled an article about it "Almost a Revolution."

To many mainstream newspapers, of course, this wartime picketing was not a sign of positive social progress. Such newspapers also referred to the changing membership profile, but not in terms of praise. The makeup of the group who attended meetings and walked the picket line provided additional evidence that suffragists were allied with the worst extremes of labor, and especially the IWW, whose leaders were being jailed for treason. The *New York World* noted that "The militant suffragists are exercising no right whatever unless it is the right to make fools of themselves. No less offensive than the I.W.W., the professional pacifists and the pro-German propagandists, they are serving the Kaiser to the best of their ability and calling it a campaign for equal suffrage" ("Comments of the Press" 12 Nov. 1917).

Although only a very few papers were willing to look beyond class arguments and discuss picketing's persuasive effect, Paul was keeping the press's and the public's attention during wartime, a difficult feat. On June 22, her colleague Katharine R. Fisher wrote to Mabel Vernon about this achievement: "The Evening Post is so charmingly naïve in saying that evidently the suffrage leaders do not stop to think what kind of publicity they are getting. We are getting the only kind the newspapers will let us have and it is good enough." Like Paul, however, Fisher expressed her dismay over the time and energy that women kept having to expend in this protracted fight for their rights: "Of course, I wish we were past the stage of blasting and could just plough and plant, but maybe we have to blast our way through to the end, even if it disturbs some of the soil already sown."

A Changing Rhetoric of Banners

As war brought changes to membership and the attitude of the press, it also changed the messages on the pickets' banners in rhetorically important ways. The war brought up an unprecedented rhetorical opportunity—to point out the contradiction between Wilson's advocacy of democracy worldwide and his failure to support it at home—and Paul seized it. To emphasize this shocking contradiction, and thus his lack of justice to women, pickets began presenting excerpts from the president's own speeches on their banners. The picketing had begun with established suffrage slogans and quotations from Milholland and Anthony. But, as Wilson worked to establish himself as an international leader, insisting that "the world must be made safe for democracy" as he stated in his declaration of war speech in Congress on April 2, the messages on the banners moved beyond those introductory themes. For example, one of Wilson's sayings, also from his war message on April 2, became a standard banner slogan: "We shall fight for the things which we have always held nearest to our hearts—for democracy, for the right of those who submit to authority to have a voice in their own governments." With Wilson's name printed beneath such a line, Paul hoped to point to the stark inconsistency, the irony, of this man touring the nation and world delivering speeches on democracy and bringing American men and women into a world war to die for democracy when at home he was keeping half his citizens from participating in democracy's most basic act (Lunardini 114). As the *Suffragist* commented about the developing banner campaign, "President Wilson is not yet candid in this manner of democracy—and women must make him see it" ("Picket and the President"). Printed without commentary, held by women standing for freedom, these banners were intended as a serious indictment of his presidency. Even years later, Paul believed that these quoted phrases had been an especially powerful choice: "It was really a big turning point. That's when the militancy really began. This going out and standing there with our beautiful banners wasn't anything very militant. But this [using Wilson's own lines] really was, I would say, the beginning of the militancy" (Fry). The banners were, in Paul's mind, militant, but their "militancy" was the use of a particularly effective kind of nonviolent rhetoric, not any form of violence.

Such banners challenged Wilson through the spring, and then Paul sought and achieved another level of aggression and publicity with her "to the Russian envoys" banner. On June 20, 1917, as representatives of the new Kerensky government of Russia drove up to the White House, Lucy Burns and Dora Lewis held out a large banner, with the following text: "To the Russian envoys:

We the women of America tell you that America is not a democracy. Twenty million American women are denied the right to vote. President Wilson is the chief opponent of their national enfranchisement. Help us make this nation really free. Tell our government it must liberate its people before it can claim free Russia as an ally" (Stevens, *Jailed for Freedom* 74). Edith Bolling Wilson wrote about this action that was so disrespectful to her husband and especially about the immediate response of the crowd: "I was indignant, but apparently no less so than a crowd of onlookers who tore the pickets' banner down" (138).

This event had a great potential for controversy, as Paul well knew. Beginning in March of that year, after the abdication of Tsar Nicholas II, Alexander Kerensky had risen through the positions of minister of justice and minister of war to provisional prime minister. His assumption of power at home and his friendship with the United States mattered a great deal to Wilson, for Kerensky intended to continue Russian involvement in the war and subdue Bolshevik leaders who were encouraging soldiers to withdraw from the battlefield. He had begun consolidating power by having Trotsky arrested and causing Lenin to go into hiding in Finland. To continue the war, American leaders felt the need of this ally, who was poised between the monarchists and the Bolsheviks. For pickets to be standing outside the White House carrying a sign arguing that these Russian diplomats could not trust Wilson—and that Wilson did not even have the support of his own citizens—was thus generally viewed as incendiary, even traitorous, an affront to the war effort and to plans for worldwide postwar democracy.

In a press release following this incident, Paul emphasized that the government had caused its own embarrassment, that it was Wilson who was responsible for women's lack of democracy and thus for the unavoidable contrast between his idealistic principles and American reality: "The responsibility . . . is with the government and not with the women of America, if the lack of democracy at home weakens government in its fight for democracy three thousand miles away" (Press Release, 20 June 1917). Some leaders agreed with her. J. A. H. Hopkins, an influential member of the Democratic National Campaign Committee of 1916 and a close associate of Wilson, wrote to Paul from New Jersey on June 22 that "Our representations to Russia that we are a democracy are certainly erroneous in fact if not in theory" and the "liberties of which we boast are not endangered, but are now nearly non-existent."

As Paul had assumed, though, when this story ran in newspapers all over the country, the analysis was not positive ("Woman's Party Appeals"). Many newspapers expressed either outrage over this traitorous act that could have an ill effect internationally or amusement that women thought any act of theirs could have any serious effect. Many newspapers that branded the act as un-American quoted governmental spokesmen like Louis Brownlow, who contended that it was being "interpreted in the newspapers of the Central Powers as a pro-German uprising" (77). At the other extreme, to denigrate the event and the women participants, the *New York Times* claimed that "the Russians went by the gate so fast that it is doubtful if even those who read English were able to see the inscriptions on the banner" ("Crowd Destroys Suffrage Banner").

With this widespread if negative press coverage, suffragists knew they had the nation's attention. On June 23, 1917, Ethel Adamson in New York wrote excitedly to Abby Scott Baker that "I am overcome with admiration and enthusiasm of the pluck and courage of these women. . . . We fairly gasped when we read it [the banner]. . . . Who is our lawyer?" Adamson recognized that additional women would be leaving the NWP as a result, but "it is a healthy pruning." One woman who was leaving, Adamson cited as an example, "never did have the real militant spirit, and so of course could not lead a group of women who really believe they are doing the Lord's service to resist tyranny." Adamson wanted Baker to understand that their maneuvers were causing excitement and determination among those who remained. "Do drop us a line of the real inside dope," Adamson continued, because these specific details would lead to greater respect and motivation within the winnowed group.

Arrests and Jail Terms Begin

After this banner appeared at the White House gates, the treatment of pickets changed dramatically: women began to be arrested for doing the same sort of picketing that had been going on since January. District of Police captain Major Pullman, who had replaced Richard Sylvester, called on Paul and ordered her to stop the picketing: her rhetoric had become too politically destructive, too publicly discussed, too embarrassing to Wilson. Paul refused; the group went out as usual on June 22. Burns and Katharine Morey were arrested for obstructing traffic, a charge that Paul found ironic because she had planned, through the picketing and the suffrage that would result from it, to obstruct the patterns of Washington's political traffic. In response to this arrest, in classic nonviolent fashion, the women offered no resistance, behavior that would continue through a long period of sentencing and jailtime.

In the next few days, Paul continued her nonviolent contest with the police. On June 23 the police warned her that the pickets would again be arrested if they went to their regular posts. On that day, Dora Lewis and Gladys Greiner were arrested, as were Mabel Vernon and Virginia Arnold, who had come to the capital to see the Russian banner unfurled. On Sunday, June 24, Pullman again telephoned headquarters to say that the group could no longer hold banners of any kind before the White House. Paul recalled his saying that "We have to say to you, if you do persist in going, and we hope you won't, that we have no alternative except to arrest you. These are our instructions." Paul replied: "Well, I think that we feel that we ought to continue and I feel that we will continue" (Fry). On June 25 twelve women were arrested, including Lucy Burns, Lavinia Dock, Mabel Vernon, Katherine Morey, Maud Jamison, and Virginia Arnold. They had gone out in defiance of Pullman's order, carrying banners with quotations from the president and from Susan B. Anthony and suffrage flags from those states where women had the vote. The twelve were arrested and ordered to appear for trial when summoned. As William R. Miller writes, this returning on these subsequent days, even to face arrest, was essential to creating an effective nonviolent presence: "In many such cases the police will intervene, often belatedly, and arrest us for 'disorderly conduct' or some other specious charge, maintaining both order and the status quo. We shall have to plan to replace the arrested cadres in successive waves as they are removed from the scene, repeat the action after an interval of hours or days, or turn to another tactic" (152). Paul chose to employ the "successive waves" method.

The situation on these days gave the pickets ample opportunity to demonstrate their strength and their commitment to nonviolent protest. Because these women were now picketing in violation of a government order, the police no longer offered them protection from the larger crowds assembling in the wake of the Russian banner. On June 26, when Lucy Burns and Alice Paul carried the banner declaring "Democracy should begin at home" by the lower White House gate, a few boys destroyed it, with the police "looking placidly on." A great crowd began to surge up and down the street while Burns and Paul "stood motionless." They spoke no words and did not attempt to defend themselves from men who were shoving and pulling on the banners. Later that day, when Paul was having lunch at the headquarters, another mob charged other pickets and tore their banners to shreds while the women stood motionless. Nine of the pickets were arrested.

In this contest of wills, from which Paul refused to withdraw, the government took the unprecedented step of imprisoning pickets. In the courtroom where this decision occurred, Paul centered her arguments against this supposedly most democratic of governments by citing the freedoms that it had been abrogating. During the trial of six of the nine who had been arrested on June 26, the pickets said they had refused to desist when the police told them to do so because picketing was legal under the Constitution and the Clayton

Act. They first quoted the First-Amendment guarantee of "the right of the people peacefully to assemble, and to petition the Government for a redress of grievances" and then reviewed the recent legislation that further secured that right. Passed in 1914, the Clayton Antitrust Act, an amendment to the Sherman Antitrust Act, had insured the right of unions and other groups to strike, boycott, and picket. Thus the court was violating basic rights of citizens when it convicted these women not for picketing, which wasn't illegal, but for "obstructing the highways." These women refused to pay the twenty-five dollar fines and were the first to be incarcerated, for a period of three days. Charges on the preceding days had all been dismissed ("Prison—and the Reaction").

With well-educated and well-connected women entering the jails, and their stories being publicly emphasized more than those of working women, Wilson faced his own rhetorical exigency. He had grown tired of having these women in front of the White House, and he certainly wanted no more banners like the Russian one. But he wanted to avoid the criticism that could erupt from his jailing of American women who were exercising their legal rights as citizens. To shape the resulting coverage, he asked Louis Brownlow, a close associate and District of Columbia Commissioner, to argue that demonstrators had to be arrested to restore order to the capital and to protect the women themselves (Brownlow 76; Stevens, *Jailed for Freedom* 140). Along with arguing that these women must be shielded from harsh crowds that the police could not control, Brownlow told a lie about Alice Paul, claiming she had promised violence if she were not arrested because she wanted to serve time in jail: "Mr. Wilson did not want them arrested, and I did not want to arrest them. But, after we entered the war, conditions became such that Major Pullman felt obligated to arrest them to protect them from the mobs who resented the insulting inscriptions on their banners; and this feeling on Major Pullman's part was supported by an ultimatum from the suffragettes themselves threatening the use of firearms if we *did not* arrest them" (76, italics in the original). To make the arrests seem more acceptable, Brownlow described Paul as militant, difficult, and wrong-headed, a German sympathizer who, as he wrongly recorded, had gone to school in Germany and formed her values there. Using the Russian banner as evidence, he even asked citizens to look more closely at her refusal to engage in war work: "to the disinterested observer the pacifism of Alice Paul was of infinitesimal dimensions" (77).

Whatever the rhetoric emanating from Wilson's forces, Paul recognized that her battle with him had little to do with the potential violence of the crowds or the behavior of the pickets. Police officials had been allowing crowds to gather and had refused to control them: they, in fact, seemed to want "sidewalk traffic" for the women to "obstruct." And, Paul believed, Wilson did not truly fear violence from her. She did constitute a danger in another sense, however, because of her opposition to him—assailing his self-proclaimed position as democracy's leader and harming his international allegiances, and doing so in wartime.

These women were, in fact, the first victims of the restricted tolerance for protest with the nation at war. During the month in which women began to be arrested for picketing, with war emotions running high, Congress passed the Espionage Act, which provided up to twenty-year sentences and ten-thou-sand-dollar fines for anyone making false statements that hindered military operations, promoted the success of America's enemies, encouraged soldiers to be disloyal, or interfered with army enlistment (Goodell 56). Wilson freely admitted that while the nation was at war there would be less patience for any form of resistance. As he said at that time: "Once lead this people into war and they'll forget there ever was such a thing as tolerance. To fight you must be brutal and ruthless, and the spirit of ruthless brutality will enter into the very fibre of our national life, infecting Congress, the courts, the policeman on the beat, the man in the street" (Baker, *Woodrow Wilson, Life and Letters, Facing War* 506–7). As Wilson's words foretold, almost two thousand pros-ecutions occurred under the Act: "nearly all concerned speeches, newspaper articles, leaflets, and books expressing opinions about the merits and conduct of the war" (Goodell 56). From 1917 to 1921, over a thousand IWW workers were arrested, and over one hundred leaders, including Bill Haywood, who was tried in Chicago along with 165 others, were given varied sentences, a few for as long as ten and twenty years. Eugene V. Debs of the Socialist Party was jailed from April 1919 to December 1921; Haywood was convicted in 1918 and served time in Leavenworth Prison until, out on bail while appealing his sentence in 1921, he fled the country and went to Moscow. As William Preston writes about this time period in *Aliens and Dissenters,* "In a war atmosphere, any 'Christian tolerance' was swept away by patriotism" (3, 6). Though the women pickets were not imprisoned under this act, but rather for blocking the sidewalk or obstructing traffic, they were actually being arrested, like Debs and Haywood, for criticizing the government: in the women's case, for standing by the president's house and challenging him through their banners. Whatever the charges made, as historians Eleanor Flexner and El-len Fitzpatrick have noted, they were "denied their civil liberties by sudden arrests" because they had expressed their view of their government (277).

The Rhetoric of the Fourth of July and Bastille Day

Whether Wilson was concerned with the city's safety, the women's inappropriate forcefulness, or his own quest for democracy, Paul felt he made a fateful error with these jail terms—and she intended to take full rhetorical advantage of it. In fact, as courts issued sentences, Paul began orchestrating visual scenes that caused larger crowds to gather, more women to be arrested, and more and longer sentences to be meted out; she believed this persecution of nonviolent protesters could only help the cause. By the end of June, she began focusing her planning on two days that would offer special rhetorical opportunities, Independence Day and Bastille Day. She restricted the regular picketing to just one day a week because she was preparing to exploit these two days, so richly symbolic of liberty and the power of the citizenry.

On July 4 a group of five women moved out from headquarters carrying banners that read "Just governments derive their power from the consent of the governed," echoing the Declaration of Independence; "Mr. President, what will you do for woman suffrage?"; and Inez Milholland's "How long must women wait for liberty," carried by her sister, Vida Milholland. In what Paul viewed as a grave misjudgment, as the five pickets crossed Pennsylvania Avenue toward the east gate of the White House, twenty-nine officers came to arrest them—and not to control what the *Suffragist* referred to as the "close-pressing crowd of men" ("Protest for Liberty" 4). As Paul's press bulletins stressed, Helen Hill Weed was arrested while wearing a DAR pin with bars that represented her fourteen ancestors who had given their lives in the American Revolution. Then, a second group of six, including Burns and Lewis, was arrested at the west gate for obstructing traffic. Kitty Marion and Hazel Hunkins were next arrested for disorderly conduct as they sold the *Suffragist* by the Belasco Theatre near headquarters. Their "disorderly conduct" occurred as Marion insisted that a man pay for the copy of the *Suffragist* he took from her and Hunkins insisted that a man return a banner because it was NWP property.

Paul and her colleagues, of course, knew the rhetorical value of the Fourth of July and the powerful symbolism, both religious and patriotic, of women seeking freedom on that day and then experiencing such cruel and un-American treatment. Maud Younger certainly recognized the publicity value of this July 4 injustice: "Monstrous as this was, it reacted to our benefit, as the newspapers for the first time since the war carried suffrage on the front page. No plea for abstract rights of thousands of women could have brought our cause to public attention as did the Government authorities by arresting us" ("Revelations" Oct., 39). The *Suffragist*'s coverage, reiterated in press bulletins, depicted the police and crowd as a mass of beasts: "With eyes that gleamed, with lips drawn back, with hoarse, ugly noises issuing from hundreds of throats" (Allender). These advocates of freedom, in the article's rhetoric, withstood the attack while holding words from the Declaration of Independence and from their own martyr Milholland, as a film about Joan of Arc, an icon of strength and sacrifice that the *Suffragist* used repeatedly, played at the Belasco Theatre, also on Lafayette Square.

In the *Suffragist* and in press bulletins, articles also fully recorded the visual and verbal scene of the trial. The pickets hung their soiled and torn yellow banner reading "Just governments derive their power from the consent of the governed" against the wall of the courtroom. Then Burns pointed out that their activities had been allowed for six months and then suddenly dubbed illegal. She argued that the police's role had been unjustly transformed from protecting to arresting and that it still varied from day to day. And, she continued, she could speak these words only to a government-appointed judge: since these women were arrested on traffic charges, they were denied the right to a jury trial. When the judge ruled, eleven pickets accepted three days in jail instead of paying the twenty-five dollar fine. Marion's case was dismissed, and Hunkins was never tried ("United States Convicts"; "Protest for Liberty Answered").

July offered Paul another day that symbolized loyalty and freedom. For Bastille Day, July 14, when speeches about liberty were being given across the country, many women came to Washington to join the picket line and the crowd of supporters. Sixteen suffrage leaders were selected to picket, including many women of high social status: Alison Turnbull Hopkins, wife of J. A. H. Hopkins; Florence Bayard Hilles, daughter of a former ambassador to Britain and secretary of state; Matilda Hall Gardner, wife of journalist Gilson Gardner; Eunice Brannan, daughter of journalist Charles Dana; and Elizabeth Seldon Rogers, wife of a prominent New York physician ("Protest for Liberty Answered"). On that day, the banners included "Liberty, Equality, Fraternity, July 14, 1789" and "Mr. President, how long must American women wait for liberty?"—another combination of a historical plea for freedom with their own. As these pickets went out, police arrested them for unlawful assembly and for obstructing traffic. Louis Brownlow said that he decided to have them arrested, even though he knew a further assumption of rhetorical martyrdom was thus possible, because "the daily riots ought to be stopped" (77).

On July 17, at the trial for these Bastille Day offenses, the government went further than before by meting out sentences of sixty days. Before the judge, the arrested pickets contested claims that huge crowds had forced policemen to make arrests to clear the traffic and assure everyone's safety.

Burns and Gardner spoke, as did their attorney Dudley Field Malone, who had represented the Democratic Party in a visit to the NWP Convention in June of 1916 and had since become Paul's ally. He countered police assertions about the size and unruliness of the crowd and labeled these as political arrests, instigated by Wilson, of women whose actions were protected by the Constitution and the Clayton Act ("United States Government on Trial"). When the judge decided on a twenty-five dollar fine or sixty days in prison, these nonviolent protestors opted for prison.

Press releases and other publicity about July 14 caught the nation's attention, especially because harsh treatment of these women protestors had occurred on another day historically designated for celebrating democracy. Because Paul had secured well-respected and well-connected women for this key day, the long sentence seemed especially shocking. Lucy Burns, in fact, wrote to Alva Belmont on July 24 concerning the first-rate publicity opportunity emanating from social position: "It was a stroke of good fortune that this was the group selected by the magistrate for the indefensible sentence of sixty days in the workhouse."

As soon as these women were sentenced, the party headquarters sprang into action to publicize these inequities. Before she began her sentence, Anne Martin, then chair of the NWP's Legislative Committee, wrote circular letters to supporters encouraging them to contact their local newspapers and to write their legislators. She sent telegrams to newspapers across the country, including those in the hometown of every participant, to tell their story. Her accounting of the event was repeated verbatim in many papers, as was the following defense of their picketing during war: "It is unpatriotic, we are told, to complain of injustice now. We believe that it is unpatriotic not to complain. We have no right to allow our representatives to act basely—to preach freedom abroad, and deny freedom at home." Men were being asked to die abroad and women to economize on their children's food and to send their sons to war, she continued, but the president and Congress would not endorse democracy at home and were instead persecuting women who fought for it.

The Rhetoric of a Pardon

Faced with the public outrage caused by this sentence for picketing on a day celebrating freedom, the government's resolve lasted only three days. Wilson had been shocked when Dudley Malone supported these pickets at their July 17 trial, as Edith Bolling Wilson remembered: "Imagine our surprise when Dudley Field Malone, whom my husband had appointed Collector of the Port of New York, defended these women. Nevertheless, they were sentenced to sixty days in the workhouse. I was blazing with anger at Malone's conduct, and my husband was deeply hurt." Malone had been a close Wilson associate: he had helped Wilson during his campaigns, worked in the Secretary of State office for William Jennings Bryan, and was Wilson's hand-picked Collector of the Port of New York. Even though Malone's choices affected his relationship with Wilson, the president still consulted him about how to end this bothersome conflict. At a meeting with Malone and J. A. H. Hopkins, whose wife was in jail, Wilson, as his wife further recalled, "suggested pardoning the women, though not because Mr. Malone had defended them. He said they must not be made martyrs. Mr. Tumulty opposed the pardon but the next day, after a round of golf with Dr. Grayson and me, the President signed the paper" (138).

At their meeting, Malone and Hopkins urged Wilson to make suffrage a war measure to assure its passage and to quickly get rid of it as a political liability (Baker, *Woodrow Wilson, Life and Letters, War Leader*, 171–72). In a hearing before a Senate committee on April 26, Anne Martin had begun arguing for suffrage as a war measure, the only type of legislation being passed in that session, since women then might "as fully-equipped, fully-franchised citizens, do our part in carrying out and helping to solve the problems that lie before the government when our country is at war" (Irwin, *Story of Alice Paul* 307–8). On May 14, Vernon, J. A. H. Hopkins, and others had visited with Wilson to advocate this amendment as part of the war program. He had not been convinced of these arguments then, and he rejected them again in July.

To Alice Paul, this pardon, as well as Wilson's consideration of suffrage as a war measure, created unprecedented rhetorical opportunities, a chance to publicly defend women's rights to make their own decisions and face the consequences on their own. The women thus affected, led by Alison Turnbull Hopkins, contested the pardon they had not requested ("Vindication of the Suffrage Pickets"; "We Ask Justice, Not Pardon"). Just as the first pickets had turned down Wilson's invitation to come into the White House parlor to escape from the rain, so in the press these imprisoned pickets said they did not want to accept this favor from Wilson or seem thus allied with him. Hopkins wrote Wilson a letter, which she also released to the press, to express her anger over his decision, which deprived her of the right to appeal her arrest. She did not want his benevolence, the letter maintained, but justice. The day after her release, Hopkins went out by herself to picket with a banner that read "We do not ask pardon for ourselves, but justice for all American women." In response to questions from reporters who trailed her, she said the pickets didn't want to be pardoned by the government for something they considered right and proper to do.

Paul extended the rhetorical advantage of the pardon in articles in the *Suffragist* and press bulletins, discussing it as an admission of guilt, as Wilson's recognition that through the arrests he had been denying freedom of speech to American citizens and breaking the law. In the *Suffragist,* Paul argued that this unsought pardon signaled the end of women's being arrested for picketing because it proved that they had been illegally charged. Thus, she wrote, this pardon "closes a chapter in the American woman suffrage struggle as ignoble as was the witchcraft chapter in the history of this country" ("Vindication of the Suffrage Pickets"). In this reference to Salem in 1692, Paul compared suffragists to other women who had been subjected to brutal treatment out of fear and prejudice, with decisions about their guilt and innocence separated from any form of evidence and made in special courts without juries. Another article described the pardon as "the government's complete and sudden surrender": "This is a victory, singular in these days of war hysteria, of the people against the United States government" ("Picket and the President"). Using the word *hysteria,* Paul constructed these arrests as part of a pattern of irrational behavior—not by women, about whom the word was frequently wielded, but by the president and government.

Encouraged by their strength in weathering arrests and jail, and especially by the rhetorical use they had made of the pardon, the group resumed regular picketing on July 23, carrying the "battle-scarred banner" bearing Milholland's last words—"Mr. President, how long must women wait for liberty?"—that had been in court with Alison Turnbull Hopkins and the other women when they were sentenced for the Bastille Day picketing. They also carried with them a banner that quoted Hopkins, "We ask not pardon for ourselves, but justice for all American women," her inclusion on the banners associating her with suffrage heroes like Anthony and Milholland.

Paul felt that these confrontations were building interest in suffrage and respect for the pickets. She especially felt that calm acceptance of jail terms was making them into nonviolent heroes and martyrs, steadfast individuals facing the worst that an authoritarian government could do. William R. Miller describes the apotheosis possible for the nonviolent protestor repeatedly attacked by the police or by a crowd: "The juxtaposition of the angry, violent attacker and the calm, unretaliating resister mobilizes spontaneous human sympathy for the latter on the part of any onlookers" (157). As he comments further, when the opponent overreacts and enacts too harsh a penalty, public evaluation may shift, because the situation places the opponent "into a position of moral disadvantage" and makes him "lose countenance" (160). In a *Suffragist* article titled "Advertising Democracy," Nina Allender argued that these women were "calm, deliberate, calculating, college-bred women" who "understand the modern value of publicity": they were well able to establish the moral high ground and appear as valiant crusaders to the press and public.

In the summer, as women entered and left jail and then repeatedly reappeared on the picket line, they knew they were making progress, proving their stamina as purveyors of nonviolence. Margaret Sanger wrote to Anne Martin in July 1917 praising women who were accepting jail time for moving the campaign forward: "It is the first bit of martyrdom the suffrage cause has extracted from its advocates in America. You will gain more for your cause and will forward its march greater by 60 days in a workhouse than any other single demonstration has ever done." She continued by declaring that "There is hope today for woman's emancipation because she has desired something and will suffer for it. A new spirit has arisen!" As Rheta Childe Dorr wrote in *A Woman of Fifty,* the public cruelty of the police seemed to be a political mistake: "And finally they committed the worst blunder politicians could possibly make, they tried to suppress the pickets. The women were arrested—for obstructing traffic!" (302). Paul certainly recognized the decision to jail these women as a surprising and very visual form of injustice, one that put these women in the national spotlight, as Lavinia Dock commented in the *Suffragist:* "Surely, nothing but the creeping paralysis of mental old age can account for the phenomenon of American men, law-makers, officials, administrators and guardians of the peace, who can see nothing in the intrepid young pickets with their banners, asking for bare justice, but common obstructors of traffic, naggers—nuisances that are to be abolished by passing new, stupid laws forbidding and repressing, to add to the old junk heap of laws which forbid and repress" ("Young Are at the Gates" 5). Paul, of course, hoped that the government's cruel overreaction would not just secure press attention and public sympathy, but action on suffrage.

Kaiser Wilson

As citizens and the press began questioning the choice of imprisoning, Wilson and his officials decided to curtail the arrests. In late July and early August, women continued to stand by the White House holding their picket signs, but no more arrests were forthcoming, so press coverage dwindled. As Paul had done before, she soon felt that she needed to increase the level of danger and controversy. In early August Paul decided on a new disruptive rhetoric that would spur arrests and create news. She chose another emotionally wrought banner, one that made another highly controversial reference to the war: given the president's unwillingness to recognize the rights of all citizens and his failure to support real democracy, he was not much better than the German Kaiser Wilhelm II. Suffragists labeled the president "Kaiser Wilson" on picket signs—and caused a well-publicized uproar, as Paul had certainly expected.

On August 10 the new banner was unfurled: "Kaiser Wilson, have you forgotten your sympathy with the poor Germans because they were not self-governing? 20 million American women are not self-governing/Take the beam out of your own eye" ("Kaiser Wilson"). Two other banners made the comparison of Wilson to the German dictator more specific: "He rules over them (Am. women) by sheer autocratic power—the very type of power he denounces in Austria and Germany" and "A President is a duly elected representative. For 20,000,000 American women Wilson Is NOT a President. A Kaiser is an autocratic ruler. For 20,000,000 American women Wilson is a Kaiser" (Faber 163). In a letter to fellow suffragist Paula Jakobi, a playwright from New York, Paul explained the action. The title "Kaiser" was not meant as a personal insult to Mr. Wilson, she maintained, but "as a simple way of stating the relation of the unenfranchised women of America to a government in which they have no voice." She viewed the banner as creating an important visually symbolic event that would secure press attention for women's disenfranchisement: "If we had given out a long, scholastic dissertation on the political status of women in this country, nobody would have paid any attention to it; but when we boiled down into one word—Kaiser—the real position of women, the people were knocked into thinking. Certainly the press would not have carried a political treatise on the enfranchisement of women, but every newspaper in the country did carry the statement that to American women the President of the United States is in the position of Kaiser."

But of course with the nation at war against Germany, with Kaiser Wilhelm constructed in the press as an evil villain, many critics viewed her actions not as an intellectual plea for equality but as a vicious attack on the president, one tantamount to treason. At that time, the Kaiser was urging the continued waging of war while many members of his Reichstag, or imperial assembly, were suggesting peace resolutions. Newspapers called him the "the Mad Dog of Europe" and "the Beast of Berlin." One cartoonist had recently portrayed him as "a cross between a Cro-Magnon primitive and a slavering crocodile" (Fleming 57). Comparing Wilson to this war-mongering emperor, the enemy's leader, was certainly incendiary. Although Paul was vilified for the decision, she felt that, especially with her movement losing momentum during wartime, this bad press was preferable to no press at all. In her letter to Paula Jacobi, she argued that criticism would expose the faults in a specious argument, but, with a principled one, the bad press would bring attention to the issue and encourage people to think about it for themselves. Katharine

Rolston Fisher in New York wrote to Lucy Burns on August 12, 1917, that indeed this incident and newspaper articles about it "must have jogged a few million inert brain cells." She sent encouragement for keeping up the pressure: "I wonder how much more of our medicine Wilson will require. . . . I hope you are mixing another stiff dose."

On August 10 through August 16, the days on which the pickets walked out with the Kaiser banners, the police offered them no protection against mounting violence and even gunshots, as articles in the *Suffragist* and press bulletins stressed. As the pickets submitted themselves peacefully to mob violence, each subsequent day helped shift public discussion from their traitorous act to their dedication and strength. Dr. Caroline E. Spencer wrote in the *Colorado Springs Gazette,* a newspaper in her home state, that on August 10 her banner was demolished by men and boys whom the police did not try to control. This newspaper and many others reported that as Wilson drove by, three sailors, part of a "mob" of five thousand, sprang onto Lucy Burns and dragged her and her banner to the curb. On each subsequent day, the pickets stood together silently as they faced repeated "attacks of excited boys and United States sailors" ("Kaiser Wilson"). Then, on August 14, after the women returned to headquarters with torn banners and placed them on the second and third floor balconies, three sailors brought a ladder and tore down the "Kaiser Wilson" banner and an American flag, and a bullet was fired through a second-floor window, all without any police response ("President Onlooker at Mob Attack"). Determined to prove their own resilience and to assert their right to picket nonviolently, Katharine Morey and Catherine M. Flanagan then took out the Kaiser banner and stood on the sidewalk for twenty minutes under attack from the crowd. They made repeated attempts to move toward the White House without police protection. Next, four women went out, one with the Inez Milholland banner, and all of their banners were destroyed, but they did make it to the White House and stood there for an hour, without banners and without police assistance. On August 15 four women went out, and all of their banners were destroyed. Paul was knocked down three times and a sailor dragged her "the width of the White House sidewalk." The *Suffragist* article and press bulletins on this incident, sent to newspapers across the country, stressed Paul's nonviolence—"Making no resistance, Miss Paul was seriously bruised in this encounter" ("Administration Versus the Woman's Party" 6). On August 16, according to the *Suffragist,* police attacked the pickets with as much cruelty as earlier mobs and in the evening watched as the mob tore their banners and shoved the women away from the White House. Lucy Burns, Virginia Arnold, and Elizabeth Stuyvesant were injured; men who tried to help the pickets were arrested ("Administration Versus the Woman's Party").

Each day the nation witnessed a contest between pickets and their opponents, one that Paul believed was demonstrating women's abuse within the current nondemocratic system as well as their strong resolve to change that system. After each incident, Paul sent out detailed press releases and asked participants to telegram their hometown newspapers, stressing that, even though their banners might be extreme, they were just cloth and words: the police were inciting physical harm. For Paul, these attacks were a silencing of the silent, a taking away of the women's chosen form of communication as too dangerous even to be seen. But, as each piece of publicity noted, even when they faced the worst of this terror, these women stood firm as "silent sentinels," as watchguards for freedom, without offering any violence in return.

With a flood of stories occurring, criticizing the banners themselves but also providing details of the attacks, the government again chose to use jail sentences to get the women away from the White House and to stifle their campaign. On August 17 Major Pullman told Paul that pickets would again be arrested because Wilson and Brownlow had lost patience with their presence, with their new offensive banners, and with the aggressive crowd that they were inciting to riot. Pullman hoped that the threat would keep Paul at home, but Paul, of course, told him that the pickets would be returning to their posts. On that day, six women were arrested, and they were sentenced to thirty days at Occuquan Workhouse in rural Virginia. None of their assailants were punished, just as no attackers from previous days had been charged ("Administration Versus the Woman's Party" 7).

Even after Paul quit using the Kaiser banner, arrests continued, and suddenly the government chose harsh sentences, especially for repeat offenders. On September 4, as punishment for banners that reminded the president that women's sons were fighting this war—"Mr. President, how long must women be denied a voice in the government that is conscripting their sons?"—thirteen women were arrested, including Lucy Burns and Abby Scott Baker. They were sent to Occuquan Workhouse for sixty days (Irwin, *Story of Alice Paul* 245). The *Boston Journal,* on September 8, 1917, compared these sentences for nonviolence—for holding banners—to the lighter sentences given to the Pankhursts: "In old England, where windows and heads were smashed in desperate suffrage demonstrations, only thirty days were given at the fourth offense" ("Comments of the Press" 12 Nov. 1917). For picketing on September 13, a day when sailors shredded the women's banners, six women were given thirty days in the workhouse when they refused to pay a fine of even five cents. For picketing on September 22, when police officers confiscated the banners, four women were given thirty days. On October 6, the day that Congress adjourned, Paul was arrested for leading ten women who protested the legislature's continuing inaction on suffrage. Their sentences were suspended. On October 15, four of the women under suspended sentences, including Rose Winslow and Maud Jamison, went out again and for this repeated offense got a sentence of six months in the workhouse. On October 20, Paul went out with three others carrying a banner quoting words Wilson had recently used on posters for the Second Liberty Bond Loan, words that applied to their campaign as well as to the war: "The time has come when we must conquer or submit. For us there can be but one choice. We have made it" (Irwin, *Story of Alice Paul* 255). Paul and Spencer were sentenced to seven months in jail; the other two were given thirty days.

* * *

From the beginning of 1917, Paul was orchestrating powerful visual rhetoric on the picket line, one of women standing together as silent nonviolent witnesses to the injustice of denying the vote to half of the population. For this campaign, they relied on their bodies and the slogans on their banners to create a nonviolent rhetoric of suffrage. Women first appeared before the White House in January, asking Wilson to pay a just bill. They kept going out after war was declared, with their actions taking on a new appearance of militancy in the new political climate. They used the Russian and the Kaiser Wilhelm banners, as well as frequent quotations from Wilson's speeches in Europe, to point out the inconsistencies within Wilson's presidency and to make clear that women were not participants in American democracy. As Paul kept choosing new banners and occasions, she attempted to assure that no technique grew stagnant or expected because that would lead to picketing no longer drawing reporters and a crowd. Starting in June, the government chose to mete out jail time—for these women's positioning themselves in front of the president's residence and holding words that supported their cause and questioned his commitment to democracy. Throughout the summer, Paul found that arrests added to her rhetoric, enabling her to further cast the government as tyrant and her pickets as heroes. They stood silently as they were handcuffed and placed into police wagons; they argued in court for the rights of citizens; they refused to pay the fines that would keep them out of jail but would signal their acquiescence to an unjust governmental authority. This extended effort brought women together, into a shared experience of strength and risk: they were true compatriots of Susan B. Anthony and Inez Milholland, of the forefathers who drafted the Constitution and honored the Fourth of July, of all men and women who not only spoke about freedom but would lay down their lives for it.

8. Hunger Strikes and Jail

To engage Americans and gain their sympathy, throughout the fall Paul was shifting the focus of her rhetoric, maintaining the picket line and banners but emphasizing the jail terms that shocked newspaper readers across the country. Women continued to picket, continued to be arrested and given sentences; and Paul seemed to be resending the same women to court the longer jail sentences that could demonstrate, to the press and the public, their determination and unity. As these women returned to the picket line, they entered prisons in large numbers. In October, for example, there were seventy women in two jails, some for just a few days on their first sentences, others for thirty or sixty days, and six for the unprecedented sentence of seven months. In total that fall, 168 women served jail sentences and at least 500 were arrested, not for picketing but on charges like "obstructing sidewalk traffic."

To involve the public, Paul exploited every rhetorical possibility inherent in these women being jailed for insisting on their equal rights as citizens. In jail that fall, in two workhouses as well as the district jail, pickets insisted on political prisoner status. They refused to work, they initiated hunger strikes, and they withstood physical assault and internment in psychopathic wards. They used their attorneys, visitors, and even sympathetic guards to get details out to the press. The story became not just the repeated appearance of pickets, but the repeated tortures enacted by a tyrannical government on its unrepresented citizens and the valor of those using nonviolent techniques to fight back.

Placing Herself in Jail

By the beginning of October, Paul decided that she needed to enter the jail on a long sentence to provide a symbol of American persecution of women. A letter written by her sister Helen from Moorestown on October 8, one that relates their religious dictates to suffrage, indicates that Alice informed her family of her plans for an extended sentence before she entered jail: "Dear beloved sister—We want to know if there is anything we can do for thee— Mamma wanted me to write thinking perhaps thee might want money for the first bail or something—or might not be well enough to stand the prison life—if we can assist in any way be sure to let us know—in the meantime all our sympathy and love is with thee" In October, Alice courted repeated sentences, knowing they would lead to the longer term—seven months— which she began serving on October 20. In embracing difficult choices, first of a long jail term and then of hunger striking, Paul involved herself not just as an organizer or executive but as a primary participant who was risking

Alice Paul leads a protest. Paul and Dora Lewis leading the picket line after police announced mandatory six-month prison sentences for pickets. The banner reads: "The time has come to conquer or submit for there is but one choice—we have made it."

her life for the cause, just as Gandhi would take on his own hunger striking for Indian independence.

During her jail term, Paul was constructed as a small and physically weak, ethereal person, yet one with the mental strength to endure torture. In its stark presentation of her arrest, the *Suffragist* declared the unthinkable in the article's first line: "Alice Paul is in jail." She had been put there, the article continued, by "Administration tools," with Wilson the ultimate controller of police and courts. Adjectives like "frail," "little," and "delicate" stressed her ill health and small size ("Seven Months Sentence"). In articles and speeches in October and November, audiences were repeatedly asked to imagine all she endured. Katharine Rolston Fisher, for example, declared at a dinner for pickets in late October: "What one of us can think of Alice Paul, of Lucy Burns, as prisoners of the National Government, and not feel on her own body, and on her own spirit, the coarse prison clothing, the galling weight of prison rules?" ("Prisoners of Freedom"). Circular letters and letters sent to politicians indicated that prison wardens were endangering Paul's life (Burns, Letter to Honorable Gwynne Gardiner). Lucy Burns asked several physicians to make statements for the press "condemning the use of forcible feeding when practiced against such a delicate woman as Miss Paul" (Letter to Caroline Katzenstein). She frequently quoted the court-appointed physician's admission of Paul's saintly fortitude as well as her vulnerability: "There is a spirit like Joan of Arc, and it is as useless to try to change it as it was to change Joan of Arc. She will die but she will never give up" (Irwin, *Story of Alice Paul* 294). As journalist Nathaniel Herbert recognized in January of 1918, Paul's determined actions and the public portrayal of them, as a persecution endured by the frailest of women, wielded great power: "Alice Paul starving in jail was bigger than the biggest enemy of the suffrage amendment, more powerful than the slipperiest friend or the bitterest rival."

A Large Group Serving Jail Terms

Although Paul was the central figure and symbol, the experience of the many women imprisoned proved that this was not just the determination or stubbornness of one woman: others suffered well-publicized indignities and cruelties that enabled the group to demonstrate their unity and wield the powerful weapons of nonviolence. Women whose detailed stories appeared in the *Suffragist* as well as the daily press included Lucy Burns, Eleanor Brannan, Sarah Colvin, Alice Cosu, Dorothy Day, Matilda Hall Gardner, Peggy Johns, Ernestine Hara Kettler, Mary Nolan, Doris Stevens, Anna Kelton Wiley, and Rose Winslow. In asking these women to picket when she knew they would be arrested, to enter prison when she knew they would be mistreated, and to instigate hunger strikes with the specter of force-feeding in front of them, Paul knew that these women's sacrifice would be huge. But she also knew that the effect on the public of the stories of this group and of each individual within it would also be huge. Jail brought on the specter of "ladies" housed with common criminals, rudely handled by male guards, choosing to starve themselves, and held down by guards who shoved tubes down their throats. Such details of long jail terms, Paul knew, would make suffrage into an unavoidable crisis for the president, even in wartime.

To staff the picket line as these longer jail terms became inevitable, by the end of the summer Paul wrote to many women to urge them to come to Washington. As they heard about this new round of confrontations, many of them, like Katharine Morey, said, "All right, then we will have to have people *willing* to be arrested, and I will come down and I will be one" (Letter to Alice Paul). As sentences lengthened, Paul made sure that new recruits knew what they might be getting into. She wrote to Mrs. C. Z. Klauder on September 5, 1917, for example, asking her to come to picket on September 8 at noon, but stressing she would face arrest and a possible sentence of sixty days. Ever the persuader, however, Paul wanted to make the effort seem worth the risk: this increasingly controversial stage of picketing, she argued, "is going to win the Federal Amendment within a short time." If Klauder could not come for that day, Paul urged, she should come for subsequent days of picketing. To Elizabeth Marot on September 22, 1917, she said that "We need people urgently to keep the picket going," and she argued that the vigor with which the administration had tried to crush the picketing testified to its effectiveness.

For those women who came in the fall, entering the picket line with jail almost assured was a very difficult choice. In her autobiography, Sarah Colvin discussed her husband's reaction to her being jailed. An army officer at Ft. McHenry, he opposed her plans to picket and accept a jail term as embarrassing for him, as a career liability. Given his oft-expressed contempt for pickets and their jail terms, she did not tell him of her intentions before she left to join the picket line one morning. They did discuss her choices, in their own way, when she returned home from jail: "The morning I was released I went back to Baltimore, and Dr. Colvin and I had a very full and frank discussion of the whole situation. After the first shock of his learning that I could possibly consider anything of more importance than his career, which had caused him really great distress, and further that, according to his estimation, I had misused the word 'principle,' we did as we have always done, finished the subject and never discussed it since. It has made no difference in our lives" (142).

Many women found their participation shocked their families and made them suspect members of their communities. Louisine Havemeyer told her comrades, and later said in her speeches, that telegrams from her family expressed their extreme shock and distaste: "From them I gleaned I had stripped the family tree, I had broken its branches, I had torn up its roots and laid it prostrate in the sorrowing dust. What had the whole treeful of innocents ever done that I should treat them thus?" ("Prison Special" 672). But as these women faced dismay and rejection, they were finding camaraderie and inspiration in the small group of women who had picketed and been arrested with them.

Because longer sentences resulted from repeated picketing, many busy wives and workers picketed once and accepted short sentences, but then did not return to the line. Ernestine Hara Kettler said that when she left jail she stayed in Washington for a week or two: "I was even tempted to go back again on the picket line, but I just couldn't stand the thought of going back to that workhouse again. After thirty days of that dreadful food and the fear of what might happen to the next contingent that was arrested, I just wasn't courageous enough to go back again. I felt horrified by the different things that could happen to you in prison" (261–62). Although Paul encouraged women to feel strong and involved, and she worked at getting them to Washington, she knew that each one had to make her own decision about returning to the line.

As she secured more pickets from across the country, Paul also tried to manage who went to jail for what length of time—to keep leaders both in and outside of prison. On November 8, 1917, for example, Lucy Burns wrote to Caroline Katzenstein in Philadelphia about deciding between going to jail and fulfilling a speaking engagement there: "I have not been able to make up my mind as to whether I would go to prison at the end of the week. Although I would go if it were necessary, because I think that this picket line is the last whack of the hammer that will drive the nail right home, on the other hand, if it is not necessary it would be silly to go. If you like you can advertise my name. It will always sound perfectly well to say that a speaker could not arrive because she is now in jail, and Miss Arnold can easily send you another."

Although it was difficult to continue staffing the picket lines and keep her organization running as jail terms lengthened, Paul was determined that only women would stand on the line: they would thus continue to develop and demonstrate their self-respect, strength, and solidarity. In September, when in a letter Miss H. E. Brennan suggested having men picket, Paul wrote back that they couldn't get enough to make a clear showing—and the women were making a clear showing on their own. Paul claimed to this supporter that each day made their position stronger and the government's position "more difficult to defend."

The Quest for Political Prisoner Status

As they entered jails and served their terms, Paul instructed the pickets to ask, in court and in the jails, for political prisoner status, for recognition that they were being jailed because they had opposed the government and not because they had interfered with sidewalks, streets, or statues. Paul wanted to emphasize that the charge of obstructing traffic was just a dodge, that these women were being arrested for opposing their government. She wanted to make clear, at the trials and in prison, that women were being denied the basic rights of citizenry, including freedom of speech.

In many European countries, as Paul had learned when she entered prison in England, political prisoners, those jailed for opposing the policies of a government, might be granted a special status: in general, they were not searched upon arrest, not housed with the rest of the prisoner population, not required to wear prison garb, and not force-fed if they engaged in hunger strikes. But this status was a European tradition, from France, Austria, Germany, and England. In the United States, the only separate status granted to those who might be considered political prisoners, like men who refused to serve in the armed services, was traditionally the right, in a federal penitentiary, to the minimum-security status afforded to other low-risk prisoners. Such incarceration might occur without high walls, barbed-wire fences, barred windows or armed guards; with less supervision and greater freedom of dress and movement; and with visitation rights. But such concessions were not guaranteed (Levy and Miller 6–7). To create a separate legal status would be to acknowledge a type of persecution the government had never recognized as occurring on American soil.

In courtrooms, Paul believed, the request for a political status that didn't exist, a request that had to be denied, could lead to a dramatic portrayal of the hypocrisies of American law and government. In making this request, these women constructed themselves as unrepresented protestors: they had not been allowed to vote on the laws and regulations for which they were being held accountable, they were often not told of the charges, they were not given access to juries because the courts were pretending that these were traffic violations, and they were not being given consistent sentences. Four women arrested on September 22 dramatically made this argument about their lack of basic civil rights when they were tried on the following day:

"We are not citizens. We are not represented. We are silently, peacefully attempting to gain the freedom of twenty million women in the United States of America. We have broken no law. We are guilty of no crime. We have been illegally arrested. We demand our freedom, and we shall continue to ask for it until the government acts" (Irwin, *The Story of Alice Paul* 251). At this trial, the four women were sentenced to thirty days in Occoquan Workhouse and granted no recognition of their political plight.

On October 8, when Paul was tried with ten other women for their picketing on October 6, she looked for a more visual representation of the court's denial of the basic rights of citizenry. This time, the women chose a silent protest to represent their own silencing through arrests and jail terms, as Inez Irwin described the scene: "They refused to recognize the Court. They would not be sworn. They would not question witnesses. They would not speak in their own behalf." Only Alice Paul spoke, to insure that everyone there understood the import of their actions. She told the judge, "We do not wish to make any plea before this Court. We do not consider ourselves subject to this Court since, as an unenfranchised class, we have nothing to do with the making of the laws which have put us in this position" (Irwin, *The Story of Alice Paul* 251).

To continue this conversation about the nature of their arrests, Lucy Burns and other suffragists housed at Occoquan Workhouse in September began asking the warden to treat them as political prisoners, backing up their demand with the threat of a hunger strike (Kettler 242–43). On October 15 they sent a petition to the Commissioners of the District of Columbia, who oversaw the jails, asking for this political prisoner status because they had been unjustly sentenced as they exercised the right of peaceful petition, a right that had been recognized in Wilson's earlier pardon. Reprinted in the *Suffragist* on November 3 and quoted in many newspapers, the petition focused on their demands and their reasons for them:

> As political prisoners we, the undersigned, refuse to work while in prison. We have taken this stand as a matter of principle, after careful consideration, and from it we shall not recede.
>
> This action is a necessary protest against an unjust sentence . . . we were exercising the right of peaceful petition, guaranteed by the Constitution of the United States. . . .
>
> Conscious of having acted in accordance with the highest standards of citizenship, we ask the Commissioners of the District to grant us the rights due to political prisoners. We ask that we no longer be segregated and confined under locks and bars in small groups, but permitted to see each other and that Miss Lucy Burns . . . be released from solitary confinement and given back to us.

We ask exemption from prison work, that our legal right to counsel be recognized, to have food sent to us from the outside, to supply ourselves with writing material for as much correspondence as we may need, to receive books, letters, newspapers, our relatives and friends. ("Political Prisoners" 8)

Much to the wardens' dismay, this protest began to influence other prisoners. Suffragist Ernestine Hara Kettler, for example, noted about the refusal to work: "All the women in that sewing room took an example from us. I think there were probably about a dozen other women in that room. When they saw that we weren't working, they took heart. They could be real courageous. They wouldn't work either. There was nothing that could be done about the whole room. I think that's what bothered the superintendent. He wouldn't have cared so much if the others had continued to work" (256–57). As Paul had hoped, this request for a nonexistent status (political prisoner), one that no American should need to pursue, was causing an uproar within the prison and leading to a serious questioning of civil rights without.

At this point, Paul entered jail for her seven-month sentence. After she went into the District Jail on October 20—authorities were separating suffragists into two spaces—Paul repeatedly made requests for political prisoner status. With Paul now involved in this debate from within an American prison, Wilson felt he had to act. He now made clear to his prison wardens that they could not even acknowledge the possibility of political-prisoner status. Wardens needed to remind the women that their arrests pertained to traffic and assembly, not to freedom of speech or opposition to the president. He then sent an associate, journalist David Lawrence, to meet with Paul in jail. Lawrence told Paul that this request had no likelihood of being fulfilled because it would then have to apply to conscientious objectors and offenders under the Espionage Act, none of whom were recognized as political prisoners: "It would be the easiest thing in the world for the Administration to treat you as political prisoners; to put you in a fine house in Washington; give you the best of food; take the best of care of you; but if we treat you as political prisoners, we would have to treat other groups which might arise in opposition to the war program as political prisoners too, and that would throw a bomb in our war program. It would never do. It would be easier to give you the Federal Amendment than to treat you as political prisoners" (Irwin, *The Story of Alice Paul* 262). Throughout the fall, Paul kept pleading for political-prisoner status, not because she expected to be granted it but because she knew that this argument kept their jailing, and thus the tyranny of the government's treatment of women, before the public.

Publicizing Prison Conditions

As she fought for political-prisoner status, Paul also insisted that her whole organization work on publicizing the details of the harsh treatment that pickets were receiving in both jails, made more poignant by their status as middle-class, educated Americans. As soon as women entered Occoquan Workhouse in Virginia, to continue the sense of outrage that their two-month sentence elicited, they publicized every shocking bodily detail of their treatment there. Matilda Hall Gardner talked with her attorney and later provided the *Suffragist* with details about having her clothing removed, being sent into showers with open doors, wearing workhouse clothes, eating unpalatable wormy food, living in enforced silence, and working—or trying to avoid working—long hours each day. In the *Suffragist,* Doris Stevens also created a stark picture of a woman stripped: "No woman there will ever forget the shock and the hot resentment that rushed over her when she was told to undress before the entire company. . . . We silenced our impulse to resist this indignity, which grew more poignant as each woman nakedly walked across the great vacant space to the doorless shower" ("Justice" 7). A complaint filed by Lucy Burns in September also concerned harsh bodily conditions: "The water they drink is kept in an open pail, from which it is ladled into a drinking cup. The prisoners frequently dip the drinking cup directly into the pail. The same piece of soap is used for every prisoner. As the prisoners in Occoquan are sometimes afflicted with disease, this practice is appallingly negligent." Virginia Bovee, who had been an officer at the Workhouse, was willing to join these suffragists in protest by signing an affidavit: "The beans, hominy, rice, corn meal . . . and cereal have all had worms in them. Sometimes the worms float on top of the soup. Often they are found in the corn bread" (Irwin *The Story of Alice Paul* 276).

Similar horrid details also came from prisoners at the District Jail. Sarah Colvin described specifics in press bulletins that she also recalled in her 1940 autobiography: "[I]t was full of rats. I minded them more than anything else. I can still hear them squealing and fighting, and the sound they made as they fell from the table to the floor and scurried away" (137). In a well-publicized maneuver, women at the District Jail had samples of food smuggled out to Dr. Harvey Wiley, who did a thorough inspection of their contents. His wife, Anna Kelton Wiley, who had been part of the club-women deputation to the president in 1914, had been sentenced to a fifteen-day term there on November 17. Harvey Wiley had become chief chemist of the United States Department of Agriculture in 1902, heading a well-publicized study of chemical preservatives. His efforts led to the 1906 Pure Food and

Drugs Act, enforced by his Bureau of Chemistry. In 1912 he had taken over the labs at *Good Housekeeping Magazine,* where he established their well-advertised *Good Housekeeping* Seal of Approval. His specific analysis of the milk, pea soup, and cornbread secured public attention, as did his final clever comparison of the suffrage campaign to a religious cause: "'A Diet of Worms won one reformation, and I expect it will win another,' Dr. Wiley declared. 'The inhuman methods of treatment accorded the women in the District jail and at Occoquan are such as justly to excite the condemnation of the whole nation'" ("Dr. Harvey Wiley Protests"). Emanating from both prison sites, such details involved readers in the plight of the group and of individuals within it, just as Sara Bard Field's specific reports of the calamities occurring on her cross-country trip had so enriched reporting of her journey.

Hunger Striking, Forced-Feeding, and the Mental Ward

To establish the women's presence in jail as nonviolent protestors, Paul and Rose Winslow immediately decided on a hunger strike, a nonviolent show of determined protest, one that Paul, like Gandhi, wanted to take on herself. When women began going to jail in June, the possibility of a hunger strike had greatly stirred press interest. The *New York Times,* for example, on June 27, 1917, had used the headline "Nine More Pickets Seized at White House" and then the subheading "Court Hearing Today—Rumors of Hunger Strike Are Revived." The article asserted that with the sentencing of these nine "the coveted goal of the American militant suffragists—a hunger strike in jail—appeared in sight today." But it took the longer sentence, when Paul and Burns were in jail in October, for women to take on this life-risking nonviolent tactic, made especially poignant through Paul's much-publicized physical vulnerability.

At the District Jail, Paul and Rose Winslow started a hunger strike, as they told their attorneys who publicized their decisions, to protest the prison's denial of their fellow inmates' diet requests—for a cup of milk at each meal and an egg a day or permission to buy both at the prison store. The assistant physician had ordered this improvement of the prisoners' diet, but the chief physician, Dr. Gannon, rescinded his order because he did not consider it his duty to maintain prisoners in sound health but only to treat those who became ill. Paul and Winslow also began the hunger strike, as they told their attorneys and visitors, to "secure for their comrades treatment accorded political prisoners in every civilized country but our own." Even in prerevolutionary Russia under the czars, they argued to the warden, in *Suffragist* articles, and in press releases, these rights had been granted to political prisoners. Besides fighting for the imprisoned women's health and their political rights,

Paul chose hunger striking to show that she was willing to give her life for suffrage. Using her own body to demonstrate her beliefs, as she knew, would have a strong effect on her comrades and on the nation. Her own sacrifice could thus constitute a powerful form of nonviolent persuasion and pressure because no warden wanted to be responsible for the severe illness or death of this well-known leader (Letter to Honorable Gwynne Gardiner).

As Paul's hunger strike continued, she was threatened with forced feeding, a terrible ordeal that she remembered well from England. In response, her supporters telegrammed commissioners and the warden and secured physicians to make statements for the press about the danger of a hard tube being forced down the throat to shove food into the stomach. Although protests appeared in newspapers, the threats of force-feeding turned into reality, shocking news that Paul wanted immediately released. After she received a letter from Paul, Dora Lewis wrote to her family members that "Miss Paul and Rose Winslow are being forcibly fed—inhuman and abominable" and asked them to circulate the news (Bacon, *Mothers of Feminism* 197). Affecting details reported by Rose Winslow and smuggled out of jail by friends and sympathetic prison employees reached many suffragists and reporters: "Yesterday was a bad day for me in feeding. I was vomiting continuously during the process. The tube had developed an irritation somewhere that is painful. . . . Don't let them tell you we take this well. Miss Paul vomits much. I do too. It's the nervous reaction, and I can't control it much. We think of the coming feeding all day. It is horrible" (Stevens, *Jailed for Freedom* 118–19).

By the time the feeding began, Paul had been separated from Winslow and put in solitary confinement, and fewer stories thus emanated from her. But her delicate health and this lack of news also made strong press. Winslow reported, in a note smuggled out by her brother, that "Alice Paul dreaded forcible feeding frightfully, and I hate to think how she must be feeling" ("Force Yard of Jail"). After word got out about Winslow and Paul, fourteen other women, both at Occoquan Workhouse and in the District Jail, began their own hunger strikes, with different women suffering different effects, all publicized in piteous detail. Dora Lewis, for example, told her friends that "Dr. Gannon then forced the tube through my lips and down my throat, I gasping and suffocating with the agony of it. I didn't know where to breathe from, and everything turned black when the liquid began pouring in" (Irwin, *The Story of Alice Paul* 288). Lucy Burns wrote of the feeding tube that "It hurts nose and throat very much and makes nose bleed freely. Tube drawn out covered with blood. Operation leaves one very sick. Food dumped directly into stomach feels like a ball of lead. Left nostril, throat, and muscles of neck very sore all night" (Stevens, *Jailed for Freedom* 125).

Washington, D.C. jail hospital. Hospital at D.C. jail where Alice Paul was held during her hunger strike.

While Paul used prison sentences to stir a debate about political-prisoner status and then secured further attention by undertaking a hunger strike joined by other inmates, she next encountered a tremendously trying experience that she used to further demonstrate what could happen to women when they lacked the basic rights of citizens. First, she was taken in a weakened condition to the prison hospital. There she was held incommunicado: no attorney and no family member or friend was allowed to see her. Prison officials threatened that if she did not end her hunger strike she would be transferred to the prison system's psychopathic ward in St. Elizabeth's Insane Asylum, a state institution for the insane. When she refused, she was taken to a cell in the prison's psychopathic ward, placed in solitary confinement, and treated like a mental patient. The specific details of this treatment, which she reported as soon as she could, were very frightening: "There were two windows in the room. Dr. Gannon immediately ordered one window nailed from top to bottom. He then ordered the door leading into the hallway taken down and an iron-barred cell door put in its place. He departed with the command to a nurse to 'observe her.'" Paul was interrupted hourly by a nurse flashing a light in her face, even during the night: "This ordeal was the most terrible torture, as it prevented my sleeping for more than a few minutes at a time" (Stevens, *Jailed for Freedom* 117). Doctors then came to tell her that she was not in a stable mental condition and needed thorough examination. When she continued her hunger striking, she was force-fed, three times a day—a further display of administrative force. Although Dr. White, the head of St. Elizabeth's Insane Asylum, would not consent to have her transferred to his hospital, she was treated as an unstable mental patient at the prison.

For Paul, this removal to a mental ward at the prison and threat of placement in a mental hospital provided strong evidence of men's power over women. In the second half of the nineteenth century, women had been frequently diagnosed as victims of hysteria, a mental illness caused by women's supposed emotional imbalance. "Hysteric" became, some historians believe, a new scientific replacement of "witch," a means of labeling "women who were in some way deviant, in some way different: women who did not fit" (Ussher 60). In homes, a primary treatment was the rest cure, involving seclusion, bland food, restraint from reading and other mental activity, and sensory deprivation, the length of the treatment determined by physicians. In asylums, to which husbands and doctors could remand women for indefinite periods, treatments included massage and application of electrical current; study of photographs of the patient to appeal to natural feminine vanity and foster self-control; management by straitjackets and leg irons meant to teach silence and decorum; and even surgical removal of the clitoris, believed to help women govern themselves (Showalter 75–86). Force-feeding, also, had been used on "lunatics in the old madhouses" (Showalter 162). In the literature of the developing field of psychiatry, the suspect behaviors that indicated the need for these treatments included many facts of Paul's life: the failure to marry and have a family, an overly zealous pursuit of education, public displays of strong opinions, unnatural desires for privacy and independence, and failure to eat regularly.

For Alice Paul, a jail sentence was something with a particular, specified duration, like one month or even seven, but remand to a mental facility could be indefinite and the treatments horrifying. Thus, although her mother and sister Helen generally stayed in New Jersey during the long suffrage campaign, when Alice was put in the psychiatric ward, Helen came from Moorestown immediately and stood in the jail yard trying to contact her sister through a window. Helen planned to hire attorneys to represent the family if Paul needed help securing release from this dangerous place ("Row Over Hunger Strike").

Through her sister and sympathetic staff, Paul publicized as many details as possible concerning this most threatening form of incarceration of women. In an article printed in the *Suffragist* on November 24, Paul declared that the physicians and nurses used various means, including the regular observation, "to make one know one's sanity was doubted." She argued that she had been subjected to this form of imprisonment and "correction" to advertise that the movement's volatile leader had lost her mind—and, if possible, to make her do so. As she complained to the doctors and wardens about this form of incarceration, the *Suffragist* reported, she was repeatedly told that "I was not in a mental condition, as I must of course know, to judge of things for myself" ("Note from Alice Paul"). As Lavinia Dock recognized in "Alice Paul in Prison," such mistreatment could have caused the effect that the doctors sought to label: "Here a conspiracy, medieval in its blind brutishness, is being carried on to make it appear that Alice Paul needs to be kept 'under observation.' Medical persecution is subtly applied, to shake, perhaps, if may be her mental serenity, or cause such signs of resentment or alarm as might be reported as evidence of mental instability." For Paul, this treatment provided a strong demonstration of women's need for control over their own lives, control that had to begin with their attaining the vote. When Dr. White of St. Elizabeth's Insane Asylum later came to see her at her headquarters, she expressed her great indebtedness to him, as she also did to her lawyer Dudley Field Malone, because of the power that the prison warden and examining doctors had over her: "I might have stayed there forever—like many, many, many, many, many women over the country" (Fry).

A Well-Planned Public Response

Instead of concluding that Paul was insane and required treatment, her colleagues knew immediately that she was being unjustly held and took well-documented action to rescue their leader. The wardens wouldn't let Malone see her, but he was allowed to speak with Rose Winslow. Malone had resigned as Collector of the Port of New York on September 7 in protest over the jail terms for pickets, causing a spate of positive press for the NWP. The suffragists were thus associated with a man who was willing to give up his own career path and his close association with the president for their cause. The *New York Post* on September 10 reported that pickets were not "getting a square deal" when they were arrested for disturbing traffic and thus "Mr. Malone's resignation is very much to his honor" ("Honorable Politician"). When Malone came to the District Jail to get Paul out of the psychopathic ward, he came as a well-known Democrat and past associate of Wilson. After she had spent a week there, he obtained a writ of habeas corpus from a U.S. District Court in Virginia, ordering her release from unlawful restraint. This writ led to her transfer back to a regular hospital ward.

While sending out press bulletins and aiding Dudley Malone, NWP members sought a visual demonstration to further publicize their belief in their leader and the injustice of her treatment. On November 10 women left headquarters in one of the longest picket lines of the campaign. Forty-one women from sixteen different states, who came to Washington in response to circular letters and newspaper articles, held signs supporting suffrage and protesting Paul's treatment. To halt such a large demonstration, the police made immediate arrests but later let the women go. When they again formed a long line the next day, however, judges decided to give the thirty-five pickets sentences ranging from six days to six months, with the longest sentence for repeat offenders, like Lucy Burns. The judge gave the lightest sentence, of six days, to Mary Nolan of Jacksonville, Florida, a seventy-three year old woman with a lame foot, and urged her to pay the fine. But she chose incarceration, an instance of bravery that was widely reported in the press. Although these women were sentenced to the District Jail, they were in fact taken to Occoquan Workhouse. Prison officials feared placing the entire group together and letting these women near Alice Paul.

Publicizing a "Night of Terror" and Other Abuse

When these pickets entered Occoquan, there occurred another well-publicized incident of horrendous treatment: the women called it the "Night of

Terror." Like Paul's confinement in a mental ward, this was certainly not a form of horror that the women sought, but it was one that made a huge rhetorical effect as their stories reached the press. Under orders from Raymond Whittaker, superintendent of the Occoquan Workhouse, as many as forty guards with clubs went on a rampage, brutalizing the jailed suffragists. According to many affidavits, women were grabbed, dragged, beaten, kicked, and choked. In the *Suffragist* and in press bulletins, Mary Nolan created a powerful account of that night, of cruel, uncontrolled men beating reserved and modest women.

When the women entered the workhouse, Nolan reported, Dora Lewis asked that they be treated as political prisoners and asked to see the warden. After keeping them waiting for hours, Superintendent Whittaker "burst in like a tornado" followed by a crowd of men, many not in uniform. When Lewis rose to address him, Whittaker said, "You shut up. I have men here to handle you." Then the men took Lewis away. Other men grabbed Nolan and dragged her through the corridors; she could hear women crying out as they suffered similar treatment, incurring injuries as they were taken to dark and filthy cells. Nolan wrote that as guards carried Dorothy Day, "a frail girl," they twisted her arms above her head and twice banged her arm down on an iron bench. Nolan lost her balance and fell against an iron bed, as did Dora Lewis as they threw her into the room: "We thought she was dead. She didn't move. We were crying over her as we lifted her to the pad on my bed, when Mr. Whittaker came to the door and told us not to dare to speak, or he would put the brace and bit in our mouths and the straitjacket on our bodies. We were so terrified we kept very still" (Stevens, *Jailed for Freedom* 123). Lewis turned out to be only stunned, but Alice Cosu suffered heart pain and vomiting. The suffragists were offered no food until three the next afternoon, a day in which they continued to insist on their status as political prisoners.

In the *Suffragist,* in interviews, and in circular letters, other participants would add their own details to this horrifying story. Dorothy Day, then a writer for the *Call* and the *Masses,* who had come down to Washington to join the picket line at the urging of a friend, noted that "there were two guards to every woman" (75). She recounted her own path to the cells: "I have no doubt but that I struggled every step of the way from the administration building to the cell block where we were being taken. It was a struggle to walk by myself, to wrest myself loose from the torture of those rough hands. We were then hurled onto some benches and when I tried to pick myself up and again join Peggy [Baird] in my blind desire to be near a friend, I was thrown to the floor. When another prisoner tried to come to my rescue, we found ourselves in the midst of a milling crowd of guards being pummeled

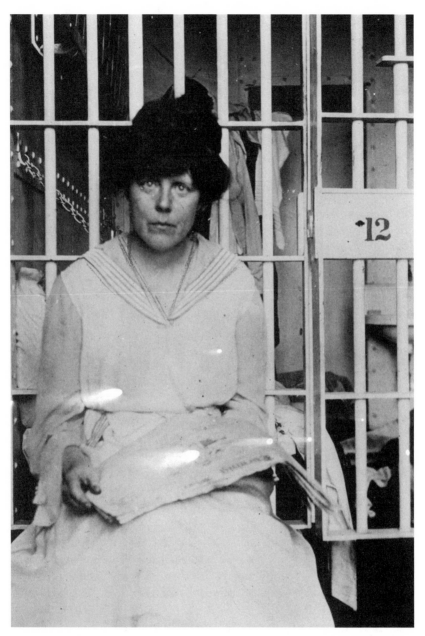

Lucy Burns at Occoquan Workhouse. Burns led most of the suffrage demonstrations and served the most time in jail.

and pushed and kicked and dragged, so that we were scarcely conscious, in the shock of what was taking place" (76). Several articles attested that Lucy Burns was held in a nearby cell, from whence she called the roll loudly to check on the other women, continuing even after guards "cuffed her wrists and fastened the handcuffs above her head to the cell door" and threatened her with a straightjacket and gag. Mrs. Henry Butterworth was taken alone into the men's cell and told that "they could do what they pleased with her" (Irwin, *The Story of Alice Paul* 283; "Move Militants from Workhouse"). Paula Jakobi, who was also dragged out of the main room, especially commented about male control and female humiliation during that night and subsequent days: there were only open toilets for these cells; the doors were uncurtained; the guards were men. Eleanor Brannan, wife of a prominent New York physician, wrote in an affadavit about the superintendent's firm control on every action: "I firmly believe that, no matter how we behaved, Whittaker had determined to attack us as part of the government's plan to suppress picketing. . . . Its perfectly unexpected ferocity stunned us. . . . Whittaker, in the center of the room, directed the whole attack, inciting the guards to every brutality" (Stevens, *Jailed for Freedom* 93–94).

As they could, weakened from their Night of Terror, some of these women began to hunger strike, led by Lucy Burns, to protest their treatment as well as Paul's placement in a psychopathic ward. On the seventh day, when Burns and Lewis were so weak that Whittaker feared for their lives, he had them forcibly fed. Other women were eating little because of the worms in the food—"old stuff that was rancid and sitting in warehouses heaven knows how many years" (Kettler 258). Burns and Lewis were then removed to the District Jail to separate them from the others, but even without them a hunger strike continued at Occoquan Workhouse. These women also kept refusing to work or wear prison clothes. Housed in separate cells, they were told that they were the only ones continuing to protest and that no news of their plight had reached the outside.

Their next ordeal occurred as these suffragists had to fight against the same threat of psychopathic wards used against Paul in the District Jail. The incident began when Peggy Johns became sick from the poor food and was hospitalized at Occoquan Workhouse. When her friend Ernestine Hara Kettler went to visit her in the hospital, she found Johns in civilian clothes, made ready for transfer to a psychopathic facility in Washington, D.C. As soon as Kettler found out, she gathered women then walking in the yard, and they forced their way into the superintendent's office, claiming that Johns could not be sent to a mental ward unless she was accompanied by her lawyer, that without such guardianship "we had no assurance what would happen to her, and that, above all things, we wanted security for our women." Superintendent Whittaker, Kettler claimed, tore the phone out of the wall to keep them from dialing their headquarters, and then he called in other prisoners and they "beat the hell out of us. I was so little that I was scared to death to get in the crowd and I was on the outside. I saw some women on the floor, being trampled" (259). Although Johns did go on to a hospital in Washington because of her weakened condition, this altercation kept her from a psychopathic ward.

As the conditions of prisoners at Occoquan grew steadily worse, Dudley Malone, along with another NWP lawyer, Matthew O'Brien, filed a writ of habeas corpus to compel the government to bring the prisoners into court and show cause why they should not be taken to the District Jail, where they had been originally sentenced. These lawyers contended that the government had no legal right to incarcerate women in Virginia who had been arrested and sentenced in the District of Columbia. Although Whittaker tried to keep his whereabouts secret to avoid being served with the writ, he was finally served at his home late at night and ordered to produce the prisoners in court on November 23.

In court, these women made quite a visual demonstration of what Doris Stevens labeled "administrative terrorism." Their physical presence demonstrated their nonviolent sacrifice: "all the people there experienced a shock when the slender file of women, haggard, red-eyed, sick, came to the bar. Some were able to walk to their seats; others were so weak that they had to be stretched out on the wooden benches with coats propped under their heads for pillows. Still others bore the marks of the attack on the 'night of terror'" (129). In a courtroom filled with journalists, faced with the palpable visual rhetoric of abused women, the judge felt required to take action: he released Eleanor Brannan, Mrs. Henry Butterworth, and Cora Weeks because they were judged too ill for further incarceration, and he allowed the twenty-five other women to transfer to the Washington District Jail.

At this second site, these women, though injured and exhausted, continued their nonviolent protest, causing further overreactions and bad publicity for the government. There, these prisoners sang suffrage songs day and night to protest the denial of books, pens, and paper and encouraged other prisoners to join them, much to the dismay of the jail's Superintendent Zinklan. They also chose continuous noise-making to illustrate their plight: "They took turns through the day and night screaming and yowling" (Brownlow 79). As a district commissioner who controlled the District Jail, Louis Brownlow now remanded them to an unused prison site filled with models and gadgets stored by the Patent Office. Brownlow had these materials removed and the place fitted with new paint, pillows, and blankets. When the women arrived, they immediately began a hunger strike, which met some very odd opposition from Brownlow. He installed two gas stoves and got "six women cooks so that each stove could be manned in eight-hour shifts around the clock." When the women went on a hunger strike, Brownlow recalled, "I kept those cooks busy day and night frying ham. I was convinced that the fragrance of frying ham was the greatest stimulus to appetite known to man. It was terribly hard on the women" (80). But they did not succumb.

Although Wilson wanted stories of women in jail, like stories about the picketing, to be ignored by Washington papers, and there was less coverage in the capital than in other cities, through the fall many newspapers were giving regular attention to these women's plight, their individual testimonies as well as their group goals. The reports drew on affidavits, press releases, *Suffragist* articles, and statements to the press made by the women themselves, their family members, and Malone and O'Brien (Stevens, Letter to Spencer Miller). Philadelphia and New York papers printed the specifics, and the Washington papers ran a less detailed version. As Dora Lewis wrote to Alva Smith Belmont on November 13, describing this coverage, it included "just the right touches—federal amendment, illegality of our arrests, treatment of our prisoners, Alice Paul in the psychopathic ward, and all the rest—just as we like to have it written." The twenty-seven papers owned by William Randolph Hearst were especially helpful, describing the choice of jail terms and the hunger striking as courageous and self-sacrificing. His *Washington Times* had at first participated in Wilson's requested boycott of coverage, but soon began to cover these courageous women on the line and in jail, as did his *Baltimore American, New York American, Daily Mirror,* and *Evening Journal.* When NAWSA, through Ida Harper, pled with Hearst to quit making martyrs of these women, Hearst refused to listen (Winkler 7).

Even staunchly antisuffragist papers reacted to these women's stories with sympathy and respect. The *New York Times* quoted John Winters Brannan, president of the Board of Trustees of Bellevue Hospital and husband of Eleanor Brannan, as he repeated the hideous stories that his wife had told him when he was finally allowed to speak with her ("Move Militants from Workhouse"). As the NWP encouraged, many stories focused on the plight of Alice Paul. During November, articles about Paul in jail occurred regularly in the *Times,* with arresting headlines such as "Miss Alice Paul on Hunger Strike" and "Row Over Hunger Strike: Militants Assert Forcible Feeding Is Unnecessary and Inhuman." The *Times'* first article about the hunger striking referred to Paul's connection with the Pankhursts, this time not to disparage her but to emphasize her understanding of the difficulties that lay ahead ("Miss Alice Paul on Hunger Strike").

This newspaper's depiction of her sister's desperate visit, after Alice had entered the psychopathic ward, ended with a scene involving the group that escorted Helen into the yard. This visit with Paul is constructed as a holy moment:

> The women walked around the jail, peering up at the window, until one of them exclaimed excitedly:
> "There's Miss Paul! There she is!"
> The delegation broke into a rush in the direction of the window, three jail guards trying vainly to stop them. . . . The women clustered beneath Miss Paul's window and called up to her, every one talking at once.
> "West Virginia greets you." "Oklahoma is with you." "New York salutes you," cried the women.
> Miss Paul raised her hand. A light flickered behind her in her room, and she was clearly silhouetted as she stood at the window. ("Force Yard of Jail")

In the *Times* and other newspapers, many articles also provided piteous details about force-feeding, along with Paul's attempts to protect herself: "I am able to prevent them from giving me half of what they bring, but I have not the strength to prevent them from forcing me to take some" ("Force Yard of Jail"). The *Times* also reported Paul's own description of being constantly observed in the psychopathic ward, hearing cries from the outside and seeing no one other than doctors and nurses: a horrifying "attempt at intimidation" ("Miss Paul Removed").

With public pressure mounting as a result of press coverage, the government felt the need to act. Wilson and his subordinates certainly had to recognize that arrests didn't stop these protestors; neither did jail terms, psychopathic wards, force-feeding, or violent attacks. Their next decision was simply to let them out. On November 27 most of the suffrage prisoners, including Alice Paul, were suddenly released. By this date, Paul had been on a hunger strike for twenty-two days. Nine who had not been on a hunger strike, including Dorothy Day, remained in jail until November 28 ("Suffrage Pickets Freed").

As these prisoners came out of their jail cells, Paul took immediate action to insure further press coverage of the details of their treatment and of their campaign. As she had done earlier with Wilson's pardon, she immediately argued in the *Suffragist* and in press releases that this sudden commutation proved the sentences had been unjust. Paul also held large, well-publicized dinners to celebrate the suffragists' release. These occasions, to which reporters were invited, provided further opportunities to define the nature of their cause and their activism. At one dinner, Katharine Rolston Fisher argued that in a true democracy these upstanding women who had broken no laws would not have been jailed. At another dinner, for three hundred people, Gilson Gardner created a definition of their heroism by considering the incendiary word *militant*: "They have not been militant in the sense that they have defied law or done anything which is illegal. They have been militants only in the sense that they had the courage to stand for that in which they believe and to put themselves—their health, their safety, and if necessary their lives into the balance for what they believed" ("Jubilee Dinner for the Pickets" 10). When Lucy Burns asked the group to thank Alice Paul, they all immediately sprang to their feet.

To take further rhetorical advantage of all that had happened, Paul also sent women across the country to give speeches that would publicize this treatment: Maud Younger to the South, Dora Lewis and Mabel Vernon to the Midwest, Anne Martin to the West, Abby Scott Baker and Doris Stevens to the East. In some cities, authorities tried to stop them from holding meetings, but they would find a hall or a home in which to draw a crowd to hear about this persecution of American women and the glorious cause for which they sacrificed.

Throughout the fall, as suffragists entered cells, participated in hunger strikes, and endured mistreatment, their much-publicized nonviolent sacrifice began to influence the public and governmental officials. As Inez Irwin commented, "this stupid persecution was proving a boomerang" (*Angels and Amazons* 388). On September 24, with suffragists regularly being arrested and accepting their sentences without any end in sight, the House voted by 181 to 107 for a committee on woman suffrage, a group that could focus attention on suffrage and force action by the Judiciary Committee and the Rules Committee ("Real Advance"). After a burial of six months, the amendment was reported out of the Senate Suffrage Committee. Then, on October 25, with Alice Paul in jail, the president changed his position on suffrage as a war measure. At his request, Democrat Edward W. Pou, chair of the House Rules Committee, added suffrage to the emergency war measures list.

Suffragists also felt very encouraged by New York's passage of state suffrage in November. Even though Paul had not worked for state legislation, the NWP felt that its involvement with socialists and with working women had helped secure suffrage in that state. Many of New York's working women had become involved with the NWP—because of NAWSA's position on war; because of the shared martyr, Inez Milholland, who had participated in shirtwaist strikes while working with Paul; and because of the publicity provided by the *Call*, which fully covered governmental persecution of pickets (Buhle 236–38; "Socialist Help to Suffrage"). Suffrage won in New York by 187,000; in 1915 it had lost by 188,200; and in those two years 1,110,000 more Socialist voters had entered the state. George Francis, a Republican representative from New York, gave the NWP credit for helping to pass suffrage there, especially by involving union and other working men and "radicals." These efforts perhaps brought the decisive vote change in New York City itself, which was responsible for the passing of the new law, not the upstate area where suffrage traditionally had its most substantial support. On November 8, 1917, in an editorial, the *New York Times* called the victory, critically of course, a "gift from Socialism, from pacifism, from those who, unconsciously or with intent, serve Germany," pointing to the new support from labor and from antiwar activists ("Non Tali Auxilio").

When the second session of the Sixty-Fifth Congress convened on December 3, 1917, a week after all prisoners had been released, the House set January 10, 1918, to vote on the amendment. Wilson didn't discuss suffrage in his annual message to Congress on December 3, 1917, but, at the end of the year, in a surprising move, he publicly acknowledged that he could "frankly and earnestly" advise representatives to vote for the federal amendment "as an act of right and justice" (Press Release, 9 Jan. 1918). Wilson met with Democrats to tell them times had changed and they should vote for the amendment if they chose to, even though it was not in the Democratic platform and even though the party officially still advocated states' rights. A committee of Democrats who called on him on January 9, 1918, publicly released this statement: "The President had not felt at liberty to volunteer his advice to members of Congress on this important matter, but when his advice was sought he very frankly and earnestly advised us to vote for the amendment, as an act of right and justice to the women of the country and of the world" ("President Wilson Comes Out" 8). The next day the amendment passed in the House with exactly the two-thirds majority, by a vote of 274 to 136. Suffragists then needed eleven votes in the Senate and felt that victory was near (Stevens, *Jailed for Freedom* 348).

Though many of her critics did not agree, Paul viewed this huge progress as a direct result of that hard year of picketing and jail terms. The *Suffragist* claimed that publicity about their commitment and their ordeal had made the difference: Wilson's "short-sighted policy of persecution" finally had led to the volatile situation in which he was "forced" to change his attitude ("Real Advance"). Given the reaction of the press and the public, as Paul explained in a speech at headquarters, Wilson had finally come to the point that he couldn't act further against suffrage with any expectation of success, so he would have to act for it. As she described their picketing, "I think that by standing in front of the White House and calling the attention thereby of all political leaders in the country from the President down and, really, calling the attention of the whole *country* to the desire and demand of women for political equality, it gradually brought it [the amendment] to having a foremost place among the different reforms that were being advocated. It impressed upon Congress. It impressed upon the President" ("Miss Paul Speaks"). The fall's political changes, Paul felt, vindicated her belief that with Wilson's backing Democrats would act and that their votes, along with those of Republicans and Progressives, would pass the amendment. But of course she knew that the battle was not fully won and that the next months would be crucial.

For Paul and her NWP, the year 1917 was certainly a difficult one, beginning with the president's rejection of their cause when he met with the deputation from the Milholland memorial. Throughout the year, to secure the attention of the press and Congress as well as the president, these women kept taking on more nonviolent risk: picketing in front of the White House, continuing to do so during wartime, using incendiary banners like the Russian banner and the Kaiser Wilson banner, facing abusive crowds and police, accepting jail sentences instead of paying fines, broadcasting their plea for political prisoner status, hunger-striking and enduring force-feeding, being threatened with incarceration in mental facilities, and suffering the Night of Terror. In taking on and enduring these trials, women developed and demonstrated the individual strength and group unity that Paul sought for them: they were even willing to risk death for suffrage. In the latter half of the year, in the movement of the rhetorical focus from the picket line to the jail, she fully illustrated what could happen to people when they had no rights. Women could not count on benevolent male protectors: as the jail experience showed, men were not always benevolent. The indignities and tortures faced by these prisoners, whose stories were detailed in the press, proved that women needed equal rights under the law to shield themselves at the most basic level: from incarceration without crime, terms in mental wards, and physical violence. In the positive actions of the Congress and the president in the fall of 1917, Paul read the impact of the visual, nonviolent demonstrations that had been escalating throughout the year.

9. At Nonviolent War

A year of picketing, arrests, punishments, and abuse, which had begun with Inez Milholland's death on November 25, 1916, had certainly given the National Woman's Party (NWP) a national audience. Alice Paul and her supporters could not be ignored. Even some conservative groups and publications had come to respect the determination of these women. More and more people were coming to feel that in dealing with them the government had moved from protection to persecution. In February of 1918 William Randolph Hearst's *Good Housekeeping*, a conservative journal for American housewives, stated that this publication supported suffrage, not picketing, but it did "bespeak for it [picketing] a fair hearing" (Wiley 123).

In the accompanying long and positive article about suffrage, Anna Kelton Wiley portrays Paul's work in Washington as a reasonable middle-class choice: winning suffrage through state-by-state campaigns might take another century of effort, which would "compel the women of the household and of the nation to go down into the alleys, the slums, and the hidden places to persuade the ignorant immigrant, the vicious, the indifferent, and the prejudiced men to give them that which they are entitled to" (124). In the difficult times of world war, when the participation of all Americans was desperately needed, that tremendous state-by-state effort would sap women's strength, keeping them from participating "in the maintenance of the governments under which they live" (125). Wiley then moved from the federal amendment to the heroism of those women who had stood in picket lines to achieve it. In refusing to pay their fines and accepting the resulting prison terms, these women had demonstrated their physical and moral strength as well as their belief in democracy.

This article reflects the country's tone in early 1918. The suffrage question seemed to have been answered: most Americans had accepted women's right to vote. After all the previous year's demonstrations, the president had even come to support suffrage as a war measure. Because the amendment had been passed by the House and Senate, Democrats now seemed to be responding positively. Paul and the NWP did not stage more public events or continue their picketing, but instead intensified their lobbying of those senators who had still not committed themselves to suffrage. A political solution seemed near.

However, when suffrage came up for a vote in the Senate on June 27 1918, Democratic Senator James A. Reed of Missouri used the filibuster to keep the vote from occurring. In lobbying sessions, he had repeatedly argued that women knew nothing about politics and needed to confine themselves to fashions, children, and housework. As H. L. Mencken commented about Reed, he had "almost unparalleled" rhetorical skills to convince other senators of his opinions: "His shoulders were thrown back, his eyes flashed; his fine head was carried superbly; his voice, when he began, was bell-like in tone."

NWP members were furious that after all their work the rhetorical posturing of a powerful senator kept suffrage from even coming to a vote; once again women had been silenced by their own government. These suffragists believed that this filibustering would end and a positive vote would occur if Wilson did more to influence Democratic senators, as he had done on many other issues such as tariffs, monopoly legislation, and war. Doris Stevens discussed Wilson's action in this way: "President Wilson was doing a little for Suffrage, but not all he could. He was not of course doing for the Suffrage Amendment a tithe of what he did for other measures in whose success he was interested. Nothing continued to happen with monotonous, unfailing regularity" (*Jailed for Freedom* 362). Alice Paul felt that Wilson was doing a bare minimum—just enough to ingratiate himself with some suffragists while still maintaining the support of conservative Democrats, especially from the South. On August 9, 1918, the *Iowa Forum* agreed: Wilson should properly be "under the suspicion of making his support of the amendment just strong enough, or just weak enough, according as the way in which one may look at it, so that it helps on the appearances of things but does not get the amendment through" ("Annoying Suffragists").

Now Paul entered a new and difficult rhetorical period. That spring, she had thought one more visit and one more argument would bring the needed Senate votes. After Reed's filibuster and the Senate's subsequent refusal to bring suffrage up for a vote again in that session, she knew nonviolent political events were again required. As the *Iowa Forum* commented, these suffragists had to hold "the President up to a pitiless publicity until the situation ultimately [got] too hot for him and he accordingly '[came] across'" ("Annoying Suffragists").

After the violence of the Night of Terror and the betrayal of the Senate filibuster, Paul felt that suffragists—if they appeared in the press at all—were being shown as victims of both physical and psychological abuse: they had been beaten in jail and betrayed in the Senate. Wilson and the nation were proceeding with war as though he had done what he could to help these women and their piteous story had concluded. Of course Alice Paul had no interest in women's being perceived as victims or as yesterday's news. It was time once again for new nonviolent approaches to move the struggle forward.

Although she still sent out pickets bearing Wilson's declarations about democracy, Paul recognized that the regular picket line was having a limited impact. With the nation fully at war, little publicity would be gained from banners or even jail sentences. After the Night of Terror, administration forces finally realized that long jail sentences and cruel treatment were creating martyrs. In 1918 the jail sentences were mild compared to the six- and seven-month terms given out before. As the *Greenwich Graphic* of April 19, 1918, commented, "The government has learned that the activities of the party cannot be suppressed by force. It has also learned that persecution also fills the ranks and coffers of the party" ("When Patience Ceases").

Paul wanted now to move away from silence into strong speech and action, strong enough to rival a president, a government, and an army at war. By the summer of 1918, she began creating a rhetoric that visually mirrored warfare, a nonviolent version of the violent, to which she brought the same level of commitment and fierceness then being devoted to war against the Central Powers. In the fall of 1917, Paul had been constructed as the martyr and victim, but in 1918 the image she wanted was not of ethereal symbol, but of general and president—of a war leader for what was more and more a war effort. Her major weaponry in this year of world war would be neither silent protest nor any form of violence. Instead, Paul chose to wage an active campaign involving manipulation of words: the suffragists would still place their own words on banners, but now they would also speak in a variety of symbolic settings across the country, and they would begin burning Wilson's words in front of the White House, physically destroying these declarations as soon as he spoke them. When Paul lost her lease on Madison Place, to wage this war on an equal status with Wilson, she sought a new site on Lafayette Square, a huge mansion directly across the park at 14 Jackson Place in which she could house the *Suffragist* office, publicity agents, and the business office while also providing lodging for workers and even a tea room. From this formidable locale, the NWP and its supporters embarked on a nonviolent war with Wilson and his Senate, one they fully expected to win: their methods were superior to the guns and tanks being deployed in Europe, they believed, and their cause was truly democracy and justice.

An Enlarging Suffrage Army

In this rhetoric of war against Wilson and his recalcitrant Senate, Paul was finally ready to fully associate her troops with women who worked in factories supporting the war effort. Early on, even though she had arranged for one deputation of working women to visit Wilson in February of 1914, it had served Paul's purpose for the group to have a middle-class image because it lent respectability to the campaign. Later, although many working-class women joined her organization in 1916 and stood on the picket lines in 1917, it had served her purposes for the women who were sentenced to Occoquan to be from the upper classes—the publicity that came from their arrests and subsequent mistreatment was invaluable. Now, as letters sent among her organizers attested, she sought highly publicized and ongoing mass activism by a select group of essential laborers: "Pressure from women engaged in war industries seems important at this moment for the action in the Senate, to create public sentiment to back the President's idea of suffrage as a war measure to our foreign policy, etc." (Organizing Letter to Alice Paul). Just as Paul had carefully planned her presentation of other groups, she now orchestrated events involving these workers so their "demand should be firm and clean cut and clear, but not threatening. (Not at the first try off, at least)" (Organizing Letter to Alice Paul). When these women were presented as both essential war-industry workers and as solid citizens with solid demands, they could sway the nation, and threaten it a bit, during wartime. To publicize its new army for suffrage, the NWP made plans to organize noon meetings near factories, to hold street demonstrations, and to get "a perfect stream of petitions, memorials, resolutions, demands etc." that could be sent to Washington. In the big ammunition plants near Newark, as letters between organizers noted, there were six to seven thousand women who were essential to production. Even if the amounts involved at other plants weren't that big, and even if only a small percentage of the women joined in any protest activity, their action for suffrage would reach the newspapers and the government (Organizing Letter to Alice Paul).

With organizational help from Paul, steel workers from Baltimore and from the Bethlehem Steel Plant in Newcastle, Delaware, went to the Capitol each day during the last week of May 1918. They wore khaki bands on their arms with the label "Munition Worker" and stood together, holding banners and waiting to see the president. Worker Isabel Aniba spoke dramatically by portraying these munitions workers as heroic members of the armed forces: "The first Americans killed after we went into the war were killed in munition factories and most of them were women. You lose weight and get sick but still you keep on working because you know they need help. We are glad to do what we can for the war but we want the government to recognize the work we are doing by giving the vote." NWP press bulletins repeated these lines and described the women's bodies as having been transformed by the TNT with which they worked: "Their skin is yellow and the hair of those who were originally blondes is now bright orange color. The powder in which they work has this effect" (Press Bulletin, 31 May 1918). Like the NWP members who had undertaken jail terms and hunger strikes, the speeches asserted, these women had been transformed by their war efforts into war-worn soldiers. On June 15, 1918, Maryland munitions workers went to Wilson as a deputation, a type of group he found hard to avoid because of their importance to the war effort. In August and September, in the president's home state of New Jersey, NWP forces helped to plan meetings in factories and streets, making front-page news ("New Jersey Munition Works").

Newspapers reacted positively to this association of women war heroes with seekers of suffrage. The *Washington Post* on July 2, 1918, for example, made a strong connection between women's role in wartime and their right for immediate recognition as citizens: "The hesitation in granting suffrage to women who are working loyally for their country's success in war is bound to have a depressing effect. The government is placed in the position of a suppliant for the services of women while it refused to acknowledge women as voters. They are asked to labor and to sacrifice and to be taxed for a country which is not their country in the sense that they have no responsible part for its government. How long would the enthusiasm and zeal of men continue under these circumstances?" ("Pass the Amendment"). Similarly, the *Richmond Evening Journal* on July 1, 1918, sarcastically quoted local men who were expressing their gratitude for the work women did during wartime but were not supporting suffrage: "These 'intelligent, capable women' are besought to carry on men's work without, however, having the male 'right' of franchise" ("Fine Words").

By 1918 the NWP was developing a stronger and more public identification, not just with factory workers but also with controversial labor leaders who had been joining its ranks since 1916 and who could help it reach a greater number of working women. During that year, the *Suffragist* repeatedly hailed Rose Winslow, who had been a hunger striker along with Paul,

as "one of the most dramatic figures in the latter phases of the fight for suffrage." At a June meeting in Detroit, Winslow spoke of women's historical
lack of power within industry and their lack of suffrage as an entwined pair.
Women had been hesitant to join trade unions, she claimed, because they
viewed themselves as, and were treated as, inferior workers. "They need the
vote to give them a sense of power," she argued, power with which they could
work more confidently in their factories ("Rose Winslow Appeals"). By that
fall, Paul's nonviolent war also involved influential members of the Socialist
Party. Louise Bryant and John Reed, who had reported from Russia on the
Russian revolution and were associated with the New York group of radicals
that included Max Eastman, began writing for the *Suffragist* and speaking at
meetings; Bryant participated in many of the year's activities. Dorothy Day, a
member of the Socialist Party and the IWW and later founder of the Catholic
Worker Movement, picketed and went to jail on the Night of Terror.

After the Senate failed to vote for suffrage in June of 1918, Paul felt it was
time to further utilize her changing group, primed for nonviolent combat. In
July Paul began planning for large protest meetings in Lafayette Square, the
first to take place on August 6, Inez Milholland's birthday, to oppose Wilson's
refusal to hold the Senate in an extra session to bring the federal amendment to a vote ("Suffrage Demonstration before White House"). In a signed
statement presented in press bulletins for the August 6 demonstration, Paul
reiterated that Wilson held the ultimate power: "nothing but his insistence
can win this victory for American democracy" (Press Bulletin, 6 Aug. 1918).
To secure publicity and participation for the event, Paul gave several speeches
associating women's lack of public demonstrations in the winter and spring
not with blind trust in Wilson but with their hard work toward the war
against the Central Powers: women had "devoted their untiring efforts to the
making of work and sacrifice the war demands of them. These efforts and
sacrifice of women continue hour by hour, while the Senate recesses." In this
construction, Paul's suffragists are strong American soldiers, working for the
war effort and for suffrage, and Wilson's Senate is the obstructionist enemy of
democracy. As the number of senators opposing suffrage decreased, women
could more clearly be presented as the true soldiers fighting nonviolently for
democracy, soldiers facing a defeatable anti-American minority.

As a site for large protest meetings, Paul chose a monument of warfare and
freedom, the statue in Lafayette Square of Marquis de Lafayette, the fierce
French warrior for liberty during the Revolutionary War. The statue's eyes, the
Suffragist pointed out, were looking toward the White House as a conscience
for modern American government ("Lafayette and Rochambeau"). As Paul
stressed in making this choice, Lafayette had come to the United States on

his own, beginning as Washington's aide-de-camp and then commanding a division of American troops before returning to France to recruit auxiliary forces. In 1781 that French support played a major role in causing the surrender of Cornwallis, the English commander. After the war, from his seat in the Estates General, Lafayette pressed the French government for the adoption of the Declaration of the Rights of Man. In 1824, the year he visited the United States, the square was named in his honor, and in 1891 a statue of him was placed at its southeast corner, honoring a hero of democracy whom the suffragists now claimed as their own compatriot.

To prepare for a new style of military "assault" event, articles in the *Suffragist* described the remaining senators who still opposed suffrage as a blockade, a lined-up force of recalcitrant Democrats determined to oppose women. In this military image, these senators stood between women and suffrage, and thus these women had to find a means of breaking through, not by adopting violent techniques but certainly by choosing aggressive ones ("Senator Sheppard"). For Americans, the term *blockade* had a strong meaning: it was Germany's submarine blockade of England that led to the sinking of the *Lusitania* in May of 1915 and ultimately to American entrance into the war (Fleming 2). Like Germans attempting to keep the English from necessary foodstuffs and from appropriate means of self-defense, these senators were cruelly keeping women from suffrage, from what they needed to achieve freedom. Thus, like the British and American armies, Paul's forces would have to break through this blockade, using words rather than guns.

In the first Lafayette Square event, Paul decided not to rely on silent picketing. It was time, she believed, for women to address the crowds and to explain the complicated actions of Wilson and his party, just as Wilson had entered Congress to convince the legislature to declare war. On August 6, 1918, one hundred women gathered at Lafayette's monument, bearing the Milholland banner as well as others condemning Wilson and the Democrats. One banner repeated Paul's positioning of the Senate in her new war rhetoric: "We deplore the weakness of President Wilson in permitting the Senate to line itself with the Prussian Reichstag by denying democracy to the people" (Press Release, 6 Aug. 1918). But Wilson's perfidy required more explanation than could occur on banners, so several women—Dora Lewis, Lavinia Dock, Helena Hill Weed, and Lucy Burns—put down their banners and gave speeches to the large crowd concerning their determination to defeat all forms of opposition and secure equal rights.

At this event, forty-eight women were arrested by the police, "acting under the orders of Colonel Ridley, President Wilson's chief military aide," as Paul wanted clearly pointed out. The charge was "congregating in the park" ("Suffragists Again Attack President"). Dora Lewis, the *Suffragist* reported dramatically, had the word *democracy* coming out of her lips when police grabbed her. After Lewis was taken away, women kept coming forward to speak and were immediately arrested, just as Paul had been in London. Others near them at the Lafayette monument who were not even speaking were also taken to police vans. As their well-known leader, Paul was arrested as she stood "perfectly still" in the street ("Women's Protest against Disenfranchisement").

For Paul, this scene had important meaning within a war of nonviolence, a meaning quite different from the earlier picketing. Women were now attempting to speak out about their president and his Senate, not just hold placards. And they were coming up against this government one at a time, in succession like marching soldiers, ready to face violence or imprisonment. The *Suffragist* labeled this strong movement as "the passive opposition of hundreds of women who have every reason to doubt the sincerity of a leader who on the one hand champions suffrage for the women of the world, and on the other, sanctions the arrests of women who dare to demand their liberty." Paul uses the labels of "passive opposition" and "passive resistance" to name their behavior in the face of the police who were silencing them and removing them from public grounds, just as the Senate was attempting to keep American women silent and outside of American political space ("Protest against Suffrage Blockade").

To make it clear that this was not one day's visual rhetoric, Paul's troops went out to the monument again on August 12, a day on which police action provided an opportunity for a new level of nonviolent war. When suffragists went out to speak for a second time that day, thirty-eight of them were taken to police headquarters. There, police took the suffragists' banners and attempted to remove their sashes. The women, in good nonviolent fashion, kept their hands tightly on the sashes while standing still, facing another assault on their bodies and property: "The women attempted to retain the sashes, which they had bought and paid for, and which they had a right to keep." They were attacked fiercely: "When released the women appeared with tears streaming down their faces, bruised throats, swollen, twisted wrists, and sprained fingers." To continue the imagery of these women facing a foreign force, at war using their own nonviolence, the *Suffragist* listed their injuries, including sprained ankles and fingers, wrenched backs, cuts and bruises, and leg and arm injuries, under the heading of "Casualty List." Lucy Burns and Dora Lewis, for example, "were bruised and twisted severely." These details in the *Suffragist* and press bulletins provided witness to the women's wartime sacrifice, to their reliance on "passive resistance" in the face of physical force, and to the enemy's perfidy ("Later Demonstrations").

On August 14 speeches at the monument connected police action to the Senate's disrespect for women and for democracy. Elsie Hill's speech involved a comparison that NWP speakers frequently reiterated, that the Senate resembled the German Reichstag insisting on its autocratic rights and denying the claims of justice and peace: "On the days our boys in khaki won their first brilliant battle in France, we, their women at home, were forced to see a few made-in-Germany Senators viciously defeat the cause of human liberty here" ("Later Demonstrations"). She continued with evidence from two days before of what the tyranny of these men meant to American women: they could be detained while they protested peacefully, could be assaulted within police stations, and could be given jail sentences on any charge and for any length of time. On that day, even while Hill was speaking, thirty women were arrested. This time, the charge was "holding a meeting without a permit."

Although the courts no longer chose to give out sentences of several months, these women, including Alice Paul and Lucy Burns, did receive sentences of ten to fifteen days, and the officials decided to isolate the women so they would not again influence other criminals. The twenty-four of them were "sick, cold, shut off from the world," in a prison that had been abandoned in 1909, in underground cells that had been declared too unsanitary for ordinary criminals. They were denied mail; they could visit with their lawyer but not with friends; and they had to endure the foul odor of this abandoned structure. As soon as they were imprisoned, they initiated a hunger strike to secure their rights as political prisoners ("In Prison"). With supporters and members of the press protesting, the women were released after five days ("Women's Protest against Disenfranchisement").

To further this theme of women at war against enemies of democracy, Paul made thorough use of the hideous details and effects of this place, which had been deemed too foul for male criminals but appropriate for these prisoners. When Maud Younger was released, Hazel Hunkins wrote in the *Suffragist*: "It was hard to realize that the same girl who carried the American flag so steadily and bravely at the head of our processions was now being brought home wrapped in a blanket and violently ill." Many women, the *Suffragist* and press bulletins claimed, became weak from fasting and from the horrible smell. Elsie Hill spoke to reporters to acquaint them with the fact that women who desired political freedom had been put in such an unusual and unacceptable locale, as though they were prisoners of war: "The crushing thought is that men should have ever built such a ghostly coffin for live people, and then that having condemned it as unsanitary for workhouse men, they should revive it for women asking for political freedom" ("Later Demonstrations"). Alva Belmont said of this incarceration: "Enemy aliens in our internment camps are treated with more consideration than these women, who are simply contending for the right of free speech" ("Mrs. Belmont Protests").

After the women were released, Colonel Ridley sent a letter to Paul granting, without her having requested this dispensation, a permit for an additional demonstration, another sure indication, in Paul's construction, of Wilson's government being in the wrong in this battle over democratic rights. In a speech that Paul gave at headquarters and printed in the *Suffragist,* she argued that "Of course the government official (it used to be the king) can do no wrong. Yet here he is almost admitting that he's committed an injustice" ("Government's Surrender"). To this offer of a permit, Paul replied that with so many women sick from imprisonment and from injuries incurred when they were arrested and in jail, they planned to wait: she did not want to mount a demonstration with approval, at a sanctioned time or place. She wanted the women to demonstrate like soldiers initiating unannounced attacks.

"Lafayette, We Are Here": Burning Wilson's Words

To make clear that in this war for suffrage the ultimate enemy was not the police but those who controlled the local officers, Paul kept seeking confrontational tactics that would keep the focus on Wilson and his Senate. On September 16 she initiated a new level of aggression in Lafayette Square. That day, the president had told a delegation of Democratic women he would work for suffrage: "I am, as I think you know, heartily in sympathy with you. I have endeavored to assist you in every way in my power, and I shall continue to do so" ("Suffragists Burn President's Words"). But then, Senator Andrieus Jones, a Democrat from New Mexico who was Chairman of the Senate Suffrage Committee, told Abby Scott Baker the amendment would not be brought up again before the Sixty-Fifth Congress adjourned in early 1919. Because legislation had to be approved by both houses in the same session, suffragists would have to begin anew in the House of Representatives in the next session (Irwin, *Story of Alice Paul* 372). So in Lafayette Square, in front of their home and Wilson's, they inaugurated a new nonviolent protest technique by burning copies of Wilson's "war for democracy" speeches in urns and dubbing the fires "Watchfires for Freedom." Lucy Branham, a Columbia Ph.D. who had participated in a hunger strike in the District Jail, was the first to step up to burn Wilson's words—to "symbolize the burning indignation of women." He gave "words, and words, and words," the women claimed, words that did not indicate real support for suffrage, words that were never backed up with real action ("President's Words Burned" 7).

On that day, the suffragists gave speeches to reinforce the message of the burning words and to emphasize their waging of a nonviolent war and the necessity of going from silence to speech to move forward. Evelyn Wainwright, wife of rear-admiral Richard Wainwright, a well-known military hero who had been on the *Maine* when it exploded in Havana harbor at the beginning of the Spanish-American War, rose to speak. She modeled her talk on what had become an epic moment in the current world war although perhaps it was already being remembered falsely. On July 4, 1917, soon after the first American army unit, the Sixteenth Infantry, arrived in France, it participated in a parade through Paris, ending at Lafayette's Tomb. There, staff colonel Charles E. Stanton gave a speech that was immediately associated with John J. Pershing, commander-in-chief of the American Expeditionary Force, who was standing by his side, in which he vilified the Kaiser and assured victory. Its reassuring ending, guaranteeing a military presence, became immediately famous: "Lafayette, we are here!" (Fleming 124). On September 6, 1918, when the 160th anniversary of Lafayette's birth was celebrated in New York, several speakers, including Teddy Roosevelt and dignitaries from the French, British, and American armies, repeated the famous line ("New York to Honor Lafayette Today"). Ten days later, in Washington, Evelyn Wainwright spoke directly to the statue, as Pershing (or Stanton) had to the tomb, and repeated the famous line—"Lafayette, we are here!"—to stress women's commitment to achieving democracy and true freedom.

Wainwright's speech presented American armies as part of worldwide struggle for liberty, heroes just as these suffragists were heroes, and asked for Lafayette's help in extending the cause of liberty in the United States, as he had during the Revolutionary War. She thus associated her comrades with the best traditions of Washington and Jefferson: these women were "a little band with no army, no power but justice and right, no strength but in our Constitution and in the Declaration of Independence." She asked the figure of Lafayette to "Speak again to plead for us, like the bronze woman at your feet, condemned like us to a silent appeal. She offers you a sword." Wainwright was referring to the figure of Columbia seated at the base of the statue and gesturing up toward him. A symbol of American democracy, this toga-clad figure holding a sword urges Lafayette to defend the new and besieged nation that would continue the best traditions of fifth-century Greece. Wainwright thus associated suffragists with Columbia: these twentieth-century women had also, through picketing and hunger strikes, silently urged their Congress and president to support true democracy.

In her speech, Wainwright then moved to these women's belief in a higher power, not of swords, but of nonviolence: "Will you not use for us the sword of the spirit, mightier far than the sword she holds out for you?" Through

Lafayette's intercession, through the public association of his commitment to freedom with theirs, women would gain the power to extend the best values of the Constitution and Declaration of Independence ("September 16 Demonstration"). As other speakers came forward, the subject continued to be words, honest and dishonest, spoken and silenced. Wilson had spoken empty words for suffrage, had been silent about it in the legislative session, and had used the police and Senate to silence these women. Other speakers also called out to this statue, urging this man and his values to become a replacement for a president who only pretended to believe in freedom.

From the President to the Senate

In Lafayette Square on September 16, with large crowds in attendance, burning the president's words and presenting a slate of resolute and vibrant speakers, Paul had certainly brought a new level of danger to the conflict, another sharpening of the suffragists' nonviolent but warlike activity. In the suffragists' construction of events, they were at war but following a superior code: they were abiding by true democratic values and Wilson was not. This strong rhetoric seemed to bear fruit. The following day, Senator Jones announced that after careful reconsideration his committee was scheduling a suffrage vote for September 26, and he vowed to keep suffrage before the Senate until it passed ("Says Suffrage Vote"). On September 30 Wilson came to the Senate to speak for suffrage, arguing that it was "vitally essential to the successful prosecution of the great war of humanity in which we are engaged." Reversing the opinion he had held since taking office in 1912, Wilson maintained that obtaining suffrage state by state was "impracticable within any reasonable length of time, if practicable at all." Here, perhaps referring to Paul and the NWP, he averred that the "voices of foolish and intemperate agitators do not reach me at all," but he was instead led by "the plain, struggling, workaday folk" who believed that a model democracy would involve both its men and its women. But when the vote occurred, even though Wilson seemed to be lending support, the amendment failed by two votes: 73 percent of Republicans voted yes, but only 57 percent of Democrats ("Defeat in the Senate").

Given his need for support from the more conservative elements of his party, Wilson was taking a risk by formally arguing for the amendment long advocated by the "foolish and intemperate." In May 1918, when a debate concerning Wilson's efficacy as a leader had occurred in Congress, Representative William Gordon of Ohio, a Democrat, had employed gendered criticism when he called the NWP "militant Amazons" who had been "coaxing, teasing and nagging the President of the United States for the purpose of inducing him by coercion to club Congress into adapting this joint resolution" (Stevens, *Jailed for Freedom* 255–56). Now many newspapers also disparaged him for listening to Alice Paul. The *Baltimore Sun,* on October 2, 1918, with the heading of "An Opponent Wonders," sarcastically criticized Wilson for this supposed new alliance: "We wonder if President Wilson has at last been able to win the distinguished approval of Alice Paul et al., and what is the next thing they will demand of him." This newspaper argued that in advocating suffrage as a war measure he had not been responding to requests from "the real womanhood of America," because the real womanhood had been working hard for the war effort; instead he was giving in to the "Shrieking Sisterhood." In this article, Wilson was compared unfavorably to the Kaiser, but on different grounds than those chosen by suffragists. The Kaiser and his quartermaster general, "disciples of frightfulness," the article maintained, "are not so easily influenced by the strident female voice as the President evidently is, and the pickets might hesitate at trying their antics in Germany whose war lord is less patient and amenable than our Chief Magistrate." In such newspapers, opposed to suffrage in general and certainly to its positioning as a war measure, Wilson often appeared as the henpecked husband, controlled by domineering women when his eyes should be fixed on war.

In his speech before Congress, Wilson came to suffrage's support, taking the criticism from the press and from conservative members of his own party that he had known would await him. Although Paul still believed that Wilson was not doing all he could for suffrage, was still stressing other issues and preserving other coalitions behind closed doors, this speech made opposition to him much more complicated. He had finally urged his party and the Senate to support this amendment; he could not be easily labeled as obstructionist.

So, after picketing the White House and burning the president's speeches, Paul turned her attention solely to the Senate, again rhetorically associating her campaign with war. After the filibuster in June, as she prepared for the August 6 demonstration in Lafayette Square, Paul began depicting those senators who opposed suffrage as anti-American. Many newspapers followed this lead, comparing the senators to Tories opposing the American Revolution or to the Germans in the current war. William Marion Reedy, in *Reedy's Mirror* (St. Louis), argued in June that it was Senate Tories who were still opposing the inevitable: "Only invincible toryism and petrified prejudice are against it. The Senate should get in step with the progress of the world" ("Get in Step with Progress"). The *Evening Journal* in Richmond, Virginia, on August 13, 1918, compared the state's two senators, both of whom opposed suffrage, to Kaiser Wilhelm, keeping a people from democracy ("Archaic Senators"). By the fall of 1918, the alignment of forces had thus shifted—from the militant suffragists versus Wilson and his Senate, to Wilson and these good Americans versus a few recalcitrant, obstructionist senators, especially Southern senators, who fundamentally opposed democracy. The *Detroit Journal* on September 11, in constructing allies and enemies, even placed Wilson aboard a train headed to suffrage and portrayed those senators as a Snidely Whiplash impeding progress: "Nothing could be more undignified, nothing could make the Senate look more like a sleepy chamber of fogies, than academic hesitation before a concrete demand for public justice. And nothing attempted in a loyal Congress would seem more to belittle the President's influence, than for the Senate to tie clotheslines across the railroad track when Mr. Wilson himself has boarded the suffrage special" ("Doddering Delay"). Similarly, in a *New York Tribune* article on October 1, 1918, the battle for full suffrage rights was depicted as occurring between a good president speaking for democracy and bad Southern Democrats ("Great and Moving Hour").

Making a difficult rhetorical choice, given her own antiwar stance and allegiance with Robert and Belle Case La Follette, Paul began labeling these senators as "willful men." Wilson had used "a little group of willful men" to describe Robert La Follette and eleven other senators whose filibuster had prevented a vote on the president's request for the authority to arm merchant ships (Fleming 27). Then Wilson and the press reiterated the term, creating a well-publicized portrayal of anti-Americanism, when La Follette and five other senators, as well as fifty members of the House of Representatives, voted against war in April of 1917. In an October 12, 1918, *Suffragist* article, Paul reiterated Wilson's term to construct both groups of senators—those who opposed war and now those who opposed suffrage—as obstructionist, anti-American, unwilling to fight for the future of democracy ("Group of Wilful Men").

Whereas recalcitrant Democrats, fighting their own leader and the nation, became the common target, some newspapers honed in especially on backwards Southerners who were hurting the national party and hindering national reform. Even southern newspapers once opposed to a federal suffrage amendment repudiated these senators, lining them up rhetorically with Tories, with Germans—with all "willful" groups that acted selfishly and unjustly. The Louisville, Kentucky, *Courier-Journal,* for example, commented that these few men had assumed the divine right of despotic kings, like the Tories or the Kaiser. The article continued with a strong regionalist tone: no one could argue that the women of Kentucky were inferior to those women who already had the vote ("'Divine Right' of Men"). "Will our Democratic senators today follow the lead of the President, or of the Prussian Diet and of Senator Reed of Missouri in opposing the extension of democracy?" asked the *Lexington Herald* on September 26, 1918 ("Prussianizing Kentucky").

To encourage this negative depiction of obstructionist senators as self-absorbed aristocrats, Paul moved to another rhetorical event, picketing the Senate and especially its willful few, an event for which she returned to the silence that would emphasize women's silencing by those men. On October 7, four banner-bearers ascended the steps of the Capitol and were immediately placed under arrest, taken to a guardroom, held for fifteen minutes, and released after their banners were confiscated. That afternoon they returned with a banner not just advocating the amendment but associating these senators with Germany: "We protest against the 34 wilful Senators who have delayed the political freedom of American women. They have obstructed the war program of the President. They have lined up the Senate with Prussia by denying self-government to the people" (Irwin, *Story of Alice Paul* 382). That afternoon, and again when they reappeared on October 10, these pickets were detained but not arrested, because the government did not want to return to issuing jail sentences ("Preserving the Peace"; "Woman's Party Protest").

But as in other events of that year of nonviolent warfare, Paul wanted more danger than simple picketing could provide. She announced to newspapers that she planned for a large group to burn words spoken by antisuffrage senators—on the Senate floor. Certainly Paul knew that there was no possibility of her being allowed to bring in an urn and light a fire there. On October 13, a huge crowd pursued them as Paul and her supporters walked to the Capitol with the urn and senators watched from the balconies. When the marchers started up the steps, the banner-bearers were taken to the guardroom immediately, as was Alice Paul, who was simply standing there. Police released these suffragists; they wanted no martyrs.

With jail terms not forthcoming, and certainly no chance of reaching the Senate floor, Paul further tightened the rhetorical aim of the banners themselves, moving the focus from the amendment or the general Senate to those specific senators who opposed suffrage. These banners pointed to their lack of support not just for the amendment, but for the nation and president. About confirmed antisuffragist Republican Senator James W. Wadsworth Jr. of New York, for example, the banners pointed out that he had chosen during this world war not to rejoin his regiment from the Spanish-American War, a specious criticism of a man of forty-one, but instead to serve obstructionist goals: "Senator Wadsworth left his regiment and is fighting against democracy in the Senate." Banners concerning Senator John Shields of Tennessee, a Democrat up for re-election in 1918, accused him of abandoning his president and, by extension, his nation at war: "Senator Shields told the people of Tennessee he would support the President's policies. The only time the President went to the Senate to ask for its support, Senator Shields voted against him. Does Tennessee back the President's war program or Senator Shields?" (Irwin, *Story of Alice Paul* 385; "Picketing Thirty-four Wilful Senators").

In the *Suffragist* and in press releases, Paul stressed the pickets' strength and determination as well as their illegal detainment—as nonviolent soldiers at war. Capitol police repeatedly took them into their guardroom, absconding with their banners but never making any charges. Coverage of the incidents stressed these officers' physical violence as well as their actions' illegality. As the suffragists' leader and symbol, Alice Paul received a great deal of coverage, but now as a determined general, not as a weakened victim of abuse. On November 21, suffragists protesting the recess of Congress without action on suffrage were thrown down the Capitol steps and dragged to the guardroom in the cellar of the Capitol. According to the *Suffragist*, these women were "held for half an hour after the thug-like police had finished hurling them against the walls of the corridors of the Capitol and had growled forth their fury against an American public that dared to express its sympathy for full suffrage." The *Suffragist* and press bulletins especially focused on these men's treatment of Alice Paul: "The guards were positively ferocious. They fell upon Miss Paul and dragged and pushed her about as if in a rage" ("Senate Recesses"). This time, the general and her troops maintained their code of nonviolence, but they did fight back. The *Suffragist* reported, on October 19, that when they were told they could not leave the guardroom, even though they had not been charged, "in a flash several of them broke the glass of the doors which the police have kept locked and guarded since the moment our arrival" ("Preserving the Peace"). Like a noble army at war, Paul's troops were protecting themselves and standing up for justice.

Influencing the Fall Election

Within this strong rhetorical environment, with Paul and her organization at war, she intensified her work to influence the fall elections. Like Wilson getting support for a world war, she was very concerned about each supportive vote. She told Maud Younger right after the negative Senate vote in September: "Come, we must find out about the short-term candidates and go into the election campaign at once." After months of comparison of the Senate to the Reichstag, newspapers were no longer so shocked by opposition to Democratic senators. The *Rocky Mount News* argued on October 2, 1918, for example, that if its readers believed in suffrage and in the president's leadership, they should "vote against the party as a party and as a whole without respect to the vote of an individual member of that party" ("Sectionalism and Suffrage"). But, given the current situation, with the president supporting suffrage, Paul was not seeking a complete boycott of Democrats. As Inez Irwin commented, she was "as fluid as water, as swift as light, to adapt that single adamantine policy to the situation of the moment" (*Story of Alice Paul* 390).

In the western suffrage states, where candidates of both parties, except the outspoken Republican Senator William E. Borah of Idaho, declared their support for suffrage, she asked supporters to continue to boycott the Democratic Party to show that women could vote their own interests and could punish this party for its refusal to pass a suffrage amendment. But in the East, she worked more specifically toward defeating candidates, regardless of party, who refused to support the amendment. In New Jersey and New Hampshire, there were short-term elections caused by deaths of senators. In both locations, her force of organizers, including Doris Stevens, Caroline Katzenstein, Maud Younger, Abby Scott Baker, and Lucy Burns, worked for Democrats who supported suffrage and against Republican candidates who did not. But in these states, the Democratic candidates received little help from Wilson, and both Republican antisuffragists won the elections. Paul celebrated, however, the defeat of Democratic Senator John Shafroth of Colorado, who had introduced the alternative suffrage amendment and still supported that choice and whose defeat resulted in a Republican Senate majority, a victory that many newspapers credited to NWP efforts in that state. The party also celebrated the election of Democrat William Pollock of South Carolina, who had pledged himself to vote for suffrage.

After the election, with the old Congress in its final session and a new one arriving in the spring, Paul knew that even gaining the Senate's attention and action, much less securing approval of a federal suffrage amendment, would be difficult. Though suffrage had Wilson's tacit support, his imprimatur carried less clout than in previous years. Many Republicans and Democrats objected to the president's trip to Europe, lasting from December 1918 to July 1919, for the peace conference; they disagreed on the terms of the treaty; they argued that events in Ireland, whose independence he opposed, revealed his tenuous position as the world's leader of democracy; they debated the worth of his League of Nations. In the new Sixty-Sixth Congress, Democrats in the House held a majority of just three seats, and the Republicans controlled the Senate by two votes. The agenda concerned treaties and postwar power, and not suffrage or any other old "war measure." With Wilson's power base much less secure, Democrats would not necessarily heed his call to join with Republicans and support the amendment.

In this environment, Paul knew that suffrage could again slip away. With events in Paris, Moscow, and Dublin vying for attention and a president under scrutiny, the postwar period would not necessarily be suffrage's hour, any more than Reconstruction had been. Senators were not clamoring for a means of repaying women; they were going on to the next debates. Foreseeing that she would have to keep national attention focused on the ongoing war for suffrage, on November 19, 1918, Paul wrote a letter to newspaper editors reviewing the women's progress, just as the president had sent wartime messages focused on moving forward and vanquishing the nation's enemies:

> By a laborious campaign, reaching over more than half a century, women have won the vote in enough states to enable them to make their political power felt in Congress. They have broken down the opposition of political parties and forced the endorsement of their measure; they have changed the attitude of the Administration from one of obstruction to one of earnest advocacy; they have won enough votes to pass the amendment through the lower house; all the great labor and business and social organizations throughout the country are its supporters; the only enemies left to be overthrown are the sectional political prejudices and autocratic traditions of the United States Senate.

To keep her momentum going, Paul planned a December demonstration at the Capitol, evincing the same faith in women acting in concert that she had in 1913: "If a thousand women would stand outside the doors of the Senate for a single day, that body would quickly act." They were mounting a demonstration, just as Wilson had entered a world war, because of the perfidy of their enemy: "The Senate's obstruction of self-government for American women must be called constantly and emphatically to the attention of the American people" (Letter to Newspaper Editors). When women stood outside of the Capitol holding banners, they made it clear that their war, which had been going on for years and which had already involved a full year of picketing, would be continuing.

To emphasize their active campaign and resolve, Paul also staged several other public events to coincide with that December's meeting of her advisory board as well as her state chairs and officers. On December 15, she held a mass meeting: "Women conducted the meeting and women made the speeches." Opened by Alva Smith Belmont, this session included speeches by Harriot Stanton Blatch, Lucy Burns, and other activists. There was also a pageant of "free women," those from suffrage states, who by their participation in a march to the Capitol demonstrated the considerable political clout that women voters already had and their determination to extend the franchise to all American women (Porritt, "Suffrage Conference at Washington"). As usual, Paul was in charge of the powerful rhetorical scene: "I was, I suppose, managing it, seeing they got there and everything, but I wasn't up making a speech. It was very beautiful, these girls that made these speeches" (Porritt, "Suffrage Conference at Washington").

A Watchfire for Freedom

By December, although Paul's forces were picketing the Senate, they felt it was time for their efforts to shift again. At Paul's urging, the NWP advisory committee decided at its December meeting to resume their pursuit of Wilson—again to burn his speeches on freedom and democracy, again to embarrass him as a champion of world liberty. Even with the war concluded, he was still advocating world democracy and simultaneously denying the rights of American women, pretending to support the amendment while paying attention to treaties and his League of Nations. He was also attempting to keep the support of conservative senators, especially key senators from the South, whose votes he would need to further his postwar plans. As the *Suffragist* constructed this reassumption of Wilson as opponent, the president was giving them no choice: "They had urged the President; they had implored him; they had picketed him. And after all this the President of the United States had said the same empty words about the women of this country 'deserving' political freedom." He had said they deserved the vote, and then with the issue pending he "had sailed serenely off to France," planning "to secure freedom for everyone but his own people" ("American Women Burn" 6). This legislative denial of women's rights was the end-of-the-war result that Paul had expected, like what had occurred at the end of the Civil War, and she wanted to call attention to it right away: women were being lauded and thanked—and denied their rights.

On December 16 Paul again publicly declared war on Wilson, a president more vulnerable to attack than he had been during wartime. She repeated some techniques to indicate that women were at the same point with the same man, but she increased the danger, drama, and participation to ensure that each technique had an increased level of impact. Paul assembled a huge group that included the working women who had helped to win the war, as the *Suffragist* listed participants: "pioneer suffragists, munition workers, women of the West, toilers, the unenfranchised women of America" ("American Women Burn" 6). To Lafayette Square came this group, headed by Anna Kelton Wiley carrying the American flag. There were speakers and fifty torchbearers, along with four hundred other marchers and a great crowd of women, all at the same time that the president was being received in France. Women to represent each state mounted the Lafayette statue and then placed "tomes and scripts of President Wilson's words on freedom" into the urn.

Vida Milholland, Inez's sister, sang the "Woman's Marseillaise," and Elizabeth Rogers spoke to explain their actions: "We burn his words on liberty today, not in malice or anger, but in a spirit of reverence for truth. This meeting is a message to President Wilson. We expect an answer. If it is more words, we will burn them again." As other speakers followed her, expanding on the day's imagery of fire, the *Suffragist* claimed that into the crowd's consciousness "had been burned the realization that the women of this country surely must have the rights that President Wilson has demanded for other people" ("American Women Burn" 6–7).

Although this event provided a meaningful demonstration of the suffragists' continuing nonviolent war, Paul then decided, as she had so many times before, that such a repetition of an earlier act would not suffice. She wanted a new type of daily reminder of the lack of justice for women; she decided to use urns not just for burning Wilson's words but also for maintaining a perpetually lit "watchfire." Many years later, Paul described this rhetorical act to an interviewer:

> We had a sort of perpetual flame going in an urn outside our headquarters in Lafayette Square. I think we used rags soaked in kerosene. It was really very dramatic, because when President Wilson went to Paris for the peace conference, he was always issuing some wonderful, idealistic statement that was impossible to reconcile with what he was doing at home. And we had an enormous bell—I don't recall how we ever got such an enormous bell—and every time Wilson would make one of these speeches, we would toll this great bell, and then somebody would go outside with the President's speech and, with great dignity, burn it in our little caldron. (Gallagher 93)

The NWP had wood brought in from all over the country to stress the unity of women in this effort; the first batch was from a tree on Independence Square in Philadelphia, thus from "liberty-consecrated ground," another connection to the Revolutionary War. These women endeavored to keep a continual fire, first near Lafayette's statue and then right in front of the White House, as a signal that they were still at war, still striving for suffrage, still having to fight for their rights.

Paul began this new level of opposition as a New Year's Day event to signal the beginning of another year in which women could not vote. As the *Suffragist* and press bulletins immediately reported, Paul came out, the bell tolled, and women marched to the White House and then to the Lafayette Monument. In an urn they had placed near the statue and dedicated to Lafayette and to liberty, they built a watchfire. It rained, but they kept the fire going. Then, in the night, to increase the danger of the event, Rose Conlan went to an ornamental urn, a large and permanent fixture on a pedestal near the White House, and lit a second watchfire, angering the police, who immediately claimed this urn was too near to the president and had cost ten thousand dollars. As Paul had foreseen, Rose Conlan was immediately arrested, and her fire tossed out. But as police took Conlan away, Paul increased the blaze with fresh wood. When she refused to desist, she was arrested. Then two more went up to relight this fire as they also kept a blaze going in the urn by the Lafayette Monument (Morris).

With publicity increasing with each hour and each new altercation, the NWP members kept the fires going for four days, with succeeding relays of women on duty ("Watchfire"). Soldiers and sailors frequently overturned the urn near the White House and stamped on the ashes, but as soon as they took action another fire would blaze up from the urn by the monument. At least one was kept continually burning even though women were arrested—on the charge of lighting bonfires between sunset and sunrise (Morris). On the third day, police began using chemicals to put the fires out, but the women relit them. Throughout these days the bell on the balcony of headquarters tolled regularly. Then on Sunday, January 5, the women brought out asbestos coils to start fires more quickly. That day, four women were given five- to ten-day sentences for trying to start a fire in the White House urn. In the District Jail, they started a hunger strike and insisted on their rights as political prisoners ("Guilty of—?"; "Impressions from the District Jail").

With this fire and with this name of "watchfire" for it, Paul was again associating her suffragists with heroic soldiers at war. She counted on press coverage of a fire in front of the president's house, but she also sought further association with American patriots. During the Revolution, towns along the coast had frequently used fires to signal the position of British ships or British troops. Towns along the western frontier had also used them to protect themselves from Indian attack. The term "watchfire" thus implied the actions of a group nonviolently safeguarding its own territory or position, not moving offensively, but staying alert to observe the opposition's movements and its treacheries. Wilson was not the hero of democracy that he portrayed himself as, and thus they were remaining vigilant against any empty declaration of good will or linguistic treacheries that he might rely on in this new year.

Burning a President in Effigy

In February of 1919 the Sixty-Fifth Congress, meeting for its final session, decided to vote again on suffrage. The NWP realized the amendment was again going down to defeat, and this defeat meant they would have to secure yet another vote in the House and Senate of the Sixty-Sixth Congress, which would convene in May. The NWP decided therefore to escalate its protest over "the threatened shame and disgrace of the Administration and to America" by furthering its war imagery, creating a symbolic depiction of war violence. Thinking that the watchfire had not gone far enough, Paul decided to burn Wilson in effigy, using a cardboard likeness that was several feet tall. His speeches had been burned; now Wilson himself would be burned symbolically, the nonviolent mirroring of violent attack on the ruler himself, not just on his home or the policies of his Senate. Paul wrote about this choice to Louisine Havemeyer, about the need to thus keep suffrage in the nation's consciousness: "We have to do something drastic, or they—the administration, who are beginning to feel uneasy under criticism of their treatment of American women—won't fight us."

In the eighteenth century, likenesses or portraits were burned to indicate the punishment that would have been appropriate for criminals who escaped. Wilson himself, Paul believed, had escaped the United States in December when he left for Europe while criminally violating the rights of women. Effigies had more commonly been used to demonstrate disapproval for leaders and their policies, especially during wartime, another NWP reference to the Revolution. In 1765, the newly forming Sons of Liberty burned Boston's stamp agent in effigy, destroying his office to get wood for the fire, an event that led to instant recruitment of members and fame throughout the colonies. This form of protest, against stamp agents and other British officials, soon spread to other towns. After the war, Independence Day celebrations often featured a likeness of George III that was paraded through a town and then burned in a central square. Although, as Paul knew, burning an enemy in effigy was an accepted and even lauded part of American history, it was a different thing to burn an image of a sitting president in front of the White House.

On the afternoon of February 9, 1919, the eve of the last senatorial vote on suffrage in the Sixty-Fifth Congress, Paul staged this most controversial of rhetorical acts. A column of thirty-six suffragists left the NWP headquarters and marched to the White House, where they burned Wilson in effigy. He could be dealt with in that form only, they told the crowd that quickly gathered, since he had left for Europe in December. In front of the White House, women put the "little figure," about two feet tall, into an urn, and then the crowd erupted. Paul's description of the uproar over this nonviolent protest against Wilson stressed the comic nature of bluecoats versus petticoats, making fun of the imperious police, men who resembled English Redcoats marching magisterially through the colonies, all insignia and injustice:

An urn about as big as a twelve-inch flower pot was produced and placed upon the ground, and a fire started in it; then the bluecoats rushed upon it, but the petticoats were too much for them. The fire brindled and kindled and crackled as if Logi the firegod himself were on our side. The bluecoats became rough and the extinguishers were called into service, and played not upon the fire but upon the women. I saw Sue White at the urn—the flames flashed. She gave me a nod; I knew the deed was done. The bluecoats were grabbing at everything in sight, hoping, I presume, to salvage the effigy, but what could you expect from those active little fire-extinguishers shooting in all directions, and so many brass buttons, so many yards of gold braid to be protected! The insignia, the great insignia, all that was left of manhood and the dignity of their rank, was to be guarded; and, not getting the effigy, they grabbed at the women and dragged their resisting leaders across Pennsylvania Avenue to the curb when another row quickly began and my attention was drawn to the curb. ("Suffragists Burn Wilson")

Here the women in battle, like Sue White of Tennessee, fight with the force of the Norse firegod Logi, who represents an unstoppable force, wildfire and lightning, one that no blockade or extinguisher can contain. Against these suffrage warriors the police appear as comic and incompetent bullies, bent on cruelty but without the true moral force to succeed. Sue White's statement once again depicts the president as a tyrant: "We burn not the effigy of the President of a free people, but the leader of an autocratic party organization whose tyrannical power holds millions of women in political slavery" ("Suffragists Burn Wilson").

That day, officers arrested thirty-nine of the one hundred participants, including Lucy Burns, Helena Hill Weed, Elizabeth Rogers, Sarah Colvin, and Louise Bryant. As requested, because of her social status, Louisine Havemeyer kept throwing bundles toward the urn to assure her own incarceration. These thirty-nine were charged with "varied and sundry" offenses, like building fires after sundown or on the sidewalk, and twenty-six were sentenced to two to five days for setting fires ("Demonstration of February 9" 10). Captain Flathers took the arrested women to the police dormitory and, to avoid the negative publicity that the NWP could easily wield, checked that the beds were clean and let Paul send in food. His actions revealed his awareness of Paul's position as leader: "Alice Paul was too good a general not to look after the welfare of her fighting forces." When the women appeared in court, they were given the choice of five days in jail or a five-dollar fine, and they refused to pay. They were then taken to the same abandoned workhouse where women had been incarcerated the previous August, where so many had become ill from poisonous gases. Otherwise it had not been used for eight years, for it was judged "unfit for human habitation" ("Suffrage Trial").

The NWP was widely rebuked for this burning of Wilson in effigy, as Paul had known it would be, but the organization was also recognized as a force at war. NAWSA leader Maud Wood Park spoke and wrote vehemently about this outrage, which she falsely claimed had been stopped by police before it could occur: "That such an insult to the official head of our government should have been contemplated, particularly while he was representing the United States in a foreign land, was shocking to all friends of the President and to many of his political opponents as well." On the next day, while admitting that the event had been "exciting," the *New York Times* asked whether, in light of their taking on such an action, the NWP really still aimed at passing the amendment—or just selfishly wanted to advertise itself in a highly controversial manner. The article depicted the NWP as a potent force, on its own aggressive path, beyond government control ("Suffragists Burn Wilson").

The Prison Special

To further dramatize the fact that the war in Europe was over but women's war continued, Paul looked for additional rhetorical actions that would focus on women's betrayal and their need for continued battle: "The great club of publicity was in our hands and we were only waiting for an opportunity to brandish it." To shape that publicity, in February of 1919, she decided to very publicly send her warriors out on a national campaign. This battle-hardened battalion ventured out on a reserved train, the Prison Special, echoing the use of the Suffrage Special in April of 1916. Whereas the first group had occupied one car of a train and had participated in a series of genial meetings, now Paul reached for a greater physical presence and more confrontational interaction for her travelers—as a war-worn battalion moving into new theatres of the fighting. Special prison wrappers, the shapeless calico dresses with washrags pinned at the belt, and oversized brogans like those women had to wear at Occoquan Workhouse served as the women's uniforms. They planned to decorate the cars with bars or cell windows to emphasize their experience as prisoners of war, but the railroad would not allow it ("Prison Special" Feb. 1).

On February 6, 1919, a press release said that the Special had been delayed a week, to February 16, so that the twenty-six women would have more complete knowledge of the suffrage situation in the Senate. All along the route, these women, including Abby Scott Baker, Mabel Vernon, Vida Milholland, Lavinia Dock, Mary Winsor, Louisine Havemeyer, Sarah Colvin, and Elizabeth Rogers, left the train to speak at meetings, accompanied by Vida Milholland's singing. Abby Scott Baker, assisted by Cora Weeks, did the press work, contacting newspapers before the train arrived in each city and sending out the story of each engagement. Helen Hill Weed made the schedule, and Lucy Burns served as manager of the tour. Paul had prepared the way to make sure that the train was met by a mayor or other city representative in each place. Their speaking followed a general plan: Havemeyer spoke first, on party methods and on the dramatic arrests; Elizabeth Rogers followed with a history of woman's suffrage; Vida Milholland sang the "Women's Marseillaise"; Mary Winsor told of the terrible conditions in jail; Josephine Bennett spoke on the status of the amendment; and Mabel Vernon asked for contributions. The train's slogan was "From Prison to People," and its appearances were quite successful ("Prison Special" Feb. 22).

Along the way, this troop spoke to immense audiences, but also involved itself in suffrage conflicts, as a battalion entering skirmishes at various battle sites. In New York the Prison Special group participated in its first volatile battle scene. Wilson had returned to the United States on February 24 to convince the Senate to pass his appropriations bills and support his League of Nations, both of which faced opposition even by Democrats. On March 4, with Congress having adjourned the previous day, he went to New York to leave for Europe again after an appearance at the Metropolitan Opera House with William Howard Taft, a supporter of an international league. Outside the opera house, women amassed with the immediate purpose of pressuring Wilson to call for a special session of Congress to vote on the suffrage amendment. As they marched to the opera house, they were met by soldiers and sailors who, assisted by police, began to assault the pickets. Doris Stevens said these two hundred officers "beat us back with such cruelty as none of us had ever witnessed before" (*Jailed for Freedom* 177). Six women were arrested, including Elsie Hill, Doris Stevens, and Alice Paul, but they were quickly released. When the women re-formed their line and started again toward the opera house, they were attacked by police: "The women were knocked down. As they attempted to keep their line intact, some were trampled underfoot and picked up later, limp and bleeding from scrapes and bruises." In this fracas, Elsie Hill spoke to make the comparison to soldiers at battle clear: "Did you fellows turn back when you saw the Germans come? What would you have thought of any one who did? Do you expect us to turn back now? We never turn back either—and we won't until democracy is won" (Irwin, *Story of Alice Paul* 425).

Then, outside of the opera house, Paul initiated another new level of aggressive response to Wilson's declarations on democracy. As Wilson spoke inside the opera house, women wrote down his words and runners brought them outside, where the group encircled an urn with a fire burning. Thus, as he continued to advocate world liberty inside the building, women standing outside, "outsiders" to his vision of the future, were consigning these words to flame. This was not a response to earlier written texts or speeches given in Europe, but an immediate refusal to accept his hypocrisies, an action widely reported by the press.

In Boston on March 9, the warlike conflicts continued, as Prison Special travelers participated in a meeting with the sixteen women who had been jailed for a public protest there. When Wilson returned from Europe, landing in Boston on February 24, Presidents' Day, women had unfurled banners for suffrage and been arrested for speaking on Boston Common without a permit and given ten days in jail; others were charged with loitering for more than seven minutes ("Reminding the President"). At the March meeting, the Prison Special travelers gave these women prison pins and a prison door replica, labeled a "war cross" by the local papers. NWP members, bearing banners reminding Wilson that he had told the Senate the government would "deserve to be distrusted" if it did not enfranchise women, marched through lines of Marines that tried to hold the crowds back. Paul wanted her troops to look as strong and determined as the United States military: they even adopted stern facial expressions to indicate that they were disciplined forces at war. Twenty-one were quickly arrested for "loitering," and most were sentenced to eight days in the Charles Street jail.

On March 10 in New York, the Prison Special travelers were again protected by "fellow" servicemen as they held a pageant at Carnegie Hall that created another warlike controversy because of attacks from a surging crowd. Under Hazel MacKaye's direction again, the pageant featured women colorfully dressed to signify "free nations," ones where women had the franchise. They were grouped around Vida Milholland, robed to represent Justice, a figure that could only reign where all citizens could vote. Following these women was a separate group in the black drapes of mourning, the color and spacing chosen to represent the tragedy of their distance from justice. As the women stepped out from the building and formed the separate groups, police couldn't or didn't control the crowd. But this time, as press bulletins and interviews stressed, servicemen in uniform stepped forward to aid the women. This development was for Paul not just an indication of kindness or chivalry but of the fellowship among warriors for freedom.

Like these servicemen, many Americans had come to respect this war for suffrage, a judgment reflected in the press in 1918. In an article concerning the August demonstrations in Lafayette Square, the *Washington Herald* on August 11, 1918, informed readers that "We are against senseless suffrage demonstrations, but, so far in their campaign, it looks as though the women have considerably the best of the argument, with the police looking puny and foolish by comparison." This paper, like other journals, commented on the rhetorical stupidity of repeated arrests: "It is impossible for a newspaper to overlook the arrest of a half a hundred women in the shadow of the White House. The suffragists know this and they are capitalizing on the stupidity of the police" ("Suffrage Demonstrations"). The *San Antonio Express,* on August 19, 1918, was even willing to reevaluate a controversial banner of the year before: "As long as we exclude women, we are, truth to tell, less a democracy than is Russia, which has enfranchised its women, many of whom are taking an active part in politics" ("Our Prestige Demands"). Of the burning of Wilson's words, the *Charleston Evening Post* commented on December 27 that "it cannot fail to penetrate the understanding of men of light, of whom the South Carolinian is one. It is highly mystical and a sign of the times. The women should kindle their faith as they have kindled the words of Wilson" ("Suffrage and the Senate"). The *Utica* (New York) *Press* compared the women to Christian martyrs and to Columbus, combining images of religion and patriotism in their praise: "Such women are like John Huss, who would not recant at the stake. Like Wycliffe, who would not take back his words. Like the early Christians, who preferred to become martyrs rather than renounce their faith. To look at these women one is impressed with the fact that not as long as life lasts will they be dismayed. Their march is onward. They are the Columbuses of a new age, who in spite of ridicule, in spite of bodily pain, in spite of all things 'sail on and on'" ("Truth about the Pickets"). This article compared NWP activists to church reformers Huss and Wycliffe as well as to early Christian martyrs in their fight against corrupt authorities, their belief in higher moral principles, and their egalitarian world view. Because of the bravery required to form a new route and enter a new world, they could also stand with Columbus.

By the spring of 1919, with changes in the public's view of women voting and with changes in the makeup of the Senate, it seemed, even more than during the previous year, that suffrage was very near to passing. Through the preceding year, suffrage had come to seem inevitable. It had certainly gotten the nation's attention, even with the war still on, as Paul waged her own war with the Senate and the president, with the enemy shifting from one to the other during the year. Paul had thus constructed women as patriotic fighters for freedom who opposed undemocratic hypocrites through nonviolence: by appealing to Lafayette as a war leader, by standing up to a Reichstag Senate, by burning a hypocritical president's words, by burning the president in effigy, by maintaining watchfires for freedom, and by sending out on a train an experienced battalion ready for further warfare. Although many of these events led to criticism, they also led to the realization that these women would not give up: they would fight for suffrage until the right was gained.

Conclusion

The Sixty-Sixth Congress convened on May 19, 1919, with the president at the Peace Conference in Versailles. The NWP worked on getting prosuffrage Democrats and the president to influence those senators who still opposed the amendment. Wilson had met, for example, with Democrat William J. Harris of Georgia, who went from Italy to France to consult with him about suffrage. With Harris and other senators, Wilson argued that the Democratic Party's future could be made or ruined by its action at that time. Many newspapers recognized the irony that Democrats, who had opposed a federal amendment for so many years, would be coming forward to take credit if the amendment passed during Wilson's presidency.

On the night of May 20, Wilson cabled a message of support for the amendment to the new Congress, and he even praised "women and men who saw the need for it and urged the policy of it when it required steadfast courage to be so much beforehand with the common conviction" (Irwin, *Story of Alice Paul* 428). He was no longer criticizing any suffrage group, and perhaps he was even recognizing the efforts of Alice Paul.

On May 21, 1919, the new House passed the suffrage amendment by 304 votes to 89, 42 more than the required two-thirds. The previous positive vote in the House had been by only one vote more than the required two-thirds.

When William J. Harris announced his intention to vote for suffrage, providing the last vote needed for the amendment to pass in the Senate, Republican senators Henry W. Keyes of New Hampshire and Frederick Hale of Maine also endorsed the amendment to join the winning side. On June 4, 1919, with little debate, the Senate passed the amendment by a vote of 56 to 25.

Alice Paul sews a star. Paul sewing a star, representing a ratifying state, on the National Woman's Party (NWP) Ratification Flag. Mabel Vernon is seated far left, and Anita Politzer is standing, right.

Immediately after the Senate vote, Alice Paul began working on securing the necessary ratification by three-quarters of the state legislatures, thirty-six of the forty-eight states. The first task was to get a vote in the seven state legislatures then convened, and then to get the remaining states to call special sessions during which the amendment could be ratified. In a race to be the first to ratify, Wisconsin, Michigan, and Illinois passed the amendment on June 10. Kansas, Ohio, and New York ratified on June 16. Kansas was the first state to call its legislature into special session to secure a vote.

The first nonsuffrage state to ratify the amendment was Pennsylvania, on June 24, following a difficult campaign in which, as in other states, a national organizer, Dora Lewis, worked with a state chair, Mary Ingham: talking to the governor and each state legislator, using press bulletins to maintain newspaper attention, and drawing crowds to meetings and to legislative sessions. In June and early July, Pennsylvania, Massachusetts, Texas, Iowa, and Missouri ratified. During those months, Alabama, Georgia, and Virginia defeated ratification, but then Arkansas, Montana, and Nebraska ratified in special sessions.

On August 14 Abby Scott Baker went to the Governors' Conference in Salt Lake to talk more governors into calling special sessions. In California, Baker worked with Elizabeth Kent, Vivian Pierce, and state chair Genevieve Allen to influence newspaper coverage concerning the vote in that state and create an "avalanche of telegrams, letters, petitions, resolutions" to legislators (Irwin, *Story of Alice Paul* 441). Governor Stevens called for a special session on November 1, and on that date the state ratified. In Wyoming in January 1920, the governor insisted that legislators pay their own way to the state capital for a special session. Telegrams from the National Republican Congressional Committee to every Republican in the legislature, sent on the request of organizer Anita Pollitzer, led to a session and to ratification on January 27.

By March 1920 thirty-five states had ratified, and only one more was needed. The motion failed in Delaware in May even though the NWP sent an impressive slate of organizers, Irish president de Valera contacted Irish members of the House, the American Federation of Labor (AFL) helped with the campaign, and Wilson telegrammed Democratic members of the state legislature. When the Republican National Convention began on June 8 in Chicago, the NWP picketed each day because Vermont and Connecticut, two likely candidates for ratification, were under Republican control and votes there were by no means secure. The banners included the threat of a boycott in the 1920 elections: "Vote against the Republican Party as long as it blocks suffrage" (Irwin, *Story of Alice Paul* 460).

With no final state vote secure, at the Democratic National Convention, Abby Scott Baker took charge of a campaign to get Democratic leaders to put pressure on the Democratic governor of Tennessee to convene a legislative session for a vote on suffrage. In Tennessee, organizers like Catherine Flanagan and Anita Pollitzer worked with state chair Sue White and Alice Paul to plan campaigns in every congressional district. Abby Scott Baker instigated regular visits to the presidential candidates, James M. Cox and Warren G. Harding, to convince them of the boon to their election hopes that a proactive role would create: they could demonstrate their leadership abilities by influencing Tennessee state legislators. In a very full Nashville, housing antisuffrage as well as suffrage forces, suffrage was ratified on August 18. After antisuffragists instituted a suit to question the validity of the Tennessee vote, Connecticut ratified on September 14.

Throughout her eight-year attempt to get the vote that finally concluded with the ratification by Tennessee and then Connecticut, Paul had insisted that women join together and stand up for themselves. They did not seek suffrage as a favor or reward. Instead, they were securing for themselves a human right—insisting that women be treated as equal human beings. They

Alice Paul hangs the flag. Paul unfurling the National Woman's Party (NWP) ratification banner after receiving word that Tennessee had ratified. Photograph printed in the *Suffragist,* Sept. 1920.

could put themselves first—their rights being equal in importance to a world war—without any self-indulgence or selfishness involved, because they had a role to fulfill in their nation.

To first create an impact on women and then on the nation, Paul made her arguments visually as well as verbally so first women could fully *see* themselves as confident activists and then all Americans could see what women could be and do. They could plan a parade on the day before a president came to town; they could also take advantage of the opportunities provided by a world's fair, a cross-country motor trip, national party conventions, a new road up Pike's Peak, and campaign trips by train. They could live and work across from the president's house, insist on entering his drawing room, follow him to other cities, and stand before his home with banners carrying his own words. And, as the ultimate symbol of their strength and sacrifice, they could withstand jail terms, hunger strikes, force-feeding, physical abuse, and incarceration in mental wards.

For Paul, the guiding force behind this new vision of American women and this visual campaign was always nonviolence. This philosophical choice, stemming from her Quaker upbringing and from the influence of writers like Thoreau and Tolstoy, stressed the building of self-respect through determined action and sacrifice, the exploitation of well-planned symbolic moments, and the dogged attempt to change the minds and thus the actions of the opposition. This moral grounding caused Paul to feel that NAWSA's meetings and compromises could not be her choice nor could she emulate the violence promulgated by the Pankhursts and their WSPU. Instead, she continued to place women within the national scene, relying on boycotts, picketing, aggressive lobbying, submission to jail terms, and other choices that, like Gandhi's campaign techniques in South Africa and India, changed how the adherents themselves and ultimately how the government and public viewed American women.

The *Hartford Post* commented on December 12, 1918, that "It was only the clever vision, the intense conviction, and the unhesitating persistence of Miss Paul and the Woman's Party that kept the amendment to the front and carried it to the point where it now stands, simply awaiting final action by the Senate" ("Persistence of Woman's Party"). Judge Walter Clark of the Supreme Court of North Carolina said of Paul that because of this effort, "Your place in history is assured. . . . There were politicians, and a large degree of public sentiment, which could only be won by the methods you adopted. It is certain that but for you success would have been delayed for many years to come" (Stevens, "Militant Campaign").

Alice Paul's place has not been assured, perhaps because she forged ahead with her work on the Equal Rights Amendment and never told her own story or perhaps because this story reveals frightening realities about American police and government. But Alice Paul, at the beginning of the twentieth century, created the first successful nonviolent campaign for social change in the United States. Like Gandhi and Martin Luther King, she used every possibility of a nonviolent rhetoric to bring both a greater sense of self and civil rights to a disenfranchised group.

Works Cited

NAWSA Papers = National American Woman Suffrage Association Papers at the Library of Congress

NWPP = National Woman Party Papers at the Library of Congress

"5000 Women March, Beset by Crowds." *New York Times* 4 Mar. 1913: 5.

Adamson, Ethel. Letter to Abby Scott Baker. 6 Nov. 1916. Reel 35, NWPP.

———. Letter to Abby Scott Baker. 11 Nov. 1916. Reel 35, NWPP.

———. Letter to Abby Scott Baker. 17 Nov. 1916. Reel 35, NWPP.

———. Letter to Abby Scott Baker. 23 June 1917. Reel 44, NWPP.

"The Administration Versus the Woman's Party." *Suffragist* 25 Aug. 1917: 6–7.

"Alice Paul Talks: Hunger Striker Describes Forcible Feeding." 22 Jan. 1917. Library of Congress American Memory Collection. Votes for Women: Selections from the National American Woman Suffrage Association Collection, 1848–1921. http://www.memory .loc.gov/cgi-bin/query/D?new:2:/temp/~ammem_6jJN

Allender, Nina E. "Advertising Democracy." *Suffragist* 14 July 1917: 5.

"Almost a Revolution." *New York Call.* Comments of the Press. *Suffragist* 8 Sept. 1917: 10.

"America Last." *New Orleans Item.* Comments of the Press. *Suffragist* 11 Jan. 1919: 10.

"American Women Burn President Wilson's Words on Democracy." *Suffragist* 21 Dec. 1918: 6–7.

"Annoying Suffragists." *Iowa Forum.* Comments of the Press. *Suffragist* 31 Aug. 1918: 10.

Annual Report of Membership Department, 1916–1917. Reel 91, NWPP.

"Archaic Senators on Par with Kaiser." *Richmond Evening Journal.* Comments of the Press. *Suffragist* 24 Aug. 1918: 9.

"An Armed Truce." *Remonstrance against Woman Suffrage* Apr. 1916: 2.

Arnold, Virginia. Letter to Maria Dean. 2 Apr. 1918. Reel 59, NWPP.

"An Artist's Work for Suffrage." *Forecast.* Comments of the Press. *Suffragist* 20 Feb. 1915: 6.

"Assemble in Convention." *Washington Post.* Press Comments on the Convention. *Suffragist* 2 Oct. 1915: 6.

"Attacks Belmont Meeting." *New York Times* 24 Aug. 1914: 8.

Bacon, Margaret Hope. *In the Shadow of William Penn: Central Philadelphia Monthly Meeting of Friends.* Philadelphia: Central Philadelphia Monthly Meeting, 2001.

———. *Mothers of Feminism: The Story of Quaker Women in America.* San Francisco: Harper, 1986.

"Bad Campaign Tactics." *New York Times* 18 May 1915: 12.

Baker, Abby Scott. Letter to Mrs. Rosenwald. 11 Dec. 1916. Reel 35, NWPP.

Baker, Ray Stannard. *Woodrow Wilson, Life and Letters, Facing War, 1915–1917.* Vol. 6. New York: Doubleday, Doran, 1940.

———. *Woodrow Wilson, Life and Letters, War Leader: April 6, 1917–February 28, 1918.* Vol. 7. New York: Doubleday, Doran, 1939.

Baker, Ray Stannard, and William E. Dodd. *The Public Papers of Woodrow Wilson: War and Peace.* Vol. 5. New York: Harper, 1927.

Barry, J. D. "The Militant Suffragists." *New York Telegram.* Comments of the Press. *Suffragist* 1 June 1918: 12.

Baumgartner, Lisa Marie. "Alice Paul, the National Woman's Party, and a Rhetoric of Mobilization." Diss. U of Minnesota, 1994.

Beard, Charles A. "The Woman's Party." *New Republic* 21 July 1916: 329–31.

———. "Woman Suffrage and Strategy." *New Republic* 12 Dec. 1914: 22–23.

Beard, Mary. "Have Americans Lost Their Democracy?" 1913. Reel 5, NWPP.

———. Letter to Alice Paul. 24 June 1914. Reel 10, NWPP.

———. Letter to Alice Paul. 15 Aug. 1914. Reel 11, NWPP.

———. Letter to Lucy Burns. 18 Jan. 1914. Reel 7, NWPP.

———. Letter to Mr. and Mrs. Phelps Stokes. 2 May 1917. Reel 42, NWPP.

"Begging for Rights." *Suffragist* 8 Apr. 1916: 6.

"Begin Police Grill." *Washington Post* 5 Mar. 1913: 3.

Belmont, Alva. "An Appeal to the Women Voters." *Suffragist* 19 Sept. 1914: 3.

Benedict, Burton, ed. *The Anthropology of World's Fairs: San Francisco Panama Pacific International Exposition of 1915.* London: Lowie Museum of Anthropology, 1983.

"A Big Lift for Suffrage." *Arizona Republican.* Comments of the Press. *Suffragist* 9 Oct. 1915: 6.

"Birthdays and the Judiciary Committee." *Suffragist* 13 May 1916: 10.

Bland, Sidney. "'Never Quite as Committed as We'd Like': The Suffrage Militancy of Lucy Burns." *Journal of Long Island History* (Summer/Fall 1981): 4–23.

Blatch, Harriot Stanton. Letter to Alice Paul. 14 Jan. 1917. Reel 37, NWPP.

———. Letter to Anne Martin. 14 Feb. 1917. Reel 39, NWPP.

Blatch, Harriot Stanton, and Alma Lutz. *Challenging Years: The Memoirs of Harriot Stanton Blatch.* New York: Putnam, 1940.

Board of Directors of the Five Boroughs of the Woman Suffrage Party. Telegram to Corporal Tanner. 8 Mar. 1913. Reel 2, NWPP.

Boeckel, Florence. "Reflections of a Picket." *Suffragist* 3 Mar. 1917: 6.

———. "Why They Put Alice Paul in Solitary Confinement." *Suffragist* 10 Nov. 1917: 7.

Borda, Jennifer L. "The Woman Suffrage Parades of 1910–1913: Possibilities and Limitations of an Early Feminist Rhetorical Strategy." *Western Journal of Communication* 66.1 (2002): 25–52.

Brandeis, Louis, Josephine Clara Goldmark, and Curt Muller. *Women in Industry*. New York: Arno, 1908.

Breckinridge, Sophonisba P. *Women in the Twentieth Century: A Study of Their Political, Social and Economic Activities*. New York: Hill, 1933.

Brock, Peter. *Freedom from War: Nonsectarian Pacifism, 1814–1914*. Toronto: U of Toronto P, 1991.

Brownlow, Louis. *A Passion for Anonymity: The Autobiography of Louis Brownlow, Second Half*. Chicago: U of Chicago P, 1958.

Buhle, Mari Jo. *Women and the American Socialism, 1870–1920*. Urbana: U of Illinois P, 1981.

"Bunker Hill Day at the Panama-Pacific Exposition." *Suffragist* 26 June 1915: 5.

Burke, Kenneth. *Language as Symbolic Action*. Berkeley: U of California P, 1966.

Burns, Lucy. "The Indomitable Picket Line." *Suffragist* 9 June 1917: 6.

———. Letter to Alva Belmont. 24 July 1917. Reel 91, NWPP.

———. Letter to Anna Howard Shaw. 21 Nov. 1913. Reel 5, NWPP.

———. Letter to Caroline Katzenstein. 8 Nov. 1917. Reel 52, NWPP.

———. Letter to Emily Perry. 22 April 1914. Reel 9, NWPP.

———. Letter to Honorable Gwynne Gardiner. 7 Nov. 1917. Reel 52, NWPP.

———. Letter to Members of the Woman's Party. 9 Nov. 1917. Reel 52, NWPP.

———. Letter to the Editor. *Chicago Post*. 11 July 1916. Reel 29, NWPP.

———. Letter to the Editor. *Washington Star*. 8 May 1915. Reel 16, NWPP.

———. "Susan B. Anthony." *Suffragist* 13 Feb. 1915: 6.

Cairns, William B. *A History of American Literature*. New York: Oxford UP, 1912.

"Can the President Help Us?" *Suffragist* 22 May 1915: 4.

"Card Index Converts." *Woman Patriot* 15 Mar. 1919: 8.

Carpenter, Alice. Letter to Alice Paul. 6 June 1917. Reel 43, NWPP.

Carter, April. *Direct Action*. London: Peace News, 1962.

"Cartooning for the Suffragist." *Suffragist* 29 July 1916: 4.

Case, Clarence Marsh. *Non-Violent Coercion: A Study in Methods of Social Pressure*. New York: Century, 1923.

Catt, Carrie Chapman. Letter to Alice Paul and Members of the Board of the Congressional Union. 26 May 1915. Reel 16, NWPP.

———. Letter to Anne Martin. 13 Mar. 1916. Reel 25, NWPP.

———. Letter to Presidents of State Suffrage Associations in Suffrage States. 12 Jan. 1916. NAWSA.

Catt, Carrie Chapman, and Nettie Rogers Shuler. *Woman Suffrage and Politics: The Inner Story of the Suffrage Movement*. New York: Scribner's, 1923.

"Chief Sylvester Out." *New York Times* 6 Mar 1915: 4.

Clarke, Pauline. "The Trial." *Suffragist* 24 Aug. 1918: 6.

Cleaver, Bob. Telephone interview with Katherine H. Adams. 16 Oct. 2002.

"Closing Session of the Woman's Party Convention." *Suffragist* 13 May 1916: 5.

Colvin, Sarah Tarleton. *A Rebel in Thought*. New York: Island, 1944.

"Comments of the Press." *Suffragist* 4 Nov. 1916: 10.

"Comments of the Press." *Suffragist* 17 Mar. 1917: 10.

"Comments of the Press." *Suffragist* 12 Nov. 1917: 10.

"The Congressional Union for Woman Suffrage." *Suffragist* 15 Nov. 1913: 2.

Congressional Union Pamphlet, 1913. Reel 92, NWPP.

"Crowd Destroys Suffrage Banner at White House." *New York Times* 21 June 1917: 1–2.

Dalton, Dennis. *Mahatma Gandhi: Nonviolent Power in Action*. New York: Columbia UP, 1993.

"A Daughter of Light." Excerpts from the *Philadelphia Ledger, L.A. Evening Express,* and *New York Evening Post*. Press Comments on the Life and Work of Inez Milholland. *Suffragist* 9 Dec. 1916: 10.

Davis, Robert. *Woodbrooke 1903–1953: A Brief History of a Quaker Experiment in Religious Education*. London: Bannisdale, 1953.

DeBenedetti, Charles. *The Peace Reform in American History*. Bloomington: Indiana UP, 1980.

"The Defeat in the Senate." *Suffragist* 12 Oct. 1918: 4.

"The Demand of the Women." *New York Evening Mail*. Comments of the Press. *Suffragist* 17 June 1916: 9.

Demo, Anne Teresa. "The Guerilla Girls' Comic Politics of Subversion." *Women Studies in Communication* 23 (2000): 133–56.

"Democrats Lose 12 Senate Seats; House is a Toss-up. *New York Times* 8 Nov. 1916: 3.

"The Demonstration of February 9." *Suffragist* 22 Feb. 1919: 10–12.

"The 'Divine Right" of Men." *Louisville Courier-Journal*. Comments of the Press. *Suffragist* 19 Oct. 1918: 9.

Dobkin, Marjorie Housepian. *The Making of a Feminist: Early Journals and Letters of M. Carey Thomas*. Kent, Ohio: Kent State UP, 1979.

Dock, Lavinia. "Alice Paul in Prison." *Suffragist* 24 Nov. 1917: 7.

———. Letter to Carrie Chapman Catt. Reel 17, NWPP.

———. "The Urgent Need of Political Equality." *Suffragist* 9 June 1917: 5.

———. "The Young Are at the Gates." *Suffragist* 30 June 1917: 5–8.

"Doddering Delay." *Detroit Journal*. Comments of the Press. *Suffragist* 5 Oct. 1918: 8.

Dorr, Rheta Childe. Letter to Alice Paul. 21 Apr. 1914. Reel 9, NWPP.

———. *Susan B. Anthony: The Woman Who Changed the Mind of a Nation*. New York: Stokes, 1928.

———. *What Eight Million Women Want*. Boston: Small, Maynard, 1910.

———. "What Would Men Do?" *Chicago News*. Comments of the Press. *Suffragist* 17 Feb. 1917: 10.

———. *A Woman of Fifty*. New York: Funk & Wagnalls, 1924.

"Dr. Harvey Wiley Protests at Treatment of Picket Prisoners." *Suffragist* 10 Nov. 1917: 9.

Dunn, Mary Maples, and Richard S. Dunn. *The Papers of William Penn*. Vol.1. 1644–1679. Philadelphia: U of Pennsylvania P, 1981.

"Eastern Missionaries." *Oakland Tribune*. The Press of the Country. *Suffragist* 29 Apr. 1916: 8.

Eastman, Crystal. "Alice Paul's Convention." *Crystal Eastman on Women and Revolution*. Ed. Blanche Wiesen Cook. New York: Oxford UP, 1978. 57–63.

———. Letter to Alice Paul. 24 July 1917. Reel 46, NWPP.

Emory, Julia. Letter to Alice Paul. 5 Sept. 1917. Reel 48, NWPP.

Enion, Ruth Charles. "The Intellectual Incubation of a Quaker College, 1869–1903." B.A. Thesis. Swarthmore, 1944.

Ewald, Donna, and Peter Clute. *San Francisco Invites the World: The Panama-Pacific International Exposition of 1915.* San Francisco: Chronicle Books, 1991.

"Excuse Him: He's Tied." *Suffragist* 16 Jan. 1915: 8.

"The Executive Committee of the Congressional Union." *Suffragist* 10 Jan. 1914: 5–6.

Faber, Doris. *Petticoat Politics: How American Women Won the Right to Vote.* New York: Lothrop, Lee and Shepard, 1967.

Faith and Practice of Pacific Yearly Meeting of the Religious Society of Friends: A Quaker Guide to Christian Discipline. San Francisco: Pacific Yearly Meeting, 1985.

"The Farewell of the Woman Voters' Envoys." *Suffragist* 2 Oct. 1915: 5.

"A Federal Amendment Now." *Suffragist* 15 Nov. 1913: 4.

Field, Sara Bard. Letter to Lucy Burns. 28 Sept. 1915. Reel 19, NWPP.

"Fine Words." *Richmond Evening Journal.* Comments of the Press. *Suffragist* 14 Dec. 1918: 10.

"First National Convention of the Congressional Union." *Suffragist* 4 Dec. 1915: 6–7.

Fisher, Katharine Rolston. Letter to Lucy Burns. 12 Aug. 1917. Reel 46, NWPP.

———. Letter to Mabel Vernon. 22 June 1917. Reel 44, NWPP.

Fisher, Mary. *A General Survey of American Literature.* Chicago: McClurg, 1899.

Fleming, Thomas. *The Illusion of Victory: America in World War I.* New York: Basic Books, 2003.

Flexner, Eleanor, and Ellen Fitzpatrick. *Century of Struggle: The Woman's Rights Movement in the United States.* 1959. Enlarged Ed. Cambridge: Harvard UP, 1996.

The Flushing Remonstrance: The Origin of Religious Freedom in America. Flushing, N.Y.: Bowne House, n.d.

"Force Yard of Jail to Cheer Miss Paul." *New York Times* 12 Nov. 1917: 8.

Ford, Linda G. *Iron-Jawed Angels: The Suffrage Militancy of the National Woman's Party, 1912–1920.* Lanham, Md.: UP of America, 1991.

Foss, Sonja K. "Framing the Study of Visual Rhetoric: Toward a Transformation of Rhetorical Theory." In Hill and Helmers, *Defining Visual Rhetorics* 303–13.

"From Ocean to Ocean Suffragists Celebrate Great Day." *Suffragist* 2 May 1914: 5.

"From San Francisco to Washington: Women Voters Bring Their Message to Congress." *Suffragist* 9 Oct. 1915: 5.

Fry, Amelia R. Conversations with Alice Paul: Woman Suffrage and the Equal Rights Amendment. November 1972 and May 1973. Suffragists Oral History Project, University of California at Berkeley. Online Archive of California. www.oac.cdlib.org/texts/

Fry, Amelia R., and Fern Ingersoll. *Rebecca Hourwich Reyher: Search and Struggle for Equality and Independence.* Berkeley: U of California P, 1977.

———. Rebecca Hourwich Reyher: Search and Struggle for Equality and Independence. Suffragists Oral History Project, University of California at Berkeley. Online Archive of California. ark.cdlib.org/ark:/13030/kt6xonb1ts

Gale, Zona. "Civic Problems in the Small City and Village." *La Follette's Weekly Magazine* 7 Aug. 1909: 12–13.

———. *Friendship Village.* New York: Macmillan, 1908.

———. *Friendship Village Love Stories.* New York: Macmillan, 1909.

———. *Neighborhood Stories.* New York: Macmillan, 1914.

———. *When I Was a Little Girl.* New York: Macmillan, 1913.

Gallagher, Robert S. "I Was Arrested, of Course." *American Heritage* Feb. 1974: 17–24+.

Gandhi, Mahatma. "Living on Spinning and Weaving." *Young India: 1924–26.* New York: Viking, 1927. 589–91.

———. *Satyagraha in South Africa.* Trans. Valji Govindji Desai. 1928. Ahmedabad, India: Navajivan, 1961.

———. *Woman's Role in Society.* Comp. R.K. Prabhu. Ahmedabad, India: Navajivan, 1959.

Garbus, Julia. "Service-Learning, 1902." *College English* 64 (May 2002): 547–65.

Gardener, Helen. *Facts and Fictions of Life.* Chicago: Kerr, 1893.

———. *Men, Women, and Gods, and Other Lectures.* New York: Truth Seeker, 1885.

———. *Plain Talk: A Pamphlet on the Population Question and the Moral Responsibility of Woman in Maternity.* Chicago: Wilson, n.d.

Glenn, Cheryl. "Silence: A Rhetorical Art for Resisting Discipline(s)." *JAC: A Journal of Composition Theory* 22 (2002): 261–91.

Goodell, Charles. *Political Prisoners in America.* New York: Random, 1973.

"The Government's Surrender." *Suffragist* 31 Aug. 1918: 5.

"A Great and Moving Hour." *New York Tribune.* Comments of the Press. *Suffragist* 12 Oct. 1918: 14.

"The Greatest Suffrage Day." *Suffragist* 9 May 1914: 2+.

Green, Martin. *Gandhi: Voice of a New Age Revolution.* New York: Continuum, 1993.

Gregg, Richard. *The Power of Non-Violence.* Philadelphia: Lippincott, 1934.

"A Group of Wilful Men." *Suffragist* 12 Oct. 1918: 6.

"Guilty of—?" *Suffragist* 1 Feb. 1919: 4.

Hallowell, Anna Davis. *James and Lucretia Mott: Life and Letters.* Boston: Houghton, 1890.

Harper, Ida Husted. Letter to the Editor of the *Chattanooga Times,* January 3, 1917. Ida H. Harper Papers, Box 2.

———. *The Life and Work of Susan B. Anthony.* Indianapolis: Hollenbeck, 1898.

———. "The National Suffrage Amendment Proposed by Senator Shafroth." *Suffragist* 11 Apr. 1914: 6.

Harper, Ida Husted, Elizabeth Cady Stanton, Susan B. Anthony, and Matilda J. Gage, ed. *History of Woman Suffrage.* 6 vols. New York: Little and Ives: 1881–1922.

———. *History of Woman Suffrage.* Vol 5. New York: Little and Ives, 1922.

Haskell, Oreola Williams. "The Invader." *Banner Bearers: Tales of the Suffrage Campaigns.* Geneva, NY: Humphrey, 1920. 1–31.

Havemeyer, Louisine W. "The Prison Special: Memories of a Militant." *Scribner's Magazine* 71 (June 1922): 661–76.

"Hearing before the House Judiciary Committee." *Suffragist* 25 Dec. 1915: 5–7.

Heck, Fannie E. S. "The Woman's Hymn." WMU Year Book 1913–14. WMU Watchwords and Hymns. 10 Dec. 2003. www.wmu.com/resources/library/watchwords.asporg _hymn

"'Heckling' the President." *Suffragist* 22 May 1915: 4.

Heckscher, August. *Woodrow Wilson: A Biography.* New York: Scribner's, 1991.

Herbert, Nathaniel. "A Victory Tribute from the Front." *Suffragist* 12 Jan. 1918: 9.

"Her Pressure on Congress." *New York Times* 2 Mar. 1919: 71–72.

Hill, Charles A. "The Psychology of Rhetorical Images." In Hill and Helmers, *Defining Visual Rhetorics* 25–40.

Hill, Charles A., and Marguerite Helmers. *Defining Visual Rhetorics*. Mahwah, NJ: Erlbaum, 2004.

Hitchcock, Virginia. Letter to Alice Paul. 5 Feb. 1914, Reel 7, NWPP.

Hocks, Mary E. "Understanding Visual Rhetoric in Digital Writing Envionments." *College Composition and Communication* 54 (2003): 629–56.

"An Honorable Politician." *New York Post*. Comments of the Press. *Suffragist* 22 Sept. 1917: 10.

"The Honor Badge." *Cambden* (NJ) *Courier*. Comments of the Press. *Suffragist* 4 May 1918: 13.

"Honor Suffrage Soldiers." *New York Tribune*. Comments of the Press. *Suffragist* 7 July 1917: 10.

Hopkins, J. A. H. Letter to Alice Paul. 22 June 1917. Reel 44, NWPP.

Hunkins, Hazel. "Prison Described by the Prisoners." *Suffragist* 31 Aug. 1918: 8.

Hutchinson, George E. *The History of Madison Place, Lafayette Square, Washington D.C.* Washington, D.C.: Federal Circuit Bar Association, 1998.

Huxman, Susan Schultz. "The Woman's Journal, 1870–1890: The Torchbearer for Suffrage." *A Voice of Their Own: The Woman Suffrage Press, 1840–1910*. Ed. Martha M. Solomon. Tuscaloosa: U of Alabama P, 1991. 87–109.

"Impressions from the District Jail." *Suffragist* 25 Jan. 1919: 12.

"Inez Milholland Boissevain." *Suffragist* 2 Dec. 1916: 6.

"In Prison." *Suffragist* 24 Aug. 1918: 7.

Irwin, Inez Haynes. *Angels and Amazons: A Hundred Years of American Women*. Garden City, N.Y.: Doubleday, 1934.

———. *The Story of Alice Paul and the Woman's Party*. New York: Harcourt, 1921.

"Itinerary of the Suffrage Special." *Suffragist* 15 Apr. 1916: 15.

Josephson, Hannah Geffen. *Jeannette Rankin, First Lady in Congress: A Biography*. New York: Bobbs-Merrill, 1974.

"A Jubilee Dinner for the Pickets." *Suffragist* 15 Dec. 1917: 10–11.

Juhnke, James C., and Carol M. Hunter. *The Missing Peace: The Search for Nonviolent Alternatives in United States History*. Kitchner, Ontario: Pandora, 2001.

"July 14—Freedom Day?" *Miami Metropolis*. Comments of the Press. *Suffragist* 17 Aug. 1918: 8.

"Kaiser Wilson." *Suffragist* 18 Aug. 1917: 6.

Katzenstein, Caroline. *Lifting the Curtain: The State and National Woman Suffrage Campaigns in Pennsylvania as I Saw Them*. Philadelphia: Dorrance, 1955.

Kearns, Edna B. Letter to Alice Paul, Aug. 1918. Reel 64. NWPP.

Keller, Helen. "Letter to a English Woman-Suffragist." *Out of the Dark: Essays, Letters and Addresses on Physical and Social Vision*. Garden City, N.Y.: Doubleday, 1913. 115–120.

Kerfoot, Anne Lindsay. "Alice Paul and the Nineteenth Amendment." Masters Thesis. Shippensburg State College, 1972.

Kerr, Laura. *The Girl Who Ran for President*. New York: Nelson, 1947.

Kettler, Ernestine Hara. "In Prison." *From Parlor to Prison: Five American Suffragists Talk about Their Lives*. Ed. Sherna Berger Gluck. New York: Monthly Review, 241–86.

Kiewe, Amos. "A Dress Rehearsal for a Presidential Campaign: FDR's Embodied 'Run' for the 1928 Governorship." *Southern Communication Journal* 64 (1999): 155–67.

Krone, Henrietta Louise. "Dauntless Women: The Story of the Woman Suffrage Movement in Pennsylvania, 1910–1920." Diss. U of Pennsylvania, 1946.

"Lafayette and Rochambeau." *Suffragist* 3 Aug. 1918: 4.

La Follette, Belle Case. "Justice for Pickets." *Suffragist* 6 Oct. 1917: 9.

"The Later Demonstrations." *Suffragist* 24 Aug. 1918: 5.

Letter to Dear Madam. 4 Mar. 1913. Reel 2, NWPP.

Levy, Howard, and David Miller. *Going to Jail: The Political Prisoner.* New York: Grove, 1970.

Lewis, Dora. Letter to Alva Smith Belmont. 13 Nov 1917. Reel 52, NWPP.

Livingston, Leota E. Notarized Account of Police Action in the 1913 Washington Parade. Reel 2, NWPP.

Link, Arthur S. *Wilson: The New Freedom.* Princeton: Princeton UP, 1956.

———. *Woodrow Wilson and the Progressive Era, 1910–1917.* New York: Harper, 1954.

"Lobbying and Political Work." *Suffragist* 10 May 1919: 5.

Lobbying Cards. April 1917. Reel 16, NWPP.

Lucaites, John Louis, and Robert Hariman. "Visual Rhetoric, Photojournalism, and Democratic Public Culture." *Rhetoric Review* 20 (2001): 37–42.

Lunardini, Christine A. *From Equal Suffrage to Equal Rights: Alice Paul and the National Woman's Party, 1910–1928.* New York: New York UP, 1986.

Lutz, Alma. *Susan B. Anthony: Rebel, Crusader, Humanitarian.* Boston: Beacon, 1959.

MacKaye, Percy. "Art and the Woman's Movement: A Comment on the National Suffrage Pageant." *Forum* 49 (1913): 680–84.

Martin, Anne. Letter to "Dear Editor." July 1914. Reel 11, NWPP.

Masel-Walters, Lynne Janet. "Their Rights and Nothing Less: The History and Thematic Content of the American Woman Suffrage Press, 1868–1920." Diss. U of Wisconsin-Madison, 1977.

McConnell. Curt. *"A Reliable Car and a Woman Who Knows It": The First Coast-to-Coast Auto Trips by Women, 1899–1916.* Jefferson, NC: McFarland, 2000.

McCormick, Ruth Hanna. Press Release. 1 Feb. 1914. NAWSA Papers.

"Members of Congress and Suffrage." *Suffragist* 18 Apr. 1914: 4.

Mencken, H.L. "James A. Reed of Missouri." *American Mercury.* April 1929. 22 Dec. 2003. pages.prodigy.net/krtq73aa/ownman.htm

Miller, Alice Duer. "Ingratitude." *New York Tribune.* Comments of the Press. *Suffragist* 17 Mar. 1917: 9.

Miller, William R. *Nonviolence: A Christian Interpretation.* 1964. New York: Schocken, 1969.

Minutes of the National Convention of the National Woman's Party and the Congressional Union, March 1917. Reel 87, NWPP.

"Miss Alice Paul on Hunger Strike." *New York Times* 7 Nov. 1917: 13.

"Miss Alice Paul Returns." *Woman's Journal* 29 Jan. 1910: 19.

"Miss Paul Removed to Prison Hospital." *New York Times* 19 Nov. 1917: 11.

"Miss Paul Speaks at National Headquarters." *Suffragist* 16 Nov. 1918: 4.

Morey, Katherine. Letter to Alice Paul. n.d. Reel 48, NWPP.

Morris, Mildred. "The New Year Demonstration." *Suffragist* 11 Jan. 1919: 4–5.

Mosier, John. *The Myth of the Great War: A New Military History of World War I.* New York: HarperCollins, 2001.

"Move Militants from Workhouse." *New York Times* 25 Nov. 1917: 6.

"Mr. Bryan at the Panama-Pacific Exposition." *Suffragist* 17 July 1915: 4.

"Mr. President, What Will You Do for Woman Suffrage." *Suffragist* 9 Dec. 1916: 7.

"Mrs. Belmont Protests." *New York Times* 20 Aug. 1918: 9.

"Mrs. Inez Milholland Bouissevain Carries Last Appeal of Eastern Women to the Women Voters of the West." *Suffragist* 7 Oct. 1916: 7.

Murdock, Myrtle Cheney. *National Statuary Hall in the Nation's Capitol.* Washington, D.C.: Monumental Press, 1955.

"Mutual Responsibility." *Suffragist* 21 Apr. 1917: 3.

"The National Memorial Service in Memory of Inez Milholland." *Suffragist* 30 Dec. 1916: 7–10.

National Woman's Party 1921 Report. Reel 87, NWPP.

"Nation Honors Inez Milholland." *Suffragist* 23 Dec. 1916: 8.

"The Nation-Wide Demonstration." *Suffragist* 11 Apr. 1914: 3, 7.

NAWSA Annual Report for 1913. NAWSA Papers.

"New Amendment Proposed." *Suffragist* 21 Mar. 1914: 4.

"New Jersey Munition Works Demand Federal Suffrage." *Suffragist* 14 Sept. 1918: 8.

"A New Leader—Alice Paul—Why She Is." *Everybody's Magazine* 25 (July 1916): 127.

"New Members of the Advisory Council." *Suffragist* 20 Feb. 1915: 3.

"The Newport Conference." *Suffragist* 5 Sept. 1914: 5–7.

"New York, Massachusetts, and Pennsylvania." *Suffragist* 6 Nov. 1915: 4.

"*New York Times* Reveals the Secret Card System Used by Suffragists to Control Congress." *Woman Patriot* 8 Mar. 1919: 1–3.

"New York to Honor Lafayette Today." *New York Times* 6 Sept. 1918: 11.

"Nine More Pickets Seized at White House." *Suffragist* 27 June 1917: 7.

Nolan, Mary A. "That Night of Terror." *Suffragist* 1 Dec. 1917: 7+.

"Non Tali Auxilio." *New York Times* 8 Nov. 1917: 14.

"A Note from Alice Paul." *Suffragist* 24 Nov. 1917: 6.

"Notes from the Prisoners." *Suffragist* 24 Aug. 1918: 8.

O'Neill, William L. *Everyone Was Brave: A History of Feminism in America.* New York: Quadrangle, 1969.

———. *The Woman Movement: Feminism in the United States and England.* New York: Barnes and Noble, 1969.

"An Opponent Wonders." *Baltimore Sun.* Comments of the Press. *Suffragist* 12 Oct. 1918: 14.

"Opposing Democrats." *Suffragist* 19 Aug. 1916: 6.

"Order of Organizations in the Processional." 1913 Parade. Reel 2, NWPP.

Organizer in Denver. Letter to Mrs. White. 23 Jan. 1915. Reel 15, NWPP.

Organizing Letter to Alice Paul. 14 May 1918. Reel 59. NWPP.

"Our—Not The." *Woman's Citizen* 28 Sept. 1918: 1–3.

"Our Prestige Demands National Suffrage." *San Antonio Express.* Comments of the Press. *Suffragist* 28 Sept. 1918: 10.

Pankhurst, E. Sylvia. *The Suffragette Movement: An Intimate Account of Persons and Ideals.* New York: Longmans, Green, 1932.

———. *The Suffragette: The History of the Women's Militant Suffrage Movement, 1905–1910.* New York: Sturgis and Walton, 1911.

"Parade Protest Arouses Senate." *New York Times* 5 Mar. 1913: 10.

"Pass the Amendment and Go on with War." *Washington Post.* Comments of the Press. *Suffragist* 13 July 1918: 8.

Paul, Alice. "Aims of the Woman's Party." *Suffragist* 30 Sept. 1916: 6.

———. "The Church and Social Problems." *Friends' Intelligencer* 20 Aug. 1910: 513–15.

———. "The Defeat in the Senate." *Suffragist* 12 Oct. 1918: 4.

———. Foreword. *Suffragist* 15 Nov. 1913: 1.

———. "The Legal Position of Women in Pennsylvania." Diss. U of Pennsylvania, 1912.

———. Letter to C. L. Hunt. January 1913. Reel 1, NWPP.

———. Letter to Crystal Eastman Benedict. 9 Nov. 1914. Reel 13, NWPP.

———. Letter to Dora Lewis. 1 June 1914. Reel 10, NWPP.

———. Letter to Edith Goode. 5 July 1916. Reel 29, NWPP.

———. Letter to Elizabeth Marot. 22 Sept. 1917. Reel 49, NWPP.

———. Letter to Elsie Hill. 10 Mar. 1914. Reel 8, NWPP.

———. Letter to Emily K. Perry. 12 Mar. 1914. Reel 8, NWPP.

———. Letter to Eunice R. Oberly. 6 Mar. 1914. Reel 8, NWPP.

———. Letter to Florence Bayard Hilles. 3 Jan. 1916. Reel 23, NWPP.

———. Letter to H. E. Brennan. 18 Sept. 1917. Reel 48, NWPP.

———. Letter to John E. Nordquit. 23 July 1913. Reel 4, NWPP.

———. Letter to Julian T. Carr. 11 July 1916. Reel 29, NWPP.

———. Letter to Kate S. Brading. 9 Dec 1916. Reel 36, NWPP.

———. Letter to Louis Brandeis. 8 Mar. 1913. Reel 2, NWPP.

———. Letter to Louisine Havemeyer. 1918 n.d. Reel 67, NWPP.

———. Letter to Lucy Burns. 17 May 1915. Reel 16, NWPP.

———. Letter to Mabel Vernon. 12 Nov. 1914. Reel 13, NWPP.

———. Letter to Mary Beard. 28 June 1913. Reel 2, NWPP.

———. Letter to Mary Beard. 9 Nov. 1914. Reel 13, NWPP.

———. Letter to Mary Ware Dennett. 11 Jan. 1913. Reel 1, NWPP.

———. Letter to Mrs. C. Z. Klauder. 5 Sept. 1917. Reel 48, NWPP.

———. Letter to Mrs. Malcolm McBride. 16 Sept. 1914. Reel 12, NWPP.

———. Letter to Mrs. P. Pendergrast. 22 Sept. 1917. Reel 49, NWPP.

———. Letter to Mrs. Robert Morton. 5 July 1916. Reel 29, NWPP.

———. Letter to Newspaper Editors. 19 Nov. 1918. Reel 65, NWPP.

———. Letter to Organizer. 19 Sept. 1916. Reel 32, NWPP.

———. Letter to Paula Jakobi. 6 Sept. 1917. Reel 48, NWPP.

———. Letter to Rheta Childe Dorr. 6 Mar. 1914. Reel 8, NWPP.

———. Letter to State Chairmen. 8 Feb. 1917. Reel 40, NWPP.

———. Letter to Vivian Pierce. 19 Sept. 1916. Reel 32, NWPP.

———. Telegram to Margaret Whittemore. 18 Oct. 1918. Reel 65. NWPP.

———. "Towards Equality." MA Thesis. University of Pennsylvania, 1907.

———. "The Woman Suffrage Movement in Great Britain." *Significance of the Woman Suffrage Movement.* Supplement to the Annals of the American Academy of Political and Social Science, May 1910. Philadelphia: American Academy of Political and Social Science, 1910. 2 3–27.

Paul, Helen. Letter to Alice Paul. 8 Oct. 1917. Reel 50, NWPP.

Paul, Mickle. Letter to Alice Paul. n.d. Reel 27, NWPP.

Paul, Tacie Parry. Letter to Alice Paul. n.d. Reel 27, NWPP.

Penn, William. *A Collection of the Works of William Penn.* Vol. 1. London: Sowle, 1726.

Perelman, Chaim, and Lucie Olbrechts-Tyteca. *The New Rhetoric: A Treatise on Argumentation.* Trans. John Wilkinson and Purcell Weaver. Notre Dame: U of Notre Dame P, 1971.

Perry, Emily K. (Chairman, Committee on Petitions). Letter to John E. Nordquit. 23 July 1913. Reel 4, NWPP.

"Persistence of Woman's Party." *Hartford Post.* Comments of the Press. *Suffragist* 11 Jan. 1919: 10.

"The Picket and the President." *Suffragist* 2 June 1917: 6.

"Picketing Thirty-four Wilful Senators." *Suffragist* 26 Oct. 1918: 8–9.

"The Pickets at the White House Gates: Have They Helped Suffrage?" *Suffragist* 28 Sept. 1918: 8.

Pierce, Vivian. "Susan B. Anthony, Militant." *Suffragist* 3 Mar. 1917: 7

"Plan Big Welcome to Suffrage Envoys." *New York Times* 25 Nov. 1915: 8.

Plante, Ellen M. *Women at Home in Victorian America: A Social History.* New York: Facts on File, 1997.

"Platform Pledges." *Suffragist* 18 Apr. 1914: 4.

"Political Prisoners." *Suffragist* 3 Nov. 1917: 8–9.

"Politics." *Crisis* 5.6 (April 1913): 1.

Ponder, Stephen. "Partisan Reporting and Presidential Campaigning: Gilson Gardner and E. W. Scripps in the Election of 1912." *Journalism History* 17.1–2 (Spring-Summer 1990): 3–12.

Porritt, Annie G. "The Suffrage Conference at Washington." *Suffragist* 28 Dec. 1918: 4–5.

———. "Woman Suffrage and Congress." *Independent* 27 Dec. 1915: 522.

"The Power of Women." *Suffragist* 21 Sept. 1918: 6.

"Preserving the Peace and Order of the Capitol." *Suffragist* 19 Oct 1918: 8.

"The President and Suffrage." *New York American.* Press Comment. *Suffragist* 11 July 1914: 8.

"The President and the Suffragists." *Literary Digest* 47 (20 Dec. 1913): 1209–11.

"The President of the United States and the Woman's Party." *New American Woman* Jan. 1917: 14.

"President Onlooker at Mob Attack on Suffragists." *Suffragist* 18 Aug. 1917: 7.

"The President's Responsibility." *Suffragist* 14 Sept. 1918: 6.

"President's Words Burned as Suffragists Protest in Front of White House." *Suffragist* 28 Sept. 1918: 6–7.

"President Wilson and Suffrage." *Suffragist* 20 June 1914: 4.

"President Wilson Comes Out for Federal Amendment." *Suffragist* 12 Jan. 1918: 8–9.

Press Bulletin. Nov. 1916. Reel 91, NWPP.

Press Bulletin. 31 May 1918. Reel 91, NWPP.

Press Bulletin. 6 Aug. 1918. Reel 91, NWPP.

Press Release. 20 June 1917. Reel 91, NWPP.

Press Release. 9 Jan. 1918. Reel 91, NWPP

Preston, William, Jr. *Aliens and Dissenters: Federal Suppression of Radicals, 1903–1933.* 2nd Ed. Urbana: U of Illinois P, 1994.

Price, Myrtle E. Letter to Alice Paul. 22 June 1917. Reel 44, NWPP.

"Prison—and the Reaction." *Suffragist* 7 July 1917: 9.

"Prisoners of Freedom." *Suffragist* 27 Oct. 1917: 9.

"The Prison Special." *Suffragist* 1 Feb. 1919: 10.

"The Prison Special." *Suffragist* 22 Feb. 1919: 3–4.

"Protest against Suffrage Blockade Continues." *Suffragist* 17 Aug. 1918: 9.

"Protest for Liberty Answered with Sixteen More Suffrage Arrests." *Suffragist* 21 July 1917: 4–5.

"Prussianizing Kentucky." *Lexington Herald*. Comments of the Press. *Suffragist* 14 Dec. 1918: 10.

"Publisher's Note." *Suffragist* 9 May 1914: 7.

Pullen, Michael G. "The Political Career of Moses Edwin Clap, Progressive and Insurgent Senator from Minnesota." MA thesis. Mankato State College, 1971.

Purvis, June. "'Deeds, Not Words': Daily Life in the Women's Social and Political Union in Edwardian Britain." *Votes for Women*. Eds. June Purvis and Sandra Stanley Holton. London: Routledge, 2000. 135–58.

Radice, Lisanne. *Beatrice and Sidney Webb: Fabian Socialists*. New York: St. Martin's, 1984.

Ramelson, Marian. *The Petticoat Rebellion: A Century of Struggle for Women's Rights*. London: Lawrence and Wishart, 1967.

"The Real Advance." *Suffragist* 29 Sept. 1917: 6.

Reedy, William Marion. "Get in Step with Progress." *Reedy's Journal*. Comments of the Press. *Suffragist* 1 June 1918: 12.

"Reminding the President When He Landed in Boston." *Suffragist* 1 Mar. 1919: 6–9.

Report of the Congressional Union for Woman Suffrage for the Year 1914 with Outline of Congressional Work During the Preceding Year. Reel 87, NWPP.

Resolution Passed by the Convention of the National Woman's Party and the Congressional Union, March 1917. Reel 87, NWPP.

Richardson, Mary R. *Laugh a Defiance*. London: Weidenfeld, 1953.

Riegel, Robert. *American Feminists*. Lawrence: U of Kansas P, 1963.

Robinson, Helen Ring. Letter to Alice Paul, n.d., 1916. Reel 36, NWPP.

———. "What about the Woman's Party?" *Independent* 11 Sept. 1916: 381–83.

Rogers, Elizabeth Selden. Letter to Alice Paul. 5 Mar. 1913. Reel 2. NWPP.

"Rose Winslow Appeals for Labor." *Suffragist* 29 June 1918: 9.

Ross, Ishbel. *Ladies of the Press: The Story of Women in Journalism by an Insider*. New York: Harper, 1936.

"Row Over Hunger Strike: Militants Assert Forcible Feeding Is Unnecessary and Inhuman." *New York Times* 10 Nov. 1917: 3.

Rudolph, Susanne Hoeber, and Lloyd I. Rudolph. *Gandhi: The Traditional Roots of Charisma*. Chicago: U of Chicago P, 1983.

Rules of Discipline of the Yearly Meeting of Friends, Held in Philadelphia. Philadelphia: Representative Committee, 1868.

Ryan, Agnes E. *The Torch Bearer: A Look Forward and Back at the Woman's Journal, the Organ of the Woman's Movement*. Boston: The Woman's Journal and Suffrage News, 1916.

Salutatory. *Suffragist* 15 Nov. 1913: 4.

Sanger, Margaret. Letter to Anne Martin. July 1917. Reel 45, NWPP.

"Says Suffrage Vote Will Not Be Delayed." *New York Times* 24 Sept. 1918: 24.

Scott, Anne Firor, and Andrew Scott. *One Half the People: The Fight for Woman Suffrage.* Philadelphia: Lippincott, 1975.

"Sectionalism and Suffrage." *Rocky Mount News.* Comments of the Press. *Suffragist* 26 Oct. 1918: 10.

Seeley, Robert A., and Aldous Huxley. *The Handbook of Non-Violence.* Westport, Conn.: Hill, 1986.

"Senate Police Inquiry On." *New York Times* 6 Mar 1913: 3.

"Senate Recesses while Women Are Arrested." *Suffragist* 23 Nov. 1918: 9.

"Senator Sheppard on 'Kaiserism' in Congress." *Suffragist* 17 Aug. 1918: 3.

"The September 16 Demonstration." *Suffragist* 21 Sept. 1918: 4.

"Seven Months Sentence for National Suffrage Leader." *Suffragist* 27 Oct. 1917: 4.

"The Seventh Week of the Suffrage Picket." *Suffragist* 3 Mar. 1917: 5.

Severn, Bill. *Free But Not Equal: How Women Won the Right to Vote.* New York: Messner, 1967.

Sharp, Gene. "A Study of the Meaning of Nonviolence." *Gandhi Marg* Oct. 1959: 265–73+.

Shaw, Anna Howard. *The Aims and Policies of the National American Woman Suffrage Association As Contrasted with Those of the Congressional Union Are Here Set Forth by Dr. Anna Howard Shaw for Information and Reference of All Suffragists.* 1916. NAWSA Papers.

———. Letter to Dora Lewis. 28 Nov. 1917. NAWSA Papers.

———. Letter to Lucy Burns. 19 Nov. 1913. NAWSA Papers.

———. Letter to M. M. Forrest. Jan. 1914. NAWSA Papers.

———. *The Story of a Pioneer.* New York: Harper, 1915.

Showalter, Elaine. *The Female Malady: Women, Madness, and English Culture, 1830–1980.* New York: Pantheon, 1985.

"Silent, Silly, and Offensive." *New York Times* 11 Jan. 1917: 14.

Simmons, Eleanor Booth. "Does Publicity Pay." *New York Sun.* Comments of the Press. *Suffragist* 2 Mar. 1918: 9.

"Socialist Help to Suffrage." *Suffragist* 17 Nov. 1917: 3.

Stanton, Elizabeth Cady. *Eighty Years and More (1815–1897): Reminiscences of Elizabeth Cady Stanton.* New York: European, 1898.

Stevens, Doris. *Jailed for Freedom: American Women Win the Vote.* New York: Boni and Liveright, 1920.

———. "Justice: As Seen at Occuquan." *Suffragist* 11 Aug. 1917: 7–8.

———. Letter to Spencer Miller. 17 Nov 1917, Reel 52, NWPP.

———. "The Militant Campaign." *Suffragist* 19 July 1919: 8–9.

Stiehm, Judith. *Nonviolent Power: Active and Passive Resistance in America.* Lexington, Mass.: Heath, 1972.

Stockbridge, Frank. "How Woodrow Wilson Won His Nomination." *Current History* 20 (July 1924): 561–72.

Stoneburner, Carol. "Drawing a Profile of American Female Public Friends as Shapers of Human Space." In Stoneburner and Stoneburner, *The Influence of Quaker Women on American History* 1–55.

"Suffrage and the Liberty Loan." *Woman's Citizen* 28 Sept. 1918: 352–54.

"Suffrage and the Senate." *Charleston Evening Post*. Comments of the Press. *Suffragist* 25 Jan. 1919: 14.

"Suffrage Demonstration before White House Planned." *Suffragist* 3 Aug. 1918: 5.

"Suffrage Demonstrations." *Washington Herald*. Comments of the Press. *Suffragist* 17 Aug. 1918: 8.

"Suffrage Goal in Sight." *Chicago Examiner*. The Press of the Country. *Suffragist* 29 Apr. 1916: 8.

Suffrage Parade: Hearings before a Subcommittee of the Committee of the District of Columbia United States Senate. Sixty-Third Congress. Washington: GPO, 1913.

"Suffrage Pickets Freed from Prison." *New York Times* 28 Nov. 1917: 13.

"The Suffrage Trial." *Suffragist* 22 Feb. 1919: 13.

"Suffragette Tells of Forcible Feeding." *New York Times* 18 Feb. 1910. 7.

"The *Suffragist*." *Suffragist* 10: Jan. 1917: 9.

"Suffragists Again Attack President." *New York Times* 7 Aug. 1918: 1+.

"Suffragists Burn President's Words." *New York Times* 17 Sept. 1918: 13.

"Suffragists Burn Wilson in Effigy." *New York Times* 10 Feb. 1919: 1+.

"Suffragists Wait at the White House for Action." *Suffragist* 17 Jan. 1917: 7.

"Suffragists Will Picket White House." *New York Times* 10 Jan 1917: 1.

"Susan B. Anthony, 1820–1918." *Suffragist* 16 Feb. 1918: 8.

Sussman, A. "The Silent Sentinels." *Suffragist* 27 Oct. 1917: 5.

Tarbell, Ida. "Organized Women Dramatic Phase in Political Flurry." *New York World* 8 June 1916: 4.

———. "Woman's Party is Made Up of Voters Wise in Politics." *New York World* 7 June 1916: 4.

Taylor, Bryan C. "'Our Bruised Arms Hung Up as Monuments': Nuclear Iconography in Post-Cold War Culture." *Critical Studies in Media Communication* 20.1 (2003): 1–34.

Thomson, Jane. "Selling the War to the People." *Woman's Citizen* 28 Sept. 1918: 357–58.

Thoreau, Henry David. "Civil Disobedience." In Witherell, *Henry David Thoreau* 203–24.

———. "A Plea for Captain John Brown." In Witherell, *Henry David Thoreau* 396–417.

Tolstoy, Leo. *The Kingdom of God Is within You*. 1894. Trans. Constance Garnett. Lincoln: U of Nebraska P, 1984.

"To Permit Women's Parade." *New York Times* 6 Jan. 1913: 9.

"To the President and Congress." *Suffragist* 30 Dec. 1916: 6.

Transcripts of Speeches Delivered at the Women Voters' Convention, Sept. 4–6, 1915. Reel 92, NWPP Papers.

"Truth about the Pickets." *Utica* (New York) *Press*. Comments of the Press. *Suffragist* 23 Apr. 1919: 10.

"The United States Convicts Eleven More Women for Demanding Democracy." *Suffragist* 14 July 1917: 4–5.

"The United States Government on Trial." *Suffragist* 21 July 1917: 7.

Ussher, Jane M. *Women's Madness: Misogyny or Mental Illness?* Amherst: U of Massachusetts P, 1991.

"Valentines Pour in upon Congress." *Suffragist* 19 Feb. 1916: 7.

Vernon, Mabel. Letter from the National Secretary. 20 June 1917. Reel 91, NWPP.

"Vassar's Head Indignant." *New York Times* 10 June 1908: 7.

"The Vindication of the Suffrage Pickets." *Suffragist* 28 July 1917: 4.

Vipont, Elfrida. *The Story of Quakerism: 1652–1952.* London: Bannisdale, 1954.

"Votes of Women and Bull Moose Elected Wilson." *New York Times* 12 Nov. 1916: 1+.

Walton, Richard J. *Swarthmore College: An Informal History.* Swarthmore, Penn.: Swarthmore College, 1986.

"War and the Suffrage Campaign." *Suffragist* 21 Apr. 1917: 6.

"War Roster of Suffrage Officials." *Woman's Citizen* 28 Sept. 1918: 355.

"Washington Hears Message of Envoys." *Suffragist* 13 May 1916: 7–8.

"The Watchfire." *Suffragist* 11 Jan. 1919: 6.

"We Ask Justice, Not Pardon." *Suffragist* 21 July 1917: 6.

Welliver, Judson. "Suffrage, A Party Issue." *Washington Times.* Comments of the Press.
Suffragist 31 Jan. 1914: 7.

Wells, Mildred White. *Unity in Diversity: The History of the General Federation of Women's
Clubs.* Washington, D.C.: General Federation of Women's Clubs, 1953.

Westermarck, Edward. *The History of Human Marriage.* London: Macmillan, 1891.

———. *The Origin and Development of the Moral Ideas.* 2 vols. London: Macmillan, 1908,
1912.

"The Western Star." *Seattle Post Intelligencer.* Comments of the Press. *Suffragist* 22 Apr.
1916: 10.

"When Patience Ceases." *Greenwich Graphic.* Comments of the Press. *Suffragist* 1 June
1918: 12.

Whitney, Charlotte. Letter to Mrs. William (Elizabeth) Kent. 24 Sept. 1915. Reel 19,
NWPP.

Whittemore, Margaret Fay. Letter to Lucy Burns (Editor of the *Suffragist*). 4 May 1916.
Reel 27, NWPP.

Wiley, Anna Kelton. "Why We Picketed the White House." *Good Housekeeping* 66 (Feb.
1918): 123–25.

"Will Quit Police Quiz." *Washington Post* 15 Mar. 1913: 2.

Wilson, A. N. *Tolstoy.* New York: Norton, 1988.

Wilson, Edith Bolling. *My Memoirs.* New York: Bobbs-Merrill, 1938.

"Wilson's Vote on Suffrage in New Jersey." *Suffragist* 16 Sept. 1916: 6.

"Wilson Won't Let Women Heckle Him." *New York Times* 1 July 1914: 4.

Winkler, John K. *W.R. Hearst: An American Phenomenon.* New York: Simon and Schuster,
1928.

Witherell, Elizabeth Hall. *Henry David Thoreau: Collected Essays and Poems.* New York:
Library of America, 2001.

Wolpert, Stanley. *Gandhi's Passion: The Life and Legacy of Mahatma Gandhi.* New York:
Oxford, 2001.

"Woman's Beauty, Grace, and Art Bewilder the Capital." *Washington Post* 4 Mar. 1913:
1+.

"A Woman's March in Washington." *Baltimore Sun* 4 Mar. 1913: 1+.

"The Woman's Party Appeals to the Russian Mission." *Suffragist* 23 June 1917: 7.

"The Woman's Party Organizes." *Suffragist* 8 Apr. 1916: 7.

"Woman's Party Protest against Wilful Senators." *Suffragist* 19 Oct. 1918: 6.

"Woman Suffrage and the War Argument." *Suffragist* 15 Aug. 1914: 4.

"Woman Voters' Convention Pledged to Anthony Amendment." *Suffragist* 25 Sept. 1915: 5–6.

"Woman Voters' Envoys Reach Unfree States." *Suffragist* 30 Oct. 1915: 3.

"Women and Politicians." *Helena* (Montana) *Record.* The Press of the Country. *Suffragist* 29 Apr. 1916: 8.

"Women Must Remain Non-Partisan." *Suffragist* 7 Oct. 1916: 6.

"The Women's Convention." *Colorado Springs Gazette.* Press Comments on the Convention. *Suffragist* 2 Oct. 1915: 6.

"Women's Protest against Disenfranchisement Broken Up by Federal Police." *Suffragist* 17 Aug. 1918: 5.

"Women Voters Hear Eastern Appeal." *Suffragist* 28 Oct. 1916: 6.

"Women Will Protest against the Thirty-four Wilful Men." *Suffragist* 12 Oct. 1918: 13.

Wood, Herbert G. "First Director of Studies." In Davis, *Woodbrooke 1903–1953* 19–30.

——. "Origins." In Davis, *Woodbrooke 1903–1953* 13–18.

Wood, Mary I. *The History of the General Federation of Women's Clubs for the First Twenty-Two Years of Its Organization.* New York: General Federation of Women's Clubs, 1912.

"The Working Women's Deputation to the President." *Suffragist* 31 Jan. 1914: 5.

"The Year's Progress." *Suffragist* 22 Mar. 1916: 6.

Young, Joy. Letter to Alice Campbell. 25 Aug. 1916. Reel 31, NWPP.

Younger, Maud. "Revelations of a Woman Lobbyist." *McCall's Magazine* (Sept. Oct. Nov. 1919): passim.

Zimmerman, Loretta Ellen. "Alice Paul and the National Woman's Party, 1912–1920." Diss. Tulane U, 1964.

Index

KATHERINE H. ADAMS is the Audrey and William Hutchinson Distinguised Professor of English at Loyola University, New Orleans. Her books include *A Group of Their Own, Progressive Politics and the Training of American's Persuaders,* and *A History of Professional Writing Instruction in American Colleges.*

MICHAEL L. KEENE is professor of English at the University of Tennessee. His books include *Writing Scientific Papers and Reports, Effective Professional Writing, A Short Guide to Business Writing,* and *Against the Grain.*

The University of Illinois Press
is a founding member of the
Association of American University Presses.

Composed in 10.5/13 Adobe Minion Pro
by Jim Proefrock
at the University of Illinois Press
Manufactured by Sheridan Books, Inc.

University of Illinois Press
1325 South Oak Street
Champaign, IL 61820-6903
www.press.uillinois.edu